DR. SAMUEL JOHNSON AND JAMES BOSWELL

Modern Critical Views

Henry Adams
Edward Albee
A. R. Ammons
Matthew Arnold
John Ashbery
W. H. Auden
Jane Austen
James Baldwin
Charles Baudelaire
Samuel Beckett
Saul Bellow
The Bible
Elizabeth Bishop
William Blake
Jorge Luis Borges
Elizabeth Bowen
Bertolt Brecht
The Brontës
Robert Browning
Anthony Burgess
George Gordon, Lord
    Byron
Thomas Carlyle
Lewis Carroll
Willa Cather
Cervantes
Geoffrey Chaucer
Kate Chopin
Samuel Taylor Coleridge
Joseph Conrad
Contemporary Poets
Hart Crane
Stephen Crane
Dante
Charles Dickens
Emily Dickinson
John Donne & the Seven-
    teenth-Century Meta-
    physical Poets
Elizabethan Dramatists
Theodore Dreiser
John Dryden
George Eliot
T. S. Eliot
Ralph Ellison
Ralph Waldo Emerson
William Faulkner
Henry Fielding
F. Scott Fitzgerald
Gustave Flaubert
E. M. Forster
Sigmund Freud
Robert Frost

Robert Graves
Graham Greene
Thomas Hardy
Nathaniel Hawthorne
William Hazlitt
Seamus Heaney
Ernest Hemingway
Geoffrey Hill
Friedrich Hölderlin
Homer
Gerard Manley Hopkins
William Dean Howells
Zora Neale Hurston
Henry James
Samuel Johnson and
    James Boswell
Ben Jonson
James Joyce
Franz Kafka
John Keats
Rudyard Kipling
D. H. Lawrence
John Le Carré
Ursula K. Le Guin
Doris Lessing
Sinclair Lewis
Robert Lowell
Norman Mailer
Bernard Malamud
Thomas Mann
Christopher Marlowe
Carson McCullers
Herman Melville
James Merrill
Arthur Miller
John Milton
Eugenio Montale
Marianne Moore
Iris Murdoch
Vladimir Nabokov
Joyce Carol Oates
Sean O'Casey
Flannery O'Connor
Eugene O'Neill
George Orwell
Cynthia Ozick
Walter Pater
Walker Percy
Harold Pinter
Plato
Edgar Allan Poe
Poets of Sensibility & the
    Sublime

Alexander Pope
Katherine Ann Porter
Ezra Pound
Pre-Raphaelite Poets
Marcel Proust
Thomas Pynchon
Arthur Rimbaud
Theodore Roethke
Philip Roth
John Ruskin
J. D. Salinger
Gershom Scholem
William Shakespeare
    (3 vols.)
    Histories & Poems
    Comedies
    Tragedies
George Bernard Shaw
Mary Wollstonecraft
    Shelley
Percy Bysshe Shelley
Edmund Spenser
Gertrude Stein
John Steinbeck
Laurence Sterne
Wallace Stevens
Tom Stoppard
Jonathan Swift
Alfred, Lord Tennyson
William Makepeace
    Thackeray
Henry David Thoreau
Leo Tolstoi
Anthony Trollope
Mark Twain
John Updike
Gore Vidal
Virgil
Robert Penn Warren
Evelyn Waugh
Eudora Welty
Nathanael West
Edith Wharton
Walt Whitman
Oscar Wilde
Tennessee Williams
William Carlos Williams
Thomas Wolfe
Virginia Woolf
William Wordsworth
Richard Wright
William Butler Yeats

These and other titles in preparation

Modern Critical Views

DR. SAMUEL JOHNSON AND JAMES BOSWELL

Edited and with an introduction by
Harold Bloom
Sterling Professor of the Humanities
Yale University

CHELSEA HOUSE PUBLISHERS ◊ 1986
New York ◊ New Haven ◊ Philadelphia

cap. 1

© 1986 by Chelsea House Publishers, a division of
Chelsea House Educational Communications, Inc.
133 Christopher Street, New York, NY 10014
345 Whitney Avenue, New Haven, CT 06511
5014 West Chester Pike, Edgemont, PA 19028

Introduction © 1986 by Harold Bloom

Printed and bound in the United States of America

∞ The paper used in this publication meets the
minimum requirements of the American National
Standard for Permanence of paper for Printed Library
Materials, Z39.48-1984.

Library of Congress Cataloging-in-Publication Data
Main entry under title:

Dr. Johnson and James Boswell.

(Modern critical views)
Bibliography: p.
Includes index.
1. Johnson, Samuel, 1709–1784—Criticism and
interpretation—Addresses, essays, lectures.
2. Boswell, James, 1740–1795—Criticism and interpretation—Addresses, essays, lectures.   3. Biography
(as a literary form)—Addresses, essays, lectures.
I. Bloom, Harold.   II. Series.
PR3534.D7   1986   828'.609   85-28070
ISBN 0-87754-678-9

Contents

Editor's Note

This volume gathers together a representative selection of the best literary criticism devoted to the works of Dr. Samuel Johnson and James Boswell. The criticism is reprinted here in the order of its publication, together with three essays that appear for the first time. Marena Fisher assisted the editor, who is grateful for her erudition and her judgment.

I have begun this book with Johnson's two most distinguished critics, W. K. Wimsatt and Walter Jackson Bate, and with Boswell's great editor and critic, Frederick A. Pottle. Wimsatt starts off with a powerful discussion of the relation of Johnson's prose style to his theory of style and diction, with its apparent emphasis upon correctness and generality. This is followed by Pottle's early but definitive treatment of Boswell as a literary artist, the equal of his greatest contemporaries. W. J. Bate, at his most admirable, writes of Johnson as a moral psychologist, and illuminates the strongest Western critic's pervasive concern with the ambivalences and ambiguities of the affective life. A second essay by Wimsatt, on Johnson's exemplary novel, *Rasselas*, reveals the abyss of nihilism that Johnson both avoids and investigates, as a precursor of Samuel Beckett.

Another generation of critics is introduced here by Paul Fussell's analysis of Johnson's remarkable achievement as an essayist in *The Rambler*, where the critic's *praxis*, as Fussell notes, evidences "his prime quality of mind: an instinctive skepticism . . . of 'systems' and unambiguous positions." Leopold Damrosch, Jr., writing upon *The Vanity of Human Wishes*, sees the poem as being at once tragedy and satire, a characteristic Johnsonian blend, difficult to find in other writers. Comparing Johnson's strategies as a biographer, particularly in the *Life of Pope* and the *Life of Savage*, to Boswell's parallel strategies, particularly in the *Tour to the Hebrides*, Frank Brady hints at a subtle link between Johnson and Boswell that might be called the prudential genre of the antiromance.

Robert Bell, chronicling Boswell's development from the *London Journal* to the *Life of Johnson,* emphasizes Boswell's mature ability "to dramatize himself in the multifaceted but unified role of biographer," an immense advance upon the early wistfulness of posing as a Macheath or an Aeneas. Boswell's search for the hero, which culminated in the *Life of Johnson,* is the center of his *Tour to Corsica,* analyzed here by William C. Dowling, who finds, in the Plutarchan figure of Boswell's General Paoli, an image of spiritual isolation. The visionary politics of Boswell's *Tour to Corsica* are countered by Johnson's realistic conservatism, which is the central emphasis in John Barrell's discussion of the relation between language and politics in the most conservative and moral of all the great critics.

This book concludes with three brilliant essays by the youngest generation of scholar–critics now writing upon Johnson and Boswell. Laura Quinney's vision of "Johnson in mourning" profoundly relates Johnson's temperament to his rhetorical stance as a critic: "He was close to suspecting that literature had imposed on him a spurious interiority, close enough to recognize such a phenomenon in theory, while regarding literary pathos, and his particular vulnerability to it, with ambivalence and distrust." Gordon Turnbull, in the most stimulating treatment yet given to the *Tour to the Hebrides,* shrewdly centers upon "Boswell's deeply perplexed national self-understanding" as a proud and patriotic Scot, who nevertheless could not resist the aura and power, cultural and political, of Johnson and London. Finally, Robert J. Griffin provides an advanced analysis of Johnson's complex critical trope of "reflection" in *The Lives of the Poets.* Griffin's exegesis of the aesthetic dimensions of Johnsonian "reflection," and of its ironic limits, is a fitting tribute to Johnson's ongoing vitality and inescapability as the central Western literary critic.

Introduction

*There lurks, perhaps, in every known heart a desire of distinction
which inclines every man first to hope, and then to believe, that Nature has
given him something peculiar to himself. This vanity makes one mind nurse
aversions and another actuate desires, till they rise by art much above their
original state of power and as affectation, in time, improves to habit, they
at last tyrannize over him who at first encouraged them only for show.*
　　　　　　—JOHNSON, in a letter to Boswell, 8 December 1763

Dr. Samuel Johnson, in the judgment of many (myself included), is the
strongest critic in the varied history of Western literary culture. In the
Anglo-American tradition, his only near rival would seem to be William
Hazlitt, who has something like Johnson's energy, intellect, and knowledge,
but lacks the full compass of Johnson's human sympathies, and is simply
not as wise. Johnson shows us that criticism, as a literary art, joins itself
to the ancient genre of wisdom writing, and so is descended from Koheleth
(Ecclesiastes) and Jesus Ben Sirach (Ecclesiasticus). If you search for Johnson's
precursor, turn from Aristotle or even from Ben Jonson, father of English
neoclassicism, and find the forerunner of *Rasselas* and *The Rambler* in
Koheleth:

> Whatsoever thy hand findeth to do, do it with thy might; for
> there is no work, nor device, nor knowledge, nor wisdom, in the
> grave, whither thou goest.

The mind of Johnson, confronting the Biblical Preacher's words, was
altered permanently. Indeed, Johnson is so strong a writer, that he nearly
achieves the metaleptic reversal of making us believe that the author of
Ecclesiastes has read deeply in Samuel Johnson. Sometimes I find myself

1

reading Ecclesiastes aloud, and become confused, believing that I am reading *Rasselas:*

> It is better to hear the rebuke of the wise, than for a man to hear the song of fools.
>
> For as the crackling of thorns under a pot, so is the laughter of the fool: this also is vanity.

Johnson teaches us that the authority of criticism as a literary genre depends upon the human wisdom of the critic, and not upon the rightness or wrongness of either theory or *praxis.* Hazlitt observed that the arts, including literature, are not progressive, and this includes criticism as a branch of the literary art. There always will be those setting rules for criticism, down to current Gallic versions of formalism, linguistic skepticism, and even psycholinguistics, but they have not given and will not give us literary criticism, which will go on being the wisdom of interpretation and the interpretation of wisdom. Johnson and Hazlitt, Ruskin and Pater, Oscar Wilde and Kenneth Burke, all in different but related ways show us that memorable criticism is experiential criticism, that there is no method except oneself, and most profoundly that it is "objectivity" which turns out to be easy, vulgar, and therefore disgusting. True critical subjectivity or personality is hardly an abandonment to self, but is a difficult achievement, dependent upon learning, intellect, and the mystery of individual vitality. "Objectivity" turns out to be a digest of the opinions of others, whether those opinions mask as philosophy, science, or the social conventions of the academies:

> Minim professes great admiration of the wisdom and munificence by which the academies of the Continent were raised, and often wishes for some standard of taste, for some tribunal, to which merit may appeal from caprice, prejudice, and malignity.
>
> *(Idler)* No. 61

Mr. Dick Minim we have in abundance these bad days; he pours forth tomes denouncing interpretation, and calling for rules, principles, methods that will turn Anglo-American criticism into a Germano-Gallic "human science." "Rigor, Rigor!" cries our contemporary Minim, while he keeps reminding us that poems and stories are written in and by language. Dr. Samuel Johnson, who had not the benefits of the Hegelian philosophy and its Franco-Heideggerian revisionists, did what he could with what he had, as here on Shakespeare's *Henry IV* plays:

> But *Falstaff* unimitated, unimitable *Falstaff,* how shall I describe thee? Thou compound of sense and vice; of sense which may be

admired but not esteemed, of vice which may be despised, but
hardly detested. . . . Yet the man thus corrupt, thus despicable,
makes himself necessary to the prince that despises him, by the
most pleasing of all qualities, perpetual gaiety, by an unfailing
power of exciting laughter, which is the more freely indulged,
as his wit is not of the splendid or ambitious kind, but consists
in easy escapes and sallies of levity, which make sport but raise
no envy.

That the balance of this judgment is admirable, and unmatched, is
palpable. But the critical magnificence surpasses mere balance, and is a
crucial insight into Shakespearean representation. Falstaff is "unimitated";
he is not a mimesis, but a supermimesis of essential nature. He is also
"unimitable," because he is a form more real than living man; he contains
us, not we him. His "perpetual gaiety," his wit of "easy escapes and sallies
of levity," a wit that exempts him from envy, testify to his unique nature
as a person without a superego. Without a superego to admonish the ego
to forsake its aggressivities (while punishing the ego all the more each time
it abandons an aggressive drive), we would be as Falstaff, in a condition of
perpetual gaiety, because our death drive, like Falstaff's, would have been
subsumed by play, by easy escapes and sallies of levity. What Nietzsche
failed to represent by his frequently bathetic Zarathustra, and what Freud
assumed was beyond representation, Johnson shows us that Shakespeare
triumphantly had accomplished in Sir John Falstaff. Johnson, greatest of
critics, can teach the rest of us that the essence of poetry is *invention*. Invention
is how meaning gets started, and Johnson implicitly demonstrates that
Shakespeare, more even than Homer or the Bible, was the work most abundant in original invention.

Yet that is only part of how superbly suggestive Johnson upon Shakespeare is. Falstaff's admirable if not estimable sense makes itself necessary
to us as well as to Hal, Bolingbroke's son, because we too lack perpetual
gaiety, because we all of us, like Samuel Johnson, are too much punished
by our superegos. Falstaff's sense, his unfailing power, is the sense and power
of how meaning gets started, of how invention is accomplished. In the terms
of Freudian reductiveness, meaning gets started rather than repeated when
the superego is overcome, but in the Freudian reduction the superego cannot
be overcome. Shakespeare, the most inventive and original of all writers,
ever, is able to generate an almost totally fresh meaning through the exuberance of Falstaff's triumphant will to power over language. Such a will,
whether in writing or speaking, can work its way only through diction,
through a choice of words that pragmatically amounts to a series of choices

For Johnson,

the essence of poetry is invention

in language. Johnson was both a critic of power (invention) and of the will
to diction, and he understood the reflection of power by choice of language
better than any critic has been able to convey since.

II

Johnson's greatest work as a critic is *The Lives of the Poets*, written
between 1777 and 1781. Yet everything about this work is peculiar, since
the *Lives* are introductions to a very odd collection of the British poets,
chosen for the most part not by Johnson, but by the booksellers. Fifty poets
are represented, with Oliver Goldsmith, Johnson's close friend, excluded
and such bards as Roscommon, Pomfret, Dorset, Stepney, Sprat, Fenton,
Yalden, and Lyttelton included, as though they were canonical. Johnson
mostly shrugs them off, even when he had suggested them, remarking
amiably enough in his *Life of Yalden:*

> Of his poems, many are of that irregular kind, which, when he
> formed his poetical character, was supposed to be Pindarick.
> Having fixed his attention on Cowley as a model, he has at-
> tempted in some sort to rival him, and has written a *Hymn to
> Darkness,* evidently as a counter-part to Cowley's *Hymn to Light.*

Alas, poor Yalden! He is remembered now, if at all, only for that
remark, and for the rather grand Johnsonian sentence that concludes his *Life:*

> Of his other poems it is sufficient to say that they deserve perusal,
> though they are not always exactly polished, though the rhymes
> are sometimes very ill sorted, and though his faults seem rather
> the omissions of idleness than the negligence of enthusiasm.

A bit earlier, Johnson had quoted Yalden's unfortunate line in which
Jehovah contemplates the new created Light:

> A while th'Almighty wondering stood.

Alas, poor Yalden! We can never forget the Johnsonian observation
upon this:

> He ought to have remembered that Infinite Knowledge can never
> wonder. All wonder is the effect of novelty upon Ignorance.

That last sentence is an epitome of the neoclassic critical stance, and
could be Ben Jonson deprecating the followers of Spenser, or Samuel Johnson himself dismissing the poetry of Sensibility, the swerve away from Pope

and back to Milton, in Gray, Collins, and the Wartons. In his *Life of Gray*, Johnson is superbly honest and direct in admitting his lack of pleasure in the poetry, and particularly in the two great Pindarics, *The Bard* and *The Progress of Poesy*. Boswell, in the *Life of Johnson*, reports the critic as dismissing Gray's Odes: "they are but cucumbers after all." The dismissal is especially hurtful if an American remembers that Johnson means the British cucumber, an ungainly and rough vegetable whose baroque outlines do suggest the shape of a Gray Pindaric upon the page.

The masterpiece of the *Lives* is the long and beautiful meditation upon Pope. Pope and Dryden, Johnson had by heart; he seems to have had total recall of their work. Swift was a profound problem for Johnson. Despite their intellectual affinities, or perhaps because of them, Johnson was unnerved by Swift. *A Tale of a Tub*, much as I myself am frightened by it, is certainly the most powerful discursive prose work in the English language. Johnson seems to have been even more frightened by it. He called it "this wild work" and wrote of it with a kind of traumatic response:

> of this book charity may be persuaded to think that it might be
> written by a man of a peculiar character, without ill intention;
> but it is certainly of dangerous example.

Scholars have surmised that Johnson feared joining Swift in madness. That seems to me a little too simple. Certainly Johnson, like many men and many women, feared dying badly:

> But few there are whom hours like these await,
> Who set unclouded in the gulfs of fate.
> From Lydia's monarch should the search descend,
> By Solon cautioned to regard his end,
> In life's last scene what prodigies surprise,
> Fears of the brave, and follies of the wise?
> From Marlborough's eyes the streams of dotage flow,
> And Swift expires a driveller and a show.

Swift's terrible irony, savage beyond measure, is antithetical to Johnson's empirical and humane stance. Neoclassical literary theory, which culminated in Johnson, emphasizes the virtues of moral instruction, imitation, and refinement, in the sense of improving the tradition without necessarily revising it. But Swift, though he agreed with this in the abstract, hardly possessed an Horatian temperament. His ferocity, perhaps unparalleled among the great writers, emerges fully only in *A Tale of a Tub*, as Johnson carefully notes:

It exhibits a vehemence and rapidity of mind, a copiousness of images, and vivacity of diction, such as he afterwards never possessed or never exerted. It is of a mode so distinct and peculiar that it must be considered by itself. . . .

That is to say, in Johnson's own terms, Swift's extraordinary nightmare of a book exhibits supreme invention, and the essence of poetry is invention, according to Johnson himself. We all of us have a favorite writer; as I grow older, Johnson is mine, as Pope was Johnson's. We tend to confederate Swift and Pope in our minds; they were close friends, political and literary allies, and they divide the glory of the British Augustans between them, in an age of satire. But Johnson was at ease with Pope, and uncomfortable with Swift. As a wisdom writer, he knew the difference between them. Pope, like Addison, has a link to Francis Bacon, as does Johnson. Swift is not a wisdom writer, but something darker and stronger.

III

Johnson, in my judgment, remains Shakespeare's best critic, precisely because Shakespeare compels Johnson to retreat from neoclassicism and to stand upon the common sense of British naturalism in order to accept and admire Shakespeare's mimetic triumphs. In his *Preface to Shakespeare,* Johnson gives us the inevitable starting point for thinking about Shakespearean representation:

There is a vigilance of observation and accuracy of distinction which books and precepts cannot confer; from this almost all original and native excellence proceeds. *Shakespeare* must have looked upon mankind with perspicacity, in the highest degree curious and attentive. Other writers borrow their characters from preceding writers, and diversify them only by the accidental appendages of present manners; the dress is a little varied, but the body is the same. Our authour had both matter and form to provide; for except the characters of *Chaucer,* to whom I think he is not much indebted, there were no writers in *English,* and perhaps not many in other modern languages, which shewed life in its native colours.

Probably Johnson underestimated Shakespeare's indebtedness to Chaucer. *A Midsummer Night's Dream* and *Troilus and Cressida* owe much to Chaucer, and possibly *Romeo and Juliet* does also. More crucially, there is a complex link between Chaucer's strongest figures, the Pardoner and the Wife of Bath, and the magnificent Falstaff. Chaucer may well have given Shakespeare something of that greatest gift they share: they are the first writers whose personages change *by listening to themselves speak*. But I add little to Johnson here, since he so massively indicates that only Chaucer and Shakespeare represent reality in reality's own colors, and one of the most essential of those colors or tropes is the effect of our words upon ourselves. It is on the central issue of Shakespeare's greatest strength, which is his mode of so representing reality as to compel aspects of reality, that otherwise we could not know, to appear, that Johnson achieves his most useful insight:

> Though he had so many difficulties to encounter, and so little assistance to surmount them, he has been able to obtain an exact knowledge of many modes of life, and many casts of native dispositions; to vary them with great multiplicity; to mark them by nice distinctions; and to shew them in full view by proper combinations. In this part of his performances he had none to imitate, but has himself been imitated by all succeeding writers; and it may be doubted, whether from all his successors more maxims of theoretical knowledge, or more rules of practical prudence, can be collected, than he alone has given to his country.

Johnson splendidly recognizes that Shakespeare's legacy is both in cognitive awareness or theoretical knowledge, and in wisdom or practical prudence. Shakespeare attained "exact knowledge," and represented it in full view; he therefore surpassed the metaphysicians in epistemological certainty, and the moralists in pragmatic measurement. An original who established a contingency that governs all writers since, Shakespeare clearly sets the standard for representation itself. This is Johnson's most complex realization about Shakespeare, and therefore about imaginative literature. To know many modes of life, and so many casts of native dispositions, is here very much a knowing indistinguishable from representation, from the allied acts of varying with multiplicity, marking by nice distinctions, and showing in full view. To vary, mark, and show is not apart from the knowing, but *is* the knowing. Shakespeare, Johnson implies, creates representations so original that conceptually *they contain us,* and continue to shape our psychology of motivation. To have created the modern representation of the mind was the achievement neither of Montaigne nor (belatedly) of Freud, but of Shakespeare alone. What Johnson teaches us is that Shakespeare invented our psychology, to an astonishing degree.

IV

Johnson's great achievement was his criticism. It is accurate to remark that *The Vanity of Human Wishes, Rasselas,* and the more general essays essentially are memorable as extensions of Johnsonian literary criticism or wisdom literature. Of Boswell, we might remark that his two greatest works were Johnson and himself, or the *Life of Johnson* and *Tour to the Hebrides,* and the *London Journal.* Frank Brady's genial observation that Boswell was the Norman Mailer of his day reminds us that "Norman Mailer," the hero of *Advertisements for Myself* and *The Armies of the Night,* probably is Norman Mailer's greatest work, surpassing *The Executioner's Song* and *Ancient Evenings.* That Boswell's "Johnson" is not quite the author of *The Lives of the Poets* is clear enough, whereas Boswell's "Boswell," like Mailer's "Mailer," leaves us in a state of wonder, which we will remember Johnson (in the *Life* of the wretched Yalden) deprecating as the effect of novelty upon ignorance.

One can prefer "Johnson without Boswell" (as I tend to do) and still reread the *Life of Johnson* endlessly as the finest literary biography in English. Boswell's own *Journal,* even the *London Journal,* seems to me not of the aesthetic eminence either of the *Life of Samuel Johnson* or the scarcely inferior *Journal of a Tour to the Hebrides,* but that is only to say that Boswell's "Johnson" is a grander fiction than Boswell's "Boswell." Still, one cannot dispute Frank Brady as to the extraordinary flexibility of style in the *Journal;* it indeed "can accommodate a wide range of material and a high degree of complexity." Brady's summary of Boswell's strengths and limitations in the *Journal* seems to me definitive:

> Boswell kept his journal compulsively, and it makes compulsive reading. The reader of journals is greedy for the actual: how do other people live, think, and feel? Of all literary forms, the journal comes closest to answering these questions directly: at its best, it realizes dramatically for the reader events and feelings in a way that seems spontaneous and true to immediate experience. Characters shift and shade off into obscurity; events are discontinuous, become prominent and disappear: even the form of the journal is comparable to living, as a day-to-day process whose outcome is unknown. But, unlike life, the journal is a written record, which in Boswell's case strings together all the unpredictable sequences of an important career, full of sharply portrayed incidents and dramatic reversals. Its length in itself draws the reader into an increasingly familiar group of figures, and a narrative which may extend a theme over many years or tell a tiny story in one or two entries.
>
> Subjectivity is both the prime value and the limitation of the journal; interest and creativity are its crucial issues. Biography

interposes the biographer between reader and subject; autobiography is liable to the corrective pull of hindsight. The journal draws the reader into another's mind without mediation or distortion. Prejudices, conscious or unconscious, the reader allows for as automatically as he does for the prejudices of the actual people he knows; whatever theoretical issues it may raise, bias is seldom a problem in practice.

But there are problems. It is at least a superficial paradox that the journal, apparently the most artless of literary forms, requires great skill to hold the reader's attention over a long stretch. It must compensate for lack of coherent narrative and character presentation by descriptive or thematic interest that depends directly on the writer's having an interesting, unusual, or powerful mind and some sense of what will entertain or involve a reader. At the same time, skill must never diminish the effect of credibility. The reader may enjoy the tall tales of Casanova more than the sober accounts of a reliable narrator, but he discounts Casanova's memoirs as in part fiction masquerading as fact.

It is possible to take the sophisticated attitude that whatever the journalist says, true or false, is revealing; but a reader is more likely to feel comfortable if he thinks he is reading a true story. And if the narrative is based on verifiable fact he is apt to think better of it; like Johnson he believes that "the value of every story depends on its being true." Boswell emphasizes circumstantial accuracy, the literal truth of matter-of-fact detail; and the credibility this gives his journal carries over to his attempts to register exact states of mind. Here inconsistency plays its part: it would be difficult to invent such vivid variations of character.

The journalist's final advantage is that, other factors being equal, the reader tends to empathize more quickly and fully with real than with fictional characters simply because they are real. For the same reason, the reader's attitude may shift sharply against a journalist, especially when, as in Boswell's case, he is extending the limits of what is permissible to say. On reading Boswell's journal after his death, his respectable executor Sir William Forbes repeatedly wrote "reprehensible passage." Often true enough, but is this the comment of inherent decorum or protective hypocrisy? Or both? Johnson paraphrases an observation in William Law's *Serious Call to a Devout and Holy Life* as, "Every man knows something worse of himself than he is sure of in others." And it is obvious that the reader who says, "Thank God, I am not like him," may be suppressing the unwelcome insight that they have a good deal in common.

But even the most sympathetically disposed can get impatient with vanity or self-pity, very likely elements in a journal since the writer so often uses it as a vent for the feelings he must repress in social life. And the unremitting subjectivity of the journal may in itself become stifling. Finally, the journalist runs the likely risk that the reader will see something in his story other than what he sees himself.

In the end, to recur to Johnson, the only way to determine literary merit is "length of duration and continuance of esteem." Like his biographies, Boswell's journal shows every sign that it will stand the test of time. But its extent and brilliance necessarily distort our perception of him because of the way in which they situate the reader within what Amiel described as "that molecular whirlwind which we call individual existence." We apprehend Boswell from inside, as we do ourselves. He is diffusive as we are; he lacks the solidity we attribute to others. The gain in intimacy is enormous, but it is easy to lose a grasp on how his contemporaries perceived him.

I have quoted all of this long judgment because it is so remarkably Johnsonian, and likely would have been accepted by Boswell himself. Brady, like his great mentor (and mine), Frederick A. Pottle, shows us implicitly that the power of the *Life of Samuel Johnson* and of the *Tour to the Hebrides* is finally the power of love, of Boswell's more-than-filial love for the capacious soul of Samuel Johnson.

W. K. WIMSATT

Johnson's Theory

What a man says about style, his theory of it, expresses a formulated, or fully conscious, preference, while what he does about style may proceed from a preference unrecognized by himself. In this sense the evidence of his theoretical pronouncements is more explicit and clearer than that of his practice. On the other hand the formulated preference suffers the disadvantage of generalization—a thing which comes partly from other minds (with the words used) and is an invasion which may set up the notions and lay out the lines which it is called in only to describe. It is not to be expected that any man should be able to define his own style adequately, even if we make the rash assumption that he is fully aware of it. We must add to this that Samuel Johnson is seldom formally addressed to the subject of his own style, that he lets fall cursory remarks, sometimes with his own style in mind, sometimes with that of others, sometimes with only a notion of style in general. The sort of evidence we are about to see is not so compelling as that already derived from Johnson's practice. It is not to be set on the same level and adduced against the practice. At best it can be but corroboratory—or, where it is contradictory, be accepted as a contradiction, or perhaps as a puzzle. No one, for example, would care to argue on the basis of the following passage that Johnson disapproved of Latin and philosophic diction, yet here we see plainly that on one occasion at least he realized the futility of the philosophic tendency to invent a name for every concept. Boswell asks him for a synonym for "transpire."

From *The Prose Style of Samuel Johnson.* © 1941 by Yale University Press. Originally entitled "Johnson's Theory—I" and "Johnson's Theory—II."

"Why, Sir (said he,) *get abroad*." BOSWELL. "That, Sir, is using
two words." JOHNSON. "Sir, there is no end of this. You may
as well insist to have a word for old age." BOSWELL. "Well,
Sir, *Senectus*." JOHNSON. "Nay, Sir, to insist always that there
should be one word to express a thing in English, because there
is one in another language, is to change the language."

In like manner it is easy to prove from a passage in the *Preface to the Dictionary*
that he understood well enough that learning in other languages could
produce corrupt English.

He that has long cultivated another language, will find its words
and combinations crowd upon his memory; and haste and neg-
ligence, refinement and affectation, will obtrude borrowed terms
and exotick expressions.

In the face of passages like these, where Johnson seems to repudiate the
preferences displayed in his own writing or to forget other critical statements
made by himself, we must parallel Boswell's decision about his eating.

His practice, indeed, I must acknowledge, may be considered as
casting the balance of his different opinions upon this subject;
for I never knew any many who relished good eating more than
he did.

But there is a more deceptive class of statements, generalities and
epithetical condemnations, where we can sometimes hardly prove what Johnson means, or where if we can, the meaning is what a reader of today might
not at first be likely to conceive. There is notably his *Idler* No. 36, on "The
terrifick diction," where he speaks of "the ponderous dictator of sentences"
and "the stately son of demonstration, who proves with mathematical formality what no man has yet pretended to doubt," and where he finds
especially distasteful "a mode of style . . . by which the most evident truths
are so obscured, that they can no longer be perceived."

This style may be called the *terrifick*, for its chief intention is to
terrify and amaze; it may be termed the *repulsive*, for its natural
effect is to drive away the reader; or it may be distinguished, in
plain *English*, by the denomination of the *bugbear style*, for it has
more terror than danger, and will appear less formidable as it is
more nearly approached.

I mean not to suggest that Johnson's own style deserves the epithets which
he here applies to other styles, but that these epithets do suggest some of
the criticisms of Johnson's style which we have quoted [elsewhere]. "Pon-

derous dictator of sentences," "stately son of demonstration," the "*terrifick*" style, "the *bugbear style*." These recall what we have heard from Archibald Campbell, Horace Walpole, Hazlitt, or Macaulay. Fortunately Johnson proceeds to give us an actual "illustrious example" of what he means. In the "*Letters concerning Mind*," he says, "the author begins by declaring, that *the sorts of things are things that now are, have been, and shall be, and the things that strictly ARE.*" It is the tone of metaphysical mystification which seems to him "terrific." He might have been surprised to learn that a later critic should find the term "terrific diction" perfectly suitable to describe so different a thing as the ranting and abusive literary criticism of Swinburne. The fact is that we all deplore terrific diction; there is scarcely anything on which we are more nearly unanimous. But we find ourselves sadly at variance when we set about comparing the objects, the phrases and words, which we actually call terrific. Epithets of this sort and all the more emphatic ways of expressing displeasure may give us a very vivid sense of what a critic dislikes in a given kind of writing if we know what kind is meant, but by themselves they are small clue to what kind is meant.

"The language is laboured into harshness," says Johnson. "The mind of the writer seems to work with unnatural violence. 'Double, double, toil and trouble.' He has a kind of strutting dignity, and is tall by walking on tiptoe." As everybody will recall, he is talking about the odes of Gray. He says of the *Memoirs of the Court of Augustus:* "Sometimes the reader is suddenly ravished with a sonorous sentence, of which when the noise is past the meaning does not long remain." Of Shakespeare: "The equality of words to things is very often neglected, and trivial sentiments and vulgar ideas disappoint the attention, to which they are recommended by sonorous epithets and swelling figures." And one of the faults of the tragedies of Johnson's own day is a "perpetual tumour of phrase."

In all these cases we know what Johnson is talking about, the work to which he is attributing the fault of excess, and from this we can infer at least approximately what form of excess is meant. If we did not know the work, we should know only that he was speaking of some form of the general fault of excess. In the following passage Johnson is speaking simply of bad writings that come under the inspection of Criticism. His range is the whole field of writing.

> Some secret inequality was found between the words and senti-
> ments, or some dissimilitude of the ideas and the original objects
> . . . incongruities were linked together, or . . . some parts were
> of no use but to enlarge the appearance of the whole, without
> contributing to its beauty, solidity, or usefulness.

Who shall ever venture to illustrate this passage, to say what concrete shapes of bombast floated before the inner eye of Johnson as he generalized?

General expressions by Johnson and general conclusions based upon such expressions can afford us no satisfaction—even when they do not seem at variance with his practice. To conclude, for example, that Johnson believed style should be "clear," "elegant," and suited to its theme is not to give Johnson a theory of style that can be distinguished from any other person's theory. Everybody believes these things—in one sense or another—just as everybody despises terrific diction. More particularly, everybody in Johnson's day believed them. To find statements we need go no farther than the best known rhetorics of the day, Kames's or Campbell's or Blair's or the routine performance of Ward. Just as in our study [previously] of Johnson's writing we were concerned to describe those characteristics of his style which distinguish it from other styles, so in this study we are most concerned to point out whatever explicit acknowledgments Johnson made of the characteristic preferences exhibited in his own writings.

Either Johnson was not specifically aware of the characters of his style which we have [elsewhere] called parallelism, antithesis, and inversion, or he thought it not worth while to discuss them. On the whole matter of the structure of sentences and paragraphs, the arrangement of ideas, Johnson makes but few statements which seem helpful to us. He has much to say, however, on the purpose of creative writing, the nature of general truth and its elaboration in writing, the relation of things and words, and the corollary question of diction.

Johnson's belief that art achieved grandeur through generality, that the streaks of the tulip were not to be numbered, is well enough known but may admit some illustration here. The tulip passage, in Imlac's account of the poet, is as follows:

> The business of a poet . . . is to examine, not the individual, but the species; to remark general properties and large appearances; he does not number the streaks of the tulip, or describe the different shades in the verdure of the forest. He is to exhibit in his portraits of nature such prominent and striking features, as recall the original to every mind; and must neglect the minuter discriminations, which one may have remarked, and another have neglected, for those characteristics which are alike obvious to vigilance and carelessness.

And Imlac makes the same application to men and manners—human nature.

He must divest himself of the prejudices of his age or country; he must consider right and wrong in their abstracted and invariable state; he must disregard present laws and opinions, and rise to general and transcendental truths, which will always be the same.

Johnson says something of this sort again and again. The metaphysicals fell short of the sublime because "great thoughts are always general, and consist in positions not limited by exceptions, and in descriptions not descending to minuteness." Shakespeare is great because "nothing can please many, and please long, but just representations of general nature."

Johnson has insisted on an important truth, that a writing should tell something more than the circumstantial or accidental, that it should not be simply representational (if it could be). To our minds it must seem that he has missed another truth, which taken with the first makes the difficulty and debate over literary art. This is that a writing must be itself, original and ungeneralized. What makes both these truths possible is that the subject in art is not things (tulips or human nature) but concepts, visions of things, in the artist's head. The question of detail in the light of this doctrine is not one of "minuter discriminations, which one may have remarked, and another have neglected," but of discrimination between detail which is relevant and that which is irrelevant to the central concept. Johnson himself once connects the notion of relevance with that of generality.

> Instead of dilating his thoughts into generalities, and expressing incidents with poetical latitude, he [Shakespeare] often combines *circumstances unnecessary to his main design,* only because he happened to find them together.

By his theory of generality Johnson could hardly account for his own experience as an artist or for the effect produced upon him by other literary art. It is not surprising to find him in occasional contradictions. In the "Essay on Epitaphs":

> There are no rules to be observed which do not equally relate to other compositions. The praise ought not to be general, because the mind is lost in the extent of any indefinite idea, and cannot be affected with what it cannot comprehend. When we hear only of a good or great man, we know not in what class to place him, nor have any notion of his character, distinct from that of a thousand others.

And he complains that he cannot find in Rowe's plays "any deep search into

nature, any accurate discriminations of kindred qualities, or nice display of
passion in its progress; all is general and undefined." In *Adventurer* No. 95
he is aware of the conflicting demands of generality and particularity and
gropes toward a reconciliation. Though the passions are few, "the alterations
which time is always making in the modes of life" are a source of variety.
"Thus love is uniform, but courtship is perpetually varying."

Thus Johnson wavered in favor of his varying immediate perceptions,
but his allegiance to the rule was none the less real. The rule itself was a
concrete and genuine part of his perception and of his performance. What
he said about the dignity of generality has its most obvious reflection in the
fact that his own writing may, as we have said, be characterized as excep-
tionally general and abstract. Johnson, the last great neoclassicist, the reactionary, was the one who most seriously attempted to put into artistic
practice the neoclassic uniformitarian ideal. Pope might speak of following
nature, of "what oft was thought," by nature he might mean only what was
universal and comprehensible to reason, unmodified by accident of time or
place, but Pope wrote about "flounce" and "furbelow," "Spadillio" and
"captive trumps," about Atticus and Sporus and the Dunces. Johnson stuck
to his principles; with relentless logic he not only theorized but practised
the generality. In his elaborate system of parallelism and antithesis, in the
"philosophic" pomp of his diction, he devised a way of lending to the abstract
an emphasis, a particularity and thickness. He made a kind of poetry of
abstraction; out of emptiness he conjured weight, out of the collapsible he
made structures. By limiting himself faithfully to the abstract, he achieved
more with it than did any other neoclassicist.

One function of Johnson's theory—though not directly a stylistic one—
appears in his estimate of certain types of literature. History he disdained.

> As ethics or figures, or metaphysical reasoning, was the sort of
> talk he most delighted in, so no kind of conversation pleased
> him less I think, than when the subject was historical fact or
> general polity. . . . "He never (as he expressed it) desired to
> hear of the *Punic war* while he lived: such conversation was lost
> time (he said), and carried one away from common life, leav-
> ing no ideas behind which could serve *living wight* as warning or
> direction."

And consistently, he "did not . . . much delight in that kind of conversation
which consists in telling stories." History, or story, tells what happened—

in some particular time at some particular place. The event is told merely as itself, for itself. History gives an idea of this event, this thing, but no generally applicable idea; it carries one away from "common life." Johnson's dislike of history is directly antithetic to his great affection for biography. Arthur Murphy mentions the two together: "General history had little of his regard. Biography was his delight." And we have the clear and authoritative record of Boswell:

> MONBODDO. "The history of manners is the most valuable. I never set a high value on any other history." JOHNSON. "Nor I; and therefore I esteem biography, as giving us what comes near to ourselves, what we can turn to use."

The events of biography are no less particular than those of history but are more generally applicable to the personal human problem, and hence may readily be thought of as more universally significant—especially if the thinker is, like Johnson, not interested in economics or government, but in private morals. Biography is what happened to a person, like oneself.

For narrative to be justified at all it must have some value as generality; it must be a "specimen of life and manners." This condition is best fulfilled in biography—in other narrative hardly at all. Events are facts, and hence narrative is an enumeration of facts, differing from other enumerations, inventories and the like, chiefly in the observance of chronological order. When we arrive at this point, at the notion of fact, of statement of fact, of a series of statements of fact, we are at the heart of what Johnson disliked in writing and by antithesis have a good indication of what he did like.

Johnson's dislike of mere fact would perhaps not have been so clearly recorded for us were it not for his extreme dislike of the prose of another writer whose style was the antipodes of his own. Perhaps some personal rancor at times stimulated Johnson to the criticism of Swift, but the criticism is too clear and too often reiterated to leave a doubt either that Swift's style was really offensive to Johnson or that there was an esthetic reason. At best Swift's style is for Johnson but an adequate vehicle for an inferior burden. In the *Life of Swift:*

> This easy and safe conveyance of meaning it was Swift's desire to attain, and for having attained he deserves praise, though perhaps not the highest praise. For purposes merely didactick, when something is to be told that was not known before, it is the best mode, but against that inattention by which known truths are suffered to lie neglected it makes no provision; it instructs, but does not persuade.

In Boswell's *Life* Johnson says of those who like and those who dislike Swift's style: "Both agree that Swift has a good neat style; but one loves a neat style, another loves a style of more splendour." There are yet other passages where Johnson is less kind—where he explains in an unreserved, unmistakable, concrete manner, what he dislikes in Swift's writing. In the *Life of Swift* he says of *The Conduct of the Allies:*

> Surely, whoever surveys this wonder-working pamphlet with cool perusal will confess that its efficacy was supplied by the passions of its readers; that it operates by the mere weight of facts, with very little assistance from the hand that produced them.

Of the same pamphlet he had earlier said:

> Swift has told what he had to tell distinctly enough, but that is all. He had to count ten, and he has counted it right.

At Mrs. Thrale's once he argued with a gentleman on the same subject.

> At length you *must* allow me, said the gentleman, that there are *strong facts* in the account of the Four last Years of Queen Anne: "Yes surely Sir (replies Johnson), and so there are in the Ordinary of Newgate's account."

Plainness of fact, not as opposed to fiction, but as opposed to elaboration—this must be understood as the opposite of what Johnson admired in writing. Swift comes no nearer to merit by the inventions of *Gulliver's Travels.* "When once you have thought of big men and little men, it is very easy to do all the rest." What *Gulliver's Travels* and the "Ordinary of Newgate's account" have in common is that they deal with things, a constant succession of different things not different aspects of the same things. It is the difference between multiplication for range ("the prince and princess") and multiplication for emphasis ("the constituent and fundamental principle"). The "so many *things,* almost in an equal number of *words*" of Sprat had been no vain exhortation to Johnson's predecessors. It had become a real and conscious rule. Swift himself praised the style of the Brobdingnagians thus: "Their style is clear, masculine and smooth, but not florid; for they avoid nothing more than multiplying unnecessary words, or using various expressions." And this was precisely the aim of Johnson, to multiply words, to use various expressions, to deal not in things but in thoughts about things. In this he is nearer to the romantic essayists than to the neoclassic. His is the more meditative, more poetic style. It pauses and develops the aspects and relations of things, works them into a thought pattern, attracts into the pattern reflections of other things.

The need for elaboration was one of the consequences of the taste for generality. There were two kinds of subject matter: things, such as Swift dealt with, which had to be new things in order to claim attention; and general truths, which being general and true must be already known and which hence must be enforced or recommended. This enforcement or recommendation was the proper scope of literary art.

> The task of an author is, either to teach what is not known, or
> to recommend known truths by his manner of adorning them;
> either to let new light in upon the mind, and open new scenes
> to the prospect, or to vary the dress and situation of common
> objects, so as to give them fresh grace and more powerful at-
> tractions, to spread such flowers over the regions through which
> the intellect has already made its progress, as may tempt it to
> return, and take a second view of things hastily passed over or
> negligently regarded.

This occurs in *Rambler* No. 3, where Johnson is explaining the plan of his work—the second alternative, "to recommend known truths by his manner of adorning them." In *Adventurer* No. 115 we find this distinction between the modes of writing repeated. If an author "treats of science and demonstration," he must have a style clear, pure, nervous, and expressive." But "if his topicks be probable and persuasory," he must "recommend them by the superaddition of elegance and imagery . . . display the colours of varied diction, and pour forth the musick of modulated periods." In *Rambler* No. 152: "Among the criticks in history it is not contested whether truth ought to be preserved, but by what mode of diction it is best adorned."

It will be noted that Johnson is an ornamentalist, at least in his terminology. But it is likely that no great writer, or even able hack writer, was ever an ornamentalist in more than terminology. As a feat of composition or as a concrete critical state of mind, ornamentalism is perhaps impossible. When Johnson speaks of things and their ornamentation, we should have no difficulty in recognizing that he is talking about things and aspects of, or ideas about, things. This is all he can be talking about. Both the things and the ideas about them are included in what we call meaning. Since Johnson was not concerned with our particular problem, he was content to look on things, truths, or facts, as solid "meaning" (though he did not employ the

but one name proper to it (though one name may by turns do service for a number of ideas), then the dignity of the idea, that is, the difference of one idea from another, is asserted, and the correct basis established for a discussion of words and meaning. Thus:

> JOHNSON. "You may translate books of science exactly. You may also translate history, in so far as it is not embellished with oratory, which is poetical. Poetry, indeed, cannot be translated."

(This is no other than the Crocean view.) If different words do correspond to different ideas—different meanings—then follows the impossibility of translating works which deal in ideas rather than in facts. Poetry and poetic prose deal in ideas. There can be no doubt that Johnson considered his own prose as leaning toward the poetic. Another step he might have taken in his dignifying of the idea and through it the term, and this would have been the identifying of the idea with the thing and hence the multiplication of as many things as there are ideas and the belief in a different thing for each word. This sort of idealism of course he never yielded to explicitly, but he may have leaned toward it wistfully. In the *Preface to the Dictionary* he wrote:

> I am not yet so lost in lexicography, as to forget that *words are the daughters of earth, and that things are the sons of heaven.* Language is only the instrument of science, and words are but the signs of ideas: I wish, however, that the instrument might be less apt to decay, and that signs might be permanent, like the things which they denote.

And in a *Rambler:* "The pebble must be polished with care, which hopes to be valued as a diamond; and words ought surely to be laboured, when they are intended to stand for things." In an Idler: "Words are but the images of things." Certainly he did believe that words could have the weight of things, or more weight, and that it was such weight that the writer ought to wield. If "a new term was not introduced, but because the former was thought inadequate," then each different term must have a justification for its existence and for its appearance in a composition. If "constituent" and "fundamental" were created to correspond to different ideas and through these ideas to stand for things, then there was no fault in saying "the constituent and fundamental principle."

II

We have referred to and disqualified as a question of style Johnson's severe canon of correctness in vocabulary [elsewhere]. From the *Plan of a*

Dictionary and the *Preface* one has no trouble whatever in showing that Johnson said he detested the adulteration of English with foreign words and uses, particularly with French, which seemed to him the most insidious threat of his own day. He would not be reduced to "babble a dialect of France." Perhaps only a wavering distinction may be drawn between Johnson's objection to certain classes of words as incorrect, not English, and his objection to others as unfit for elegant composition, inexpressive of what he thought most worth expressing. And certainly correctness was for him one of the conditions of expressiveness. But an opinion about correctness is an opinion about the limitation of a language, about what liberties may be taken with a conventional medium of expression. This is to be distinguished from an opinion about how language may be most effectively used as an expressive medium, which is an opinion about style.

First we may notice what kind of word was stylistically objectionable to Johnson. "Low" is perhaps his most generic term of censure. He makes his use of the term very clear.

> We are all offended by low terms, but are not disgusted alike by the same compositions, because we do not all agree to censure the same terms as low. No word is naturally or intrinsically meaner than another; our opinion therefore of words, as of other things arbitrarily and capriciously established, depends wholly upon accident and custom. . . . Words become low by the occasions to which they are applied, or the general character of them who use them; and the disgust which they produce, arises from the revival of those images with which they are commonly united.

Or, as we might say today, low words are those which have low meanings. Since the meaning of words depends precisely upon "the occasions to which they are applied," we should have no difficulty in admitting that words applied to low occasions are to that degree low. Our essential quarrel with Johnson would be over what meanings should be called low, or whether any meaning is so low as to be irredeemable, whether, in fact, lowness or familiarity is not one of the elements that transform most readily into the poetic. When in the same *Rambler* Johnson goes on to pick out as low terms the *"dunnest* smoke of hell" and *"knife"* and *"peep through the blanket* of the dark," we know full well that our difference is not about diction but about the very center of meaning. What makes is possible for the question to seem one of diction is Johnson's habit, already noted, of speaking as if things were meaning, and diction (with its accompanying ideas) but the dress of meaning—or, more accurately, as if there were a part of thought that was central and determined, according to the things denoted by words, and this was meaning, while the connotation of the words, the ideas about things conveyed in the names given them, was not meaning. In this way it is quite possible to form a thorough-going theory of lowness in diction.

> Language is the dress of thought; and as the noblest mien or
> most graceful action would be degraded and obscured by a garb
> appropriated to the gross employments of rusticks or mechanicks,
> so the most heroick sentiments will lose their efficacy, and the
> most splendid ideas drop their magnificence, if they are conveyed
> by words used commonly upon low and trivial occasions, debased
> by vulgar mouths, and contaminated by inelegant applications.

And it follows that there is also a poetic diction, that is, a body of words never applied to low occasions and hence felt to be suited to the lofty occasions of poetry.

> There was . . . before the time of Dryden no poetical diction:
> no system of words at once refined from the grossness of domestick
> use and free from the harshness of terms appropriated to particular
> arts.

The concept of low diction and lofty diction and of low thoughts (or matter) and lofty thoughts (or matter)—four separate things—leads to some interesting consequences. It has to be conceded, for example, that some "thoughts by their native excellence secure themselves from violation, being such as mean language cannot express." Again, low diction is sometimes suitably employed when the matter is low. "Yet ne'er looks forward farther than his nose." Boswell "objected to the last phrase, as being low. JOHN-SON. 'Sir, it is intended to be low; it is satire. The expression is debased, to debase the character.' " And lofty diction—this may be debased by application to low matter. "To degrade the sounding words and stately constructions of Milton, by an application to the lowest and most trivial things [as in the *Splendid Shilling*], gratifies the mind with a momentary triumph over that grandeur which hitherto held its captives in admiration." On the other hand lofty diction may be successful in disguising low matter. "When the matter is low or scanty [as in Addison's *Battle of the Pigmies and Cranes, Barometer,* and *Bowling Green*] a dead language, in which nothing is mean because nothing is familiar, affords great conveniences; and by the sonsorous magnificence of Roman syllables the writer conceals penury of thought and want of novelty, often from the reader, and often from himself."

In the passage quoted above from the *Life of Dryden* "the grossness of
domestick use" is coupled with "the harshness of terms appropriated to
particular arts." Low terms and terms of art are condemned together. It is
even possible that many words were to Johnson objectionable on both counts.
The following passage which he quotes from Blackmore would seem to be
full of examples.

> I am not free of the Poets' Company, having never kissed . . .
> [their] governor's hands [. . .]: mine is therefore not so much as
> a permission-poem, but a downright interloper. Those gentlemen
> who [. . .] carry on their poetical trade in a joint stock would
> certainly do what they could to sink and ruin an unlicensed
> adventurer, notwithstanding I disturbed none of their factories
> nor imported any goods they had ever dealt in.

"Language such as Cheapside easily furnished," says Johnson in introducing
this passage. And he follows it with the laconic comment, "He had lived
in the city till he had learned its note." These terms of commerce were
objectionable to Johnson as such, and used in facetious analogy as they are,
they seem to us, as well as to him, expressions of a cheap meaning.

It had been part of the diversitarianism of the Renaissance, just as it
is part of romantic and modern local-color technique, to cultivate terms of
art. Ronsard spoke out for them. English Elizabethan plays are full of them.
Dryden and Milton were still using them—though at moments with rather
sour effect, and with misgivings on the part of Dryden. Rymer implied such
terms were "gross and trumpery." Pope criticizes their use in Dryden.
Addison criticizes it in both Milton and Dryden. From his "Dictionary of
Rhyme" Edward Bysshe omits without argument "all uncommon Words,
and that are of a generally unknown Signification; as the *Names* of Distempers
that are unusual; most of the terms of Arts and Sciences." Johnson's objection
to terms of art is something of his age, though something in which he
outdoes the age.

"Words too familiar or too remote," he continues in the passage from
the *Life of Dryden,* "defeat the purpose of a poet." And of the second case
he explains: "Words to which we are nearly strangers, whenever they occur,
draw that attention on themselves which they should transmit to things."
In another part of the *Life of Dryden* he said: "It is a general rule in poetry
that all appropriated terms of art should be sunk in *general* expressions,
because poetry is to speak an universal language." The italics are mine. Here
we find the notion of generality invested with another value for Johnson—
that of comprehensibility. Swift's particularities about the reign of Queen

Anne were poor writing because as particularities they lacked the significance or importance of general truth. Push particularity further—to the degree of technicality—and to insignificance is added incomprehensibility. Or, since technicality is but an extreme of particularity, incomprehensibility is an extreme of insignificance. Johnson's objection to technical terms in poetic use is clearly expressed again and again in the *Lives,* and exemplified. From Dryden's *Annus Mirabilis* he quotes three stanzas, underlining the nautical terms. It will suffice to quote but two lines here:

> Some the *gall'd* ropes with dawby *marling* bind,
> Or sear-cloth masts with strong *tarpawling* coats.

"I suppose," says Johnson, "here is not one term which every reader does not wish away."

What Johnson disliked in poetry there is every reason to believe he disliked also in the creative prose of the general and moral essay. Even in essays of technical literary criticism he strove to deny himself the use of critical terms. In the first of the *Ramblers* on Milton's versification he realizes the difficulty of the feat but resolves upon it.

> I am desirous to be generally understood, and shall therefore studiously decline the dialect of grammarians; though, indeed, it is always difficult, and sometimes scarcely possible, to deliver the precepts of an art, without the terms by which the peculiar ideas of that art are expressed, and which had not been invented but because the language already in use was insufficient. If therefore I shall sometimes seem obscure, may be imputed to this voluntary interdiction, and to a desire of avoiding that offence which is always given by unusual words.

In the last *Rambler* he ranked "criticism . . . among the subordinate and instrumental arts." He said elsewhere: "An art cannot be taught but by its proper terms, but it is not always necessary to teach the art."

It is a truth verging on paradox that Johnson's favorite words, the "philosophic" or scientific words which we discussed [previously], should be special and technical just as much as the hated words of art. Both terms of art and philosophic terms have a tone of recondite currency; they suggest the accuracy of a special familiarity or erudition. This much "marling" and "tarpawling" have in common with "adscitious" and "equiponderant." Johnson himself is aware of the affinity in the following important passage from the *Idler* in defence of "hard words."

> The state of every . . . art is the same; as it is cursorily surveyed or accurately examined, different forms of expression become proper. In morality it is one thing to discuss the niceties of the casuist, and another to direct the practice of common life. In agriculture, he that instructs the farmer to plough and sow, may convey his notions without the words which he would find necessary in explaining to philosophers the process of vegetation.

Here "morality" as well as "agriculture" is considered as an art, and the experts in agriculture are "philosophers."

The same passage is further important as it suggests the question how Johnson himself thought he was using words in his essays. Was he discussing the "niceties of the casuist" in philosophic terms, or was he directing the "practice of common life" in common terms? The answer must be that he conceived himself as doing neither simply, but as combining the means of the former with the purpose of the latter: that is, he was turning philosophic diction to the purpose of moral instruction or discussion of general truths. We have his own word for it, unmistakably, in the last *Rambler*.

> When common words were less pleasing to the ear, or less distinct in their signification, I have familiarized the terms of philosophy, by applying them to popular ideas.

Johnson, therefore, approved philosophic terms in elegant prose, though terms of art he did not. The antithesis lies in the various degrees of generality and hence comprehensibility, significance and dignity, which the various arts, sciences, or philosophies, possess. If we construct a scale of four examples, sailing, agriculture, chemistry, morals, it is impossible to say that the terms of any upper group of these sciences would have been for Johnson "philosophic" and those of the lower, "terms of art." But it may be said that he would have tended to use the terms of the upper end of the scale, accepting the whole vocabulary of morals, picking and rejecting in chemistry and agriculture, and shunning nautical terms, as he wished that Dryden and Milton had done. The point is that the less a set of principles and facts and their terms were the business of practical and active men and the more they were the object only of study and the creation of learning, the more generally comprehensible and applicable were the terms—and of course the more worthy of the attention of learned or intelligent men outside the particular science. Further, and not so obviously, the comprehensibility of such scientific terms had a kind of inevitability and sanction—whereas the words growing from the rub of active life, the need to refer to this or that thing or part of a special business, were adventitious and bastard; they came from without the authority and tradition. "These accidental and colloquial senses are the disgrace of language, and the plague of commentators," Johnson once wrote. And while he was not referring here to terms of art, the association of "accidental" and "colloquial" is telling. He made this even clearer in the *Preface to the Dictionary*.

> Of the laborious and mercantile part of the people, the diction
> is in a great measure casual and mutable; many of their terms
> are formed for some temporary or local convenience, and though
> current at certain times and places, are in others utterly unknown.
> This fugitive cant, which is always in a state of increase or decay,
> cannot be regarded as any part of the durable materials of a
> language, and therefore must be suffered to perish with other
> things unworthy of preservation.

If meanings which arose colloquially, from the actual use of men, were "accidental," what kind of meanings were not accidental? What kind existed by prescription or inherently? One must presume that Johnson had in mind meanings fixed or derivable from the etymology of words—that is, meanings determined by *ancient* rather than by *recent* colloquial use. These were meanings so long established that they were capable of modulation, combination and extension into new meanings that demanded recognition, were not accidental, but inherent in the word roots. "It is my serious opinion," Johnson once said, "that our living languages must be formed quite slavishly on the model of the classics, if our writings are to endure." This attitude of Johnson's is part of an attitude general among eighteenth-century grammarians, that language is a logical institution, pristinely perfect but debased through usage and needing to be restored and preserved by reason. Johnson is here closely akin to Horne Tooke, who would by etymology reduce all parts of speech to nouns and verbs; to George Campbell, who attempts (despite his disavowal of the principle) to determine by etymology the "proper signification" of words.

The meaning of a word like "marling" depended on the usage of sailors, and hence was accidental, limited, insignificant, undignified, and incapable of modulation and extension. The meaning of a word like "adscititious" depended on a form of the Latin verb *adsciscere,* which in turn was an inceptive form of the verb *scire,* whose meaning was one of the most basic and simple of our ideas. Such a word as "adscititious" may itself not have been current

in any science, but it might have been or ought to have been; it was formed
on the pattern of scientific words; it was a term of the most universal science,
that of generality, *Allerlei-Wissenschaft;* it was of the native vocabulary of
philosophers. "Marling" was a word which many might understand but
which few needed or ought to understand. "Adscititious" was a word which
few might understand, but which all should understand—all who knew the
roots of the language and could put two and two together. For the same
reason the learned man might invent his "three or four" words, provided
they were of the philosophic language, not inventions at all, but extensions.

> Et nova fictaque nuper habebunt verba fidem si
> Graeco fonte cadant, parce detorta.

And it followed that philosophic words, being of inherent literal validity,
should have a strong claim to metaphorical use, and hence that their currency
in the language should increase. "As by the cultivation of various sciences,
a language is amplified, it will be more furnished with words deflected from
their original sense; the geometrician will talk of a courtier's zenith, or the
eccentrick virtue of a wild hero, and the physician of sanguine expectations
and phlegmatick delays." Johnson himself, as we have seen in our analysis
of his writing, relied continually on both the literal and figurative use of
philosophical diction, on "inundations" and "momentaneous excursions,"
on "catharticks of vice, or lenitives of passion." As Boswell puts it, "He
delighted to express familiar thoughts in philosophical language."

More simply Johnson accounted for his usage with the formula: big
words for big meaning. "He that thinks with more extent than another will
want words of larger meaning." Thus he expresses it in the *Idler* in defence
of "hard words." And Mrs. Piozzi writes; "though he was accused of using
big words as they are called, it was only when little ones would not express
his meaning as clearly, or when perhaps the elevation of the thought would
have been disgraced by a dress less superb." Johnson's notion is echoed at
length by Boswell in conversation with a young Scotch friend.

> He mentioned the Ridicule . . . called *Lexiphanes,* written by
> one Campbell. "Sir," said I, "nothing can be more unfair. Mr.
> Johnson's language is suitable to his sentiment. He gives large
> words because he has large ideas. If Campbell clothes little paultry
> ideas with these big words, to be sure the effect must be ridic-
> ulous. The late King of Prussia's tall Regiment looked very stately
> with their large grenadier caps. If Campbell had taken these caps
> and clapped them on the heads of a parcel of blackguard children

in the street, it would be highly ridiculous; but does that prove anything against the caps when properly applied? No, Sir, Mr. Johnson has gigantick thoughts, and therefore he must be allowed gigantick words." This was quite in Mr. Johnson's own stile.

And "We may," says Boswell also, "with the utmost propriety, apply to his learned style that passage of Horace, a part of which he has taken as the motto to his Dictionary." A smaller part of the same passage had been taken already by Johnson as the motto of *Rambler* No. 88, on Milton's versification. And part of this we may quote:

> Audebit quaecunque minus splendoris habebunt,
> Aut sine pondere erunt, et honore indigna ferentur,
> Verba movere loco.

and with it the translation by Creech, which Johnson adds:

> what words appear
> Too light and trivial, or too weak to bear
> The weighty sense, nor worth the reader's care,
> Shake off.

For the big thoughts and the big words the proper organ was the big voice, a part of Johnson's technique well recognized by his contemporaries. "His *bow-wow way*," Lord Pembroke called it. Boswell described it more respectfully. "He had a loud voice, and a slow deliberate utterance, which no doubt gave some additional weight to the sterling metal of his conversation." And in a note he offers another figure:

> The *Messiah,* played upon the *Canterbury organ,* is more sublime than when played upon an inferior instrument. . . . *While therefore Dr. Johnson's sayings are read, let his manner be taken along with them.*

On the island of Skye, Ulinish heard Johnson talk of tanning and milk and making whey and said: "He is a great orator, Sir; it is musick to hear this man speak."

FREDERICK A. POTTLE

The Life of Boswell

"I will venture to say," wrote James Boswell at the beginning of his great biography of Samuel Johnson, "that he will be seen in this work more completely than any man who has ever yet lived." The claim thus confidently asserted has stood against all possibility of assault for a century and a half, but it must now be called in question. The recovery during the last twenty years of Boswell's own journal and the mass of documents which, with it, made up what he characteristically called his archives, has put him in the unique position he claimed for Johnson. It is now James Boswell whom we are in a position to know more thoroughly than any other human being. Pepys's diary is unsurpassable for cool frankness and the accurate and lavish recording of historical detail, but it covers something less than ten years of his life and is not remarkable for self-analysis. Rousseau's *Confessions* are unsurpassable for self-analysis, but they were written from memory when he was past fifty and show everywhere the distortion to which recall is subject if its not controlled by contemporary records. Boswell's journal stands between the poles of Pepys and Rousseau. In certain important respects it yields to both: it is less even in texture than Pepys, being fragmentary and passing abruptly from brief entries which are hardly more than a string of names to entries of several pages. But it is as frank as Pepys, and, like Pepys, is a trustworthy contemporary record, not remolded by the interests of a later stage of development. And it covers the whole of Boswell's adult life. It is less eloquent and piercing than Rousseau, but it shows a comparable skill in the dissection of motives, with a superior power of detachment.

From *The Yale Review* 35 (Spring 1946). © 1945–1946 by Yale University.

The Boswellian materials now placed at our disposal are so extensive and varied as to embarrass and perplex the biographer. A chronicle biography is rendered unnecessary by the journal, which, with editorial patching here and there, furnishes a day-by-day record from his twenty-first to his fifty-fourth year. Some principle of selection, some device for focussing and interpreting the chronicle must be adopted. Several biographies of Boswell could be written from different points of view; no doubt several will be written. Since Boswell's record contains so much that is joyously animal, one might suppress the painful and disgusting aspects of it and give a selective account of his caperings and carousals: Boswell the Satyr. Or one could reverse the process of selection, fix upon all that is abnormal, morbid, and perverse in the evidence and give the world an extended clinical analysis: Boswell the Neurotic. Or one might present him as the man whose honest confession and unflinching self-analysis show us ourselves: Boswell the Revealer of the Unregenerate Human Heart. All these have their attractions, but surely there is another approach that should be made first. What Boswell needs most of all at present is a biographer who will assume that he is writing the life of a great man of letters, who will come to his task just as though he were writing a life of Burns or Dickens: Boswell the Author.

But clearly an author of an unusual sort, an author whose variety of greatness has been imperfectly analyzed. Macaulay more than a hundred years ago stated and did much to fix the fundamental paradox from which Boswellian criticism has been unable to escape: "His fame is great; and it will, we have no doubt, be lasting; but it is fame of a peculiar kind, and indeed marvellously resembles infamy." Ask anyone to make a list of the ten greatest prose works in English and the chances are high that the *Life of Johnson* will be included; ask the same man to name the ten greatest authors of English prose and he will never think of Boswell.

This, as I have said, is sheer paradox, for one can hardly imagine any proposition more completely self-evident than that the author of a great book is a great author. Either the case of Boswell has not been thought through and people are giving wrong explanations of sound intuitions, or else the general impression as to the relation in which he stands to his book is mistaken in matters of fact.

Now that we have recovered Boswell's journal and a portion of the other materials on which the *Life of Johnson* is based, we can indeed say with finality that the general conception of Boswell's method is mistaken. In assigning him his degree of literary merit readers of the past have tended to think of him as little more than a capable stenographer with no sense of good manners or reticence. The essential parts of the *Life*—the portions that

differentiate it from hundreds of capably written but forgotten biographies—
are Johnson's conversations. These conversations really occurred. Boswell,
it was assumed, heard them and wrote them down in a notebook on the
spot. His artistic activity in this view consisted of nothing more exacting
than trimming them and fitting them together, something, we are asked
to suppose, that any really capable stenographer could do.

A man who had read many shorthand transcriptions would decline to
suppose any such thing, but it is unnecessary to qualify this view, for it is
totally wrong. We know now that Boswell never recorded conversations on
the spot. He worked them up days, months, or even years afterwards from
brief and cryptic notes jotted down in the privacy of his own room soon
after the events described. Very little rote memory was involved in the
process. For the conversations elaborated long after the events, he had merely
written cues containing a good deal of circumstantial detail, a fading memory
of a few more details, and a mental organism unparalleled among biographers
and historians for its power to reconstruct the past selectively and vividly
within the strict limits of historical fact. This construction was, in the full
sense of the term, imaginative: may, in fact, be compared with the imaginative activity of Shakespeare when he turned the hints of Plutarch into a
play. The difference (it is the difference between fiction and imaginative
recall) is that though both were using their imaginations, they were subject
to very different controls. Shakespeare's source was a book which recorded
transactions in which he had played no personal part, in which, for that
matter, Plutarch had played no personal part. No detailed memory of the
events or the personages rose to direct or limit him. Consequently, the
control of history was of the broadest and most general sort, the more
important control being his own artistic preferences. It was not important
that his play should correspond in any thoroughgoing way with historical
circumstance. Boswell was creating, but as he created he remembered; that
is, he was able to refer every stage of his construction to a whole active mass
of organized past reactions or experience. His picture had not merely to be
lifelike and dramatic, it had also to be "true." That is, it had to keep within
the bounds of historical circumstance.

General criticism has been wrong in not assigning to Boswell a high
degree of imaginative power, in making him merely a kind of recording
machine. This has been due partly to an ignorance of facts that could not
hitherto be known, partly to a failure to think through the implications of
the extraordinary reputation of his book with critics of all degrees of austerity.
But without a change in our reigning definitions of what constitutes literary
greatness, I am not sure that a recognition of Boswell's imaginative powers

will make much difference. When we name great books we trust to a direct impression which depends very little on definition; when we name great authors we trust to formulas. And our present formulas assign a decisive role to invention. When a man creates a great fiction, a fiction in which his characters say wise and witty things, we properly give him credit not only for the power of expression that makes the whole vivid and absorbing but also for personal powers of wit and wisdom. When a man by similar exercise of the imagination presents us with dramatic dialogues filled with wit and wisdom which we know he was constructing with the aid of memory, wit and wisdom which we know he could not have invented, we feel that he deserves a more qualified kind of praise. And, other things being equal, he does. In *imaginative* power Boswell is the peer of Scott and Dickens; in *inventive* power he is nowhere in comparison with them. But it is wise to remember that outside the realm of theory other things are never equal. A great work of literature need not have in a high degree all the values which we demand in the very highest. There is only one quality which a work of literature must have in a high degree and that is the power to heighten consciousness. Beyond that it wins its way by a process of barter. Great power of expression in practice can make up for comparative weakness of moral content; profound moral value can make up for comparative coarseness of expressive technique; great power of imaginative realization can make up for lack of invention. Our academic identification of literature with fiction is narrow and unserviceable in that it leads so often to judgments of the brain which belie the testimony of the heart. The intuition which has placed the *Life of Johnson* among the greatest of English prose works is sounder than the critical theory which finds no place of honor for its author.

It is in that fashion, or one like it, that the complex of critical paradoxes surrounding the name of Boswell must be handled. We should first look to the facts to see if they have been correctly apprehended, and then we should consider whether an explanation other than that in vogue will not remove the paradoxes without denying validity to the critical intuitions. Since the essence of paradox is simplicity, we should expect our preferred explanations to be more complicated than those which they replace.

"Look to the facts to see if they have been correctly apprehended." Has anyone ever stopped to think how slender a basis Macaulay had for his generalizations? The biographer of Boswell now has at his disposal Boswell's own journal extending from 1761 to 1794, a vast autobiography crammed with detail. At least nine hundred of his letters are known; over five hundred of them have been published, and the bulk of the remainder have been calendared. Over thirteen hundred letters to Boswell have been catalogued.

It is my impression that when Macaulay in 1831 first set himself to the characterization of Boswell in a slashing review of the edition of the *Life of Johnson* brought out that year by John Wilson Croker, the Tory politican and essayist who had trimmed him so painfully in the House of Commons, he had practically no source of information concerning Boswell except Croker's text, which presented in the notes a small quantity of biographical fact and a larger quantity of orally transmitted gossip, much of it apocryphal. Croker found and printed, I think, not more than a dozen of Boswell's letters, and the best of these were not in the edition of 1831. When in 1856 Macaulay returned again to Boswell in the "Essay on Johnson," the situation had been altered only by the publication of the diary of Fanny Burney, who had first-hand knowledge but is a treacherous authority, for the Boswell of her brilliant and amusing sketches has been simplified and exaggerated by the satirical gift which made her eminent as a writer of novels, The work which for the first time laid a solid foundation for a biography—the first printing of the confidential letters of Boswell to his most intimate friend, W. J. Temple—did, indeed, appear in the same year as Macaulay's essay but too late for him to make use of it.

It is sometimes possible to deduce the character of an author satisfactorily from his publications, without recourse to outside information. One would naturally suppose that if there ever was a man of whom this would be true, it would be Boswell. It is my wish to resolve the paradoxes of Boswellian criticism, not to add to them, and I therefore regret the necessity of recording my conviction that the *Life of Johnson* by itself gives a very imperfect and misleading notion of its author. Boswell was all his life a conscious and irrepressible exhibitionist; like others not unknown to fame he thought bad publicity better than none. He displayed himself in improvised Corsican costume at the Shakespeare Jubilee of 1769; he appeared on the top of a hearse at an execution at Tyburn; he knelt and kissed the Shakespeare manuscripts, recently forged by a seventeen-year-old lawyer's apprentice, William Henry Ireland, audibly thanking God that he had lived to see the day. (Add: he sent accounts of the first two performances to the newspapers.) Though better inhibited mortals could and did call him a fool for such posturings, they were aware that they were impeaching his judgment, not necessarily his intelligence. We all know shrewd and brilliant men who have doubts about the finality of the injunction that when one becomes a man one should put away childish things. But there is inherent in the very plan of the *Life of Johnson* a kind of exhibitionism that is not generally characteristic of Boswell and has always looked like sheer fatuousness to people who have not had information that the book does not contain. Boswell himself in his "Dedication" warned his readers that they ought to suppose that he knew what he was about, but in vain. You cannot present conversations without giving both sides, and the majority of the conversations he had to record were *tête-à-têtes* between himself and Johnson. They were real conversations, everyday conversations, and there was seldom anything in his share in them that deserved publication on its own account. In many of them he was the butt of Johnson's sarcastic wit, as all but one or two of Johnson's friends were if they insisted on opposing him in argument. Now there is abundant reason to conclude that Boswell was vain, that he welcomed any excuse to magnify himself, especially to proclaim his intimacy with great men. There is a good deal of what might be called peripheral vanity in the *Life of Johnson*. But in the central matter of Johnson's conversations the decision as to what to include and what to reject was artistic to a really remarkable degree. Boswell goes in because without Boswell speaking directly and animatedly there can be no drama, only a set of disjointed apothegms. But in the Johnsonian drama Boswell plays a consistently minor role: Boswell presents no part of Boswell that is not pertinent to the dramatic effect. Compare the *Life of Johnson* with another vivid book written by a vain man, the *Life of Shelley* by Shelley's college chum and intimate associate, Hogg. It is not too much to say that Hogg's so-called biography is an autobiography of Thomas Jefferson Hogg with numerous glances at Percy Bysshe Shelley. It takes only a brief sampling of Boswell's journal to see how much good Boswellian matter could have got into the *Life* if its author had not exercised a remarkable degree of restraint. His tact is never so conspicuous as when he is presenting the scenes in which Johnson retorted on him. Yet his refusal to spoil a joke by explaining it has resulted in people's concluding that he was simply too dimwitted to know when he was being made a fool of. "I have been undoubtedly informed," he says, "that many persons, especially in distant quarters, not penetrating enough into Johnson's character, so as to understand his mode of treating his friends, have arraigned my judgment [in my terminology this would be "intelligence"], instead of seeing that I was sensible of all that they could observe."

Furthermore, as everyone knows, he had found early in his association with Johnson that some of Johnson's most memorable remarks could be elicited by trifling or perverse questions. It is natural to assume, if we have only the *Life* to go on, that he pestered every distinguished man of his acquaintance with questions about the care of new-born infants and the uses of dried orange peel. A reading in the journal of his conversations with David Hume, Voltaire, Rousseau, Pasquale Paoli, General of the Corsicans, and Lord Kames, the redoubtable Scots litterateur and judge, will soon dispel that notion. Boswell's questions always took their color from his interlocutor. If they were odd or perverse it was because he had found an area of oddity or perversity to explore.

And the genuine self-revelation that does appear in the *Life*—the gratuitous and garrulous flaunting of the Boswellian ego—is not always representative of Boswell at his best. It has been too little realized that though the greater part of the materials were safely recorded during Boswell's prime, the book was written in his decline. The careful reader of the journal can detect a permanent loss of elasticity in his mind after 1785, not a decline of intellectual power but a marked stiffness of accommodation. During the whole period of the composition of the *Life* he was fighting with frustration and succumbing to despair. His daydream of success at the English bar, so long and ardently pursued, clearly revealed itself as a mirage; his wife died slowly and painfully; his last hope of political preferment was brutally beaten down. The self-assertion of the *Life* is more than mere vanity, it is a defensive mechanism. We forget too, unless we read the journal, that the *Life* was written and published in the awful shadow of the French Revolution. No man was ever more robust in his sympathies or more tolerant of opposed opinion than Boswell in his best years, but the *Life* contains a distressing number of stiff and angry notes, the object of which is not so much to affirm his own political and religious orthodoxy as to insult those who differ with him. He was terrified at what might happen and no longer had the energy to repel his fears. Had the *Life* been written ten years earlier, hardly one of those extravagantly Tory passages which gave Macaulay his animus would have been in it.

What, then, is the result of supplementing the *Life* with the vast stores of information now at our command? What differences do the new materials make?

First and foremost, they ought not to make much difference in our view of Boswell's vices, but they seem to make a great difference. We have always known that he was a drunkard, and the journal makes this explicit. We can see now (what we should have been able to guess) that the progress of his enslavement was gradual: that in his youth he drank little; that he first took to heavy drinking in the convivial society of young advocates of his set where excess was a commonplace; and that his addiction to alcohol became morbid only after an inner conviction of failure had established itself. I do not know whether he can properly at any time be called an alcoholic; certainly he never—even at the end of his life—resorted to solitary drinking. He was a social drunkard who came increasingly to look on a dinner invitation as an excuse for intoxication. Good humor and high spirits were his most valuable contributions to social gatherings, and he came more and more to depend on alcohol for their release.

Nor does the journal really change much the conception of his sexual morals which emerged with the unexpurgated publication of his letters to Temple in 1924. He was—it is best to put it bluntly and without palliation—given both before and after his marriage to sexual indulgence of the most gross and venal sort. He was not a Don Juan but a whoremonger, one whose "wayward but simple inclinations," as Geoffrey Scott has said, "led him down paths where joys were undelayed and vanity secure from rebuff." But here the detailed and usually contrite records in the journal *seem* to make a great difference. It is actually not a matter of morals but of taboo. Say that a man is a rake, implying that that means habitual association with prostitutes but not *saying* so; then say that a man is a rake, give the details of several of his sexual escapades, and add that he contracted gonorrhea— there is not a grain of moral difference in the two cases, but unless one is very alert and careful in his judgments, the first will seem venial and the second very bad indeed. Boswell does give details (though within the decorum of the eighteenth century) and he records many attacks of venereal disease. We are not accustomed to finding in autobiographies the kind of record he has provided, and it shocks us more than in reason it should. Moral revulsion is proper, but what we take to be moral revulsion is really based in large part on considerations that are not moral at all. It may be that the present state of public speech makes it impossible to analyze this matter frankly and objectively without alienating the reader's sympathy: I should hope not. It is certain that an honest biographer can neither omit all mention of it nor treat it flippantly.

We have, as a matter of fact, a parallel case in which the world's judgment has at last been properly adjusted. Robert Burns shared both of Boswell's major vices; indeed, if we had a full journal of his life, it would resemble Boswell's strikingly. His intemperance and incontinence are abundantly established, and no serious critic would think of trying to explain them away or would even feel moved to palliate them. But the writer on Burns—thanks to a developed tradition of sound criticism—is no longer able to forget for a moment that he is dealing with a formidable literary artist. He may speak of Burns's frailties of conduct as severely as he pleases, but he is bound to respect the qualities of his mind.

The great difference that the new Boswell material does make is to render untenable any simple formula for handling him. Most of the Macaulayan adjectives are properly applicable, but one must be very careful to tie them up to the right portions of the evidence. He was one of the most complex literary characters on record, combining in uneasy equilibrium a host of contradictory traits. The easy way out is to say that he thought he was, or pretended to be, this and was really that. Nothing is farther from the truth. He was a well instructed and sincerely religious man with an unusual capacity for worship, and he was also a notable fornicator. He savored as few others have the delights of intellectual conversation, and he was a sensualist. He was weak of will, and he sat up all night through four nights in one week to record Johnson's conversation. He loved Scotland deeply, and he preferred to live in England. He was inordinately proud of his ancestry and his status as a gentleman, and he associated with the lowest of low people. He was an affectionate husband, painfully dependent on his wife, and he was unfaithful to her and kept her sitting up for him when he knew she was mortally ill. He was a thoughtful and indulgent father who found it difficult to endure his children's company. He was dissipated and restless, and he carried on an extensive legal practice. He was often gloomy to the point of suicide, and Mrs. Thrale gave him a perfect score in good humor. (Johnson got zero.) He was stately and Spaniard-like in his bearing, and he played the clown with or without provocation. He was proud and he deferred to Johnson. He was independent and he licked Lonsdale's boots. He did and said many foolish things but he was not a fool.

I have put it that way because the shortcomings of the English language make it necessary, but of course Boswell *was* a fool in a quite legitimate sense, a sense that Johnson employed freely. He was the kind of fool we have in mind when we say, "I don't see how Jones could be such a fool." The condemnation implies a compliment. We mean by it, "I don't see how Jones, whom I know to be an intelligent man, could make such a mistake in practical judgment." The biographer of Boswell must be clear and must make clear to others that when he calls Boswell a fool he is concerned with his judgment or his will and not with his intellect. A great author may make bad choices and be silly in his conduct, but he must by definition have powers of mind adequate for the production of his works. Boswell did not have a great intellect, but he had a good one. The proof is the *Life of Johnson* itself, a proof so obvious that it is always overlooked. If he was no stenographer, he had not only to understand the things that Johnson said, but also to reconstruct them in his own mind from the very scanty hints that his notes afforded. Those conversations have great intellectual range and are sometimes of considerable subtlety. Though he was incapable of inventing them by himself (that is, though he lacked the original creative power of Johnson), the easy and delighted comprehension which his dramatic record shows at every point can be explained only by assuming that he had a mind that stretched parallel to Johnson's throughout the whole range of the topics discussed.

The inference is inescapable and ought to be decisive, but if more proof were called for, it could be found in the testimony of those of his contemporaries who really knew him; it is not difficult to show that when they called him a fool (as they did) they were expressing surprise that a man of his parts should so demean himself. Boswell was a lawyer, who for the twenty years of his association with the Scottish bar practised his profession with complete regularity and a fair degree of assiduity. He never attained a commanding reputation at the bar but he kept up a competent practice— better, it may be added, than Walter Scott, who practised in the same courts for fourteen years. It would be possible, after a glance at the half dozen cases reported in the *Life of Johnson,* to conclude that he was seldom trusted with a really sound brief, but the induction would have a rather narrow base. One might, indeed, suspect that those cases were referred to Johnson not as typical but precisely because they were bad; because Boswell, having exhausted his own powers of sophistry, felt the need of help from the master. We can, if we choose, investigate several hundred more that he tried, and can read a large number of his printed legal papers. I have made only a sampling, but have reason to suppose that the sampling is fair and indicates clearly enough the conclusions that would emerge from a wider survey. Though criminal pleadings formed only a small part of his business, he did sometimes exert himself strenuously and indiscreetly for clients with desperately bad cases who had appealed to his sympathies. (He sometimes even won their acquittal.) The bulk of his work, however, from first to last, was in straightforward humdrum litigations concerning property. In these, assuming as we ought that the decisions of the judges of the Court of Session were sound, he was more often on the "right" than on the "wrong" side. I am not qualified to judge the extent of his legal knowledge and am willing to credit his own admission that it was nothing extraordinary, but his legal papers, judged simply as arguments, are luminous, ingenious, and sober. One of them drew special praise in open court from Lord President Dundas, who said it was drawn "with moderation, precision, and firmness." "I have not seen," he added, "a paper that pleased me more." Lord Mansfield (the Chief Justice) praised Boswell for his speech at the bar of the House of Lords in one of those "bad" cases recorded in the *Life of Johnson.* Lord Thurlow (the Chancellor) praised him at the same bar for another speech. That Boswell had constant and respectable legal business for twenty years does not, of course, prove that he was a great lawyer, but it does prove that he was *compos mentis.* Legal agents, who have a considerable stake in the cases they manage, do not continue for so long to employ an advocate of weak and diseased intellect.

If we are puzzled by conflicting testimony about a man's character and want really to know what we should think about him, we consult the men who know him best—that is, we do if we have reason to respect *their* judgment. The men who knew Boswell best—Sir William Forbes, Johnson, Paoli, Sir Joshua Reynolds, Edmond Malone, John Courtenay—never disparage his intellect. They deplore his restless exhibitionism and misplaced ambition, his drinking and drabbing (concerning which, it should be added, they were completely informed), they are sometimes fretted by his demands for sympathy and wearied by his boisterousness, but they unite in considering him a uniquely pleasant companion, one whose friendship is to be sought and cultivated, not merely because of his infectious good humor and appealing helplessness but also because of the interesting qualities of his mind. Forbes, shrewd and successful banker, more highly respected for probity and public spirit than any other man in Edinburgh; Paoli, distinguished general and lawgiver of a nation; Johnson, great author and moralist; Reynolds, most honored painter of the century; Malone, one of the greatest of Shakesperian scholars; Courtenay, man of fashion and politician, the most dreaded wit in the House of Commons—these form a varied and very respectable jury. Nobody is under the necessity of lifting Boswell to the extent of feeling that he would have chosen him for a personal friend, even though these men did. Such choices are legitimately arbitrary. But a biographer who professes an intention to weigh historical evidence must consider their verdict more significant than that of the poet Gray, who never met him, or Horace Walpole, who may have met him half a dozen times, or of the host of contemporary newspaper writers and satirists to whom he was merely the author of two books whose unusual method invited ridicule.

I began with the statement that we have reached the time when the great Boswellian paradox must yield to a more complicated kind of analysis. May I end with one illustration of the patient and relativistic way in which particular Boswellian problems must be dissected and laid out for judgment? I have selected what is probably the hardest of the lot, one of those minor writings of Boswell which tempt even the most sympathetic critic to consider him a fool in every sense of the word: the *jeu d'esprit No Abolition of Slavery,* which was published just before the *Life of Johnson.* For Boswell to write verse at all was foolish; he did it badly. For him, even under a technical veil of anonymity, to glory in some obscure amatory adventure was foolish. For him to use this adventure as a figure for introducing arguments in a deeply serious debate on the abolition of the slave trade was worse than foolish. For him to print the strange farrago was, in view of his literary pretensions, the most foolish act of all. We know from the abundant evidence of the journal and letters that when he was called on to analyze a difficult situation he could generally be counted on to do it fairly, shrewdly, in an adult fashion, with a minimum of self-deception. What he could not be counted on to do in certain areas was to follow consistently the course of action which his analysis showed to be appropriate. *Video meliora proboque, deteriora sequor* ("I see and approve the better action, but I perform the worse") was a test he once quoted and could have quoted many times more. There was no department of his behavior in which he was more likely to sin knowingly against decorum than in the publication of occasional verses which were quite unworthy of his genius. The complacency of his references indicates pretty certainly that he did not know how unworthy they were (prose men are often bad judges of their own performances in verse), but if he had known it he would have printed just the same. All this shows that he woefully lacked good practical judgment, the kind of judgment that should keep any man from writing a compromising or abusive letter—or at least from posting it. So far we shall set him down a fool. But it is not safe to jump the whole way and conclude that a man who in 1791 argued against the abolition of the slave trade was convicting himself of feeble-mindedness. The *ideas* concerning slavery which the pamphlet embodies can be called imbecile only if one is prepared to convict of imbecility the great majority of the British Parliament in 1791, including nearly the entire bench of bishops. Boswell's poem was printed and circulated just before Wilberforce's motion to bring in a bill to abolish the trade was to come up in the House of Commons. The motion was rejected, 163 to 88. After being defeated again and again in both houses, it finally passed in 1807, twelve years after Boswell's death.

The matter is of biographical importance because a too hasty and unhistorical reading of *No Abolition of Slavery* would be likely to make anyone think that all Boswell's talk about liberty (especially in *An Account of Corsica*) was sheer speculative moonshine. Actually his behavior on this point was laudably consistent. He supported the rebels in Corsica practically by raising a subscription and sending them a considerable shipment of artillery and gunpowder. He supported the rebels in America by firm, manly, and outspoken criticism of the policy of the government, which was as far as he could go without absolutely incurring the charge of treason. A sincere belief in the policy of self-determination for civilized political groups (which was what he meant by "liberty") does not necessarily entail a belief in the immediate abolition of the status of slavery for African savages. There is nothing original in his views on the subject: they are simply the respectable conservative views of his time, as a glance at the debates in Parliament will show. Those same arguments were to be advanced in the United States for seventy-five years more by men whom we have a right to call mistaken but should hesitate to call fools.

The importance of all this separation of epithets is that it concerns, as few other guiding principles do, the really central issue, Boswell as Author. The nature and degree of Boswell's practical follies need to be frankly exposed, for they are pertinent to the story of his troubled and unhappy life. Literary criticism is not much concerned with them. The method of paradox was never a good one and should not have been tolerated so long. The method of defense served a necessary purpose in persuading scholars and men of letters that an author too generally held in contempt was worth their serious attention, but it is now defeating itself. Interest produced knowledge, and we now know far too much to engage in special pleading with any hope of success. The present-day biographer will suppress nothing and will feel defense to be an impertience. He will take the final step, which is merely to assume that Boswell, as a great literary artist, is to be treated exactly like his peers.

WALTER JACKSON BATE

The Treachery of the Human Heart
and the Stratagems of Defense

The majestic opening of *The Vanity of Human Wishes* pictures "wav'ring man, *betray'd* by vent'rous pride," lost on paths, dreary and monotonous as well as puzzling, where he "shuns fancied ills, or chases airy good." It then moves on to suggest the massive scale of the intense, blindly destructive hopes, ambitions, and enmities that "helpless man" begins almost unintentionally to project, noting

> How nations sink, by darling schemes oppress'd,
> When Vengeance listens to the fool's request.
> Fate wings with ev'ry wish th' afflictive dart . . .
> With fatal heat impetuous courage glows,
> With fatal sweetness elocution flows . . .

And so the poem develops panoramically, sweeping vertically up and down history, and horizontally through every condition of life, to its climax: "Pour forth thy fervours for a healthful mind."

The same generality and sweep pervade the prose writings as they touch on the self-destructive reactions that are native to the human mind, preventing it from being a happy and "free agent," and creating traps that close on ourselves as well as others. This clairvoyance could disturb more than reassure. We all know that man only too often turns his short life into a state where "many of his faculties can serve only for his torment" or the torment of others. But we do not like to dwell on the extent of it. It is too hard a thing to digest; it leaves us feeling rather hopeless; and where "there

From *The Achievement of Samuel Johnson.* © 1955 by Oxford University Press.

is no hope," as Johnson said, "there can be no endeavour." But the moving question of *The Vanity of Human Wishes* continues to reverberate throughout the later prose works;

> *Must helpless man,* in ignorance sedate,
> Roll darkling down the torrent of his fate?

Behind the question is the confidence that the sprawling complexity of man's unwitting self-betrayal can be seen for what it is, and that in some way it can be "managed" or replaced by something else. In Johnson, the pressing sense of the caged and bewildered struggle of the human heart for freedom prevents him from turning to any quick answer or cheap panacea. His practical humanism grows step by step from a clear-eyed exploration of the nature of this cage and this bewilderment.

In the work of Freud, the principal problem is not, of course, sex, but repression. Johnson's own sense of the working of the human imagination probably provides us with the closest anticipation of Freud to be found in psychology or moral writing before the twentieth century. With the professional compartmentalizing of knowledge during the last century, psychologists, even when they are concerned with the history of their subject, quite understandably do not consult literary works—except for Shakespeare and recent novels—unless their titles suggest that they are immediately relevant to psychology. But Johnson is an exception. The frequency with which he is quoted is a tribute to his clear-sightedness and power of phrase. On the other hand, the remarks generally used are little more than aphorisms in the vein of Hobbes, La Rochefoucauld, and Swift. In fact, their ancestry goes back at least two thousand years to the Greek cynics and sophists. Thus one psychiatrist speaks of the Freudian character of Johnson's thought, and then cites such statements as: "Children are always cruel. . . . Pity is *acquired* and improved by the cultivation of reason"; "Abundant charity is an atonement of imaginary sins"; "Nothing is more common than to call our own condition the condition of life." We could easily multiply the list. For example: "There is a kind of *anxious cleanliness* . . . characteristic of a slattern; it is the superfluous scrupulosity of *guilt,* dreading discovery, and shunning suspicion." But that part of Johnson—and it should be stressed that it is only a part—that really anticipates the psychoanalysis of the twentieth century is not to be found in simple thrusts that cut through a sentimental and complacent idealism about human nature. It is to be found in Johnson's studied and sympathetic sense of the way in which the human imagination, when it is blocked in its search for satisfaction, doubles back into repression, creating a "secret discontent," or skips out diagonally into some form of projection. The result, of course, is not a series of formal analyses. The essays of the *Rambler, Idler,* and *Adventurer* are brief and informal reflections on a wide variety of topics. The insights they contain are to be interpreted by the frequency of themes and the pattern into which they fall as Johnson touches on problems only superficially different.

He had "studied medicine diligently in all its branches," said Mrs. Thrale, "but had given particular attention to the *diseases of the imagination,* which he watched in himself with a *solicitude destructive of his own peace,* and intolerable to those he trusted." We know something about the range of what Johnson studied—particularly that remarkable book, George Cheyne's *English Malady* (1733). What is most significant in Cheyne is his recognition of the value of counter-activity, of using the dynamic and vital capacity of the human being, instead of suppressing or throttling it. Johnson, who had so fitfully thrown himself into activities that he thought might cleanse or at least "regulate" his mind, when he had been left stranded from Oxford, could appreciate the insight and develop it outward into a more generalized and more sensitive understanding of the need to exploit and re-direct human energies.

II

The starting-point, in short, is the commonplace we all seem to forget in practice: that the mind is an *activity,* and that if it is not used in one way it will seek satisfaction or at least outlet in other ways. Joined with this is Johnson's sense that growth of "the healthful mind" consists in establishing active links of sympathy and understanding with what is outside. Conversely, the "treachery of the human heart" is what isolates the individual. We are using the phrase out of context. It occurs in a discussion of literary criticism, and the opportunity criticism can give us to "gratify our own pride or envy *under the appearance* of contending" for some standard of excellence that has been violated. But our use of it for more general purposes is justified. It expresses exactly the unwitting betrayal by man of his own ultimate interests which is the theme of *The Vanity of Human Wishes.* The "treachery" arises from the fact that the natural human desire for security, importance, or reassurance can so easily become snarled by panic or chronic discontent that our attention is then switched to ourselves. The heart then concentrates solely on what relieves or confirms its own personal ambitions or fears; it begins instinctively to regard others as rivals to be feared or means to be used, and to wall itself still more firmly behind barriers through which only a warped perception of reality filters. The whole range of misunderstandings, rivalries, and resentments that divide human beings from each other is viewed, in short, as the product of imagination acting upon what we now call "anxiety," or the chronic, crippling preoccupation with our own problems and fears. Johnson himself uses the word, as when he states that "anxiety" tends to increase itself. By keeping a man "always in alarms," and looking at all costs for safety, it leads him "to judge of everything in a manner that least favours his own quiet, *fills him with perpetual stratagems of counteraction,*" and, by wearing him out "in schemes to obviate evils which never threatened him," causes him to contribute unwittingly to the very situations he fears.

As Johnson discloses them, the recourses most of us take in the face of chronic anxiety may be called—to use current terms—regression, fixation, and the various forms of hostility. But they rarely remain unmingled. Thus the consuming need to simplify life into one all-engrossing ambition or hard-and-fast interpretation—the single-minded fixation on wealth, position, the obsession of being persecuted, or the clinging to a fixed system that will brook no departure in morality, in literary criticism, or anything else—is also shot through with hostility. Certainly most fixations, from secret societies to vested professional interests, from nationalism to militant moral or intellectual systems, are exclusive rather than inclusive. They are a means of keeping others out, of asserting one's own self-hood. Finally, the fixed projections that extend to others what our own inner fears or demands suggest tend more frequently to be hostile than benevolent.

It is reassuring to see Johnson avoid the usual liabilities of a static terminology and at once penetrate to the insights that have been only gradually rediscovered by psychology, during the last half-century, in its long, patient siege of human nature. His ability to do so rounds out and justifies confidence in other aspects of his thought. Too often, moralists, educators, and poets who preach the vision of man's development are not inclined to look deeply into the darker, more complex side of human life. They pick up their trousers or skirts and tip-toe past it. On the other hand, the sharp-eyed exploration of human motives—especially in the richly analytic psychology that began at the time of Thomas Hobbes, and has flowered during the past fifty years—has not always, in its clinical preoccupations, been kept supple by the large flexible knowledge that only the history of the arts and sciences—only the informed and immediate sense of human greatness, in all its variety—can give us. What we really want, of course, is the union of hope with complete practicality—the union of the vision of ideals, which have haunted the mind of man in its most awake moments, with the clear knowledge of the pitfalls that embarrass or betray this vision.

III

There is a simple-minded innocence in General Paoli's idle talk of a South-Sea paradise where there would not be the same "causes of dissension" that divide husband and wife in a "civilized state," though Johnson cannot refrain from puncturing it: "they would have dissensions enough, though of another kind. One would wish to go a hunting in this wood, the other in that"; and he goes on to imply that if their bickering were not long enough drawn-out to lead to a deep-rooted rancor, it is only because the husband could quickly dispose of the wife in a way in which he could not in a civilized state; or, at the very least, they would simply part company. There is innocence in Cowley's desire for rural retreat; in the author, outwardly nonchalant, who walks about expectantly on the day he is published in the hope of catching stray comments about his work; and, to a less degree, the desire for riches has a certain innocence. On the whole, "There are few ways in which a man can be more innocently employed than in getting money." Unless his rapacity has obviously injured others, and has involved gross injustices, it will be generally found that he has only "disburdened the day" in an activity that is ultimately unrewarding. What he has accumulated will in time be spent or dissipated by others. So, too, with the works of scholars or writers, whose original motives may be far from disinterested, or whose attention seems locked to the means rather than the end. For their exclusive concentration on "secondary" pursuits of learning may disclose what will benefit others if not themselves. Also, original motives can be purified or enlarged simply by being exposed enough to other values. Finally, a man's self-respect is never to be cheaply swept aside. Few efforts of any sort, Johnson always recognizes, would ever be carried out if we inquired too scrupulously into every possible motive or incentive. The cumulative process of Johnson's thought is thus diagonally upward. For he zig-zags back and forth from one positive and lucid perception to another, correcting or modifying one assertion, rooted though it is in human experience, by sympathetically tapping another view of experience equally genuine and giving it an assertion just as vigorous. But in this large sweep of sympathy there is a partial pause, a cooler and more careful probing of the "hunger of imagination" as it ricochets or bounds aside into other emotions.

For frustration is rarely simple and final. It can quickly grow fresh horns and claws. In Freudian terms, it commonly transforms itself from suppression—from mere blocking of the end desired or imagined—into *repression*, into a pressing back of the imagination, and the tunneling of desire into new and unexpected veins. The imagination of even the old man in *Rasselas*, for whom everything has "lost its novelty," and who believes that "Nothing is now of much importance beyond myself," is not at rest. In no one, without the most dangerous risks, can the hate and fear created by constant frustration be turned solely against himself for very long. The mad astronomer, also in *Rasselas*, who has ended believing that he regulates the weather, is only one picturesque outcome of the need for every man to "conceal his own unimportance from himself."

But there are subtler methods of concealing our own unimportance which take other forms of projection. The projection may show itself in that constant and uneasy suspicion by which—unless we have been extraordinarily victimized by others—we really betray our own inclinations or guilt. Another familar reaction is found in the sort of person who, consciously or unknown to himself, tries to inflict "on others what he had formerly endured himself," as if to gain some assurance, as Johnson said, that his own suffering and trials have not been wasted. More insidious, because less obvious, are those who seek to enforce on other people moral or legal obligations that they themselves have broken or secretly resent having to follow. They begin to "extenuate their own guilt" or resentment by making "vague and general charges upon others," or by circulating more particular suspicions in the hope that their own attention as well as that of others will "be employed on any rather than themselves." But the imagination can take still more "artful subterfuges." An individual can ease his guilt by magnifying or dwelling on faults or habits that seem different from his own: "He then triumphs in his comparative purity, and *sets himself at ease*." Even here Johnson notes how commonly the quality we censure in another is the counterpart to an "opposite fault" in ourselves, as if we hoped to transform our own lack into a virtue.

Yet in the hue and cry on others the principal relief is not so much that it distracts public attention from what we fear in ourselves as that it distracts our own. Repeatedly Johnson supplements his probing of human malice by recalling that it is "not so much the desire of men . . . to deceive the world as themselves." But exactly this charity of understanding points up the greater seriousness of what is implied. For self-deception can lock itself up—at least from one's own scrutiny—into a closed cell of apparent virtue, and become water-tight to outside influence or correction. Few human beings, at least consciously, and however uncertain they may be underneath, place any but a favorable interpretation on their own motives. "It is natural to *mean well,* when only abstracted *ideas* of virtue are proposed to the mind." We can constantly see the temptation in others—if not ourselves—to substitute "single acts for habits." From the reproaches of others or of our own conscience, we can then make an appeal to direct actions, however rare, and interpret our faults not as "habitual corruptions, or settled practices, but as . . . single lapses." The practice is evil simply because it involves self-deception. For self-delusion, of whatever sort, tends to grow rather than diminish; there are always "so many more instigations to evil, than incitements to good." But the practice of substituting acts for habits, in our estimate of ourselves, is almost universal. If men differ here, the difference is largely one of degree. Even those whose intention is comparatively pure forget the difference between abstract agreement and conduct, "between approving laws, and obeying them." So willing is "every man to flatter himself," that, by acknowledging "the obligations of morality, and . . . enforcing them to others," he "concludes himself zealous in the cause of virtue."

In this light, Johnson also discusses slander and most gossip. We do not usually recognize the less attractive feelings that gossip releases, as he suggests, until we find ourselves the subject of it. Often we unavoidably snatch at gossip because of a "vacuum" or lack of acquaintance with anything else to say. In fact, even among the more intelligent, it is understandably dragged out as a stock resource. But if gossip serves as a helpful means of enlivening neutrality—we may think of the wits he pictures as glaring at each other and then returning to less challenging and more receptive company, where they are free from the sense of rivalry and "recover their good humor"—it also provides opportunities for displaying a sort of spurious superiority. Like the countryman who returns from London, eager to mention names with which the villagers are unacquainted, or have heard only indirectly, some are always pushing into the foreground of conversation a "real or imaginary connexion with a celebrated character," and "desire to advance or oppose a rising name." Johnson's almost obsessive dislike of gossiping or telling stories should be regarded as a conscientious attempt to carry out the opposite of a practice he so distrusted. In all the recorded conversations, there are few remarks that can be interpreted as gossip. When pressed to give an account of someone, he would make a clear, concise statement, and then try to turn to other matters. *Rambler,* No. 188—written when Johnson was at work on the *Dictionary*—provides a perceptive analysis of the eagerness to be accepted that leads us to recount stories or incidents about others, although even here a large arch of sympathy reaches out to recognize the hunger for acceptance and the need of the heart not so much to be "admired" but to be "loved." And one of the ways in which Johnson differs from those romantics of his own period and a generation later who extol a primitive state, is in pointing out that, if rural or solitary people seem to escape this temptation, it is not from superior virtue but only from lack of opportunity.

But the need to be loved, to be accepted, can awaken desires of which we are not always completely aware, and which no longer permit us to be a "free agent." Gossip, for example, rarely remains in that uneasy neutrality in which we are able to avoid commitment while trying to "disburden the day." It may quickly become a way of "disburdening" *ourselves,* of giving outlet to that "ill-humour or peevishness" which is usually "the symptom of some deeper malady" and suggests an inner poverty that cannot afford generosity.

For example, most falsehoods, especially those that are successful, are really the result of vanity. In lies inspired by malice or the hope of gain, "the motive is so apparent, that they are seldom negligently or implicitly received; suspicion is always watchful." But vanity pleases itself "with such slight gratifications" that its unconscious strategems are less obvious. Also it takes so many forms that he who would watch her motions can never be at rest: "fraud and malice are bounded . . . some *opportunity* of time and place is necessary . . . but scarce any man is abstracted one moment from his vanity." The hidden hunger in this case is not so much to "impose on others as on ourselves"—to replace our sense of inadequacy by recounting incidents that give us a more vital sense of our own importance. Again, we see how rarely secrets are kept. And yet "the negative virtues at least"—such as the ability to keep another's confidence—are theoretically within everyone's power. Though it may be difficult for a man to speak or do well, it is "still easy for him *not* to speak." But the explanation is simple enough. "Most men seem rather inclined to confess the want of virtue than of importance," and "the vanity of being known to be trusted with a secret, is generallly one of the chief motives to disclose it." The reactions that lead us to betray another's trust ultimately sprout from our sense of our own inadequacy. Speaking of the habit of projecting guilt on others—of acquiring excuses for what he elsewhere calls the "general hostility, which every part of mankind exercises against the rest"—Johnson states that "No man yet was ever wicked *without secret discontent*"; and the method of easing this chronic discontent must be either to "reform" ourselves or else to lower others.

IV

As the aim of morality is to "reform" or redirect human appetites and needs toward healthful ends, *envy,* as Johnson treats it, suggests the oppo-

site—the destructive result that occurs when human desires, left to themselves and lacking healthful satisfaction and development, begin to turn into
an appetite for "lowering others." This desire to relieve "the sense of our
disparity by lessening others, though we gain nothing to ourselves," is easily
the principal "treachery of the human heart" discussed by Johnson. In fact,
the theme of envy crawls like a tortoise through the moral essays, giving
way at times to other subjects, but always emerging at the end. In the
Rambler alone, fifty-seven issues—or well over a fourth—contain either the
word itself or the idea. It appears in every context, from the ingrown rancor
of rural and village life to the "stratagems of well-bred malignity" in fashionable life. In professional life, the discussion ranges from the mutual
animosity of rival callings—such as the "malignity of soldiers and sailors
against each other," often "at the cost of their country"—to the far more
alert and individual envy among writers, scholars, and critics. In a sense,
the frequency of the term alone becomes almost comic. Even the first paragraph of the *Preface to Shakespeare* is unable to avoid it. That praises are
lavished on dead rather than living writers is one of the consolations of those
who feel that "the regard which is yet denied by *envy,* will be at last bestowed
by time." And in the second paragraph following, the idea again shows up:
"his works support no opinion with arguments, nor supply any faction with
invectives; they can neither indulge vanity, nor gratify malignity . . ."

But the large place given envy by Johnson is perhaps logical. For the
bottle from which this genie is ready to spring and grow is always open.
All vices except indolence and envy, as he says, at least need special opportunities. But just as "to do nothing is always in every man's power," so
envy can operate "at all times, and in every place." The direct pursuit of
self-interest, if it is to get very far, usually requires "some qualities not
universally bestowed." It demands some perseverance or effort. "But envy
may act without expense or danger. To spread suspicion . . . to propagate
scandal, requires neither labour nor courage." The ease with which almost
every stir of pride or discontent can begin to turn into envy explains its
universality, not only among all people, in different ways, but in every stage
or aspect of one individual's life. Even in the innocence of the Happy Valley,
where all desires are satisfied, Rasselas—in the chapter called "The Wants
of him that Wants Nothing"—finds himself envying the animals if only
because, unlike them, he has nothing "to desire." The very frequency of
envy "makes it so familiar that it escapes our notice." Only when a man,
who has "given no provocation to malice, but by attempting to excel," and
who finds himself pursued "with all the implacability of personal resentment," and discovers how his habits and misfortunes, or those of his family
have been discussed or laughed at,—only then does he learn to "abhor those

artifices at which he only laughed before," and discover "how much the happiness of life would be advanced by the eradication of envy from the human heart."

But most of us are fortunately spared such experiences; we struggle with the effects of envy piecemeal, without knowing our opponent, fencing with it as it appears behind different masks. Thus in professional as well as social life, Johnson notes the motives that create the cult of mediocrity— that smooth the path for those who make us better "pleased with ourselves," who never "harass the understanding with *unaccustomed* ideas"—and, at the same time, the antagonism felt toward those whose strong commitment to ideas, or whose probing queries or skills in argument, disturb our complacency. Our acceptance of those who make us pleased with ourselves, and our resistance to others who do not, may be easily rationalized: we may justify our response in terms of stability of institutions, conventions, or principles. But in the conservative Johnson the treacherous ability of the human imagination to project or rationalize is never forgotten. There is always the salutary reminder—in our moral judgments or in the criticism of literature—that what we may be rushing forward to defend is not so much institutions in society, in literature, or in anything else, as it is ourselves. Perhaps inevitably, Johnson's sensitive insight into the innumerable "stratagems of self-defense," to which all of us devote so much of our time, pauses most often for examples among authors and philosophers, scholars or critics. To some extent, his own personal experience vivifies his consideration of this, which contains as much bitterness as Johnson was ever to show. The strong phrasing occurs repeatedly: "so universal is the dread of unconscious powers"; critics "whose acrimony is excited mostly by the *pain of seeing others pleased,* and of *hearing applauses which another enjoys*"; people of genuine wit, unless they have enough reputation to shed luster on their hosts, are seldom re-invited to social gatherings, "being dreaded by the pert as rivals, and hated by the dull as disturbers of the peace"; "*merit rather enforces respect* than attracts fondness"; such is "the unwillingness of mankind to admit transcendent merit" that, to "malice and envy," a single failure "gratifies"; he pleases most whose talk is full of "*unenvied* insipidity." The Emperor Seged, in the *Rambler* allegory, innocently hoping "to avoid offense," awards liberal prizes to everyone, greater than any had ever expected. But all the recipients found their own "distinction" unhonored, and "wanted an opportunity to triumph in the mortification of their own opponents." We see how commonly even the "slight mistakes" and personal habits of great men, who may be completely unknown to us personally, are still singled out and dwelt on with obvious relish. If in this, as in other respects, "mankind is in general more easily disposed to censure than admiration," it is partly because "more can detect petty failings than can distinguish or esteem greater qualifications." Others hope to shock their hearers or simply to "fill the moment" more vividly for themselves. But underneath, in most cases, there is at least some desire to lessen "the sense of our disparity." The logical and drastic result of envy is finally to feel an uneasy rivalry with everyone in every way.

Explaining his early life to Rasselas, who is still in the Happy Valley, Imlac tells how his companions, when he first joined a caravan, exposed him to frauds, and led him into situations where he had trouble with officials, "without any advantage to themselves, but that of rejoicing in the superiority of their own knowledge." Rasselas cannot believe that man is so depraved as to wish to "injure another without benefit to himself." Also, though men are certainly pleased by feeling superior, yet Imlac's ignorance and naïveté being "merely accidental," could afford his fellow merchants "no reason to applaud themselves; and the knowledge which they had, and which you wanted, they might as effectually have shown by warning, as betraying you."

Something of Rasselas' incredulity seems to persist in Johnson himself, joining with the surprise that men can treat each other so in a world "bursting with sin and sorrow," where all of us await the same doom. Nor can Imlac give any answer except to say that "Pride is seldom delicate, it will please itself with very mean advantages; and envy feels not its own happiness, but when it may be compared with the misery of others." The most blatant pursuit of self-interest is in a sense preferable to envy. Self-interest simply disregards the rights or feelings of others. But envy leads us into something worse and essentially more destructive—into a state of actually desiring to "pull others down" for no other reason than that they are not already down. "I have hitherto," says Johnson in one of the *Ramblers,* (No. 183), "avoided that dangerous and empirical morality, which cures one vice by means of another. But envy is so base . . . that the predominance of almost any other quality is to be preferred. . . . Let it therefore be constantly remembered, that whoever envies another, confirms his superiority, and let those be reformed by their pride who have lost their virtue." Almost every other "crime," as he says, is carried out by the help of some quality which *might* have produced esteem or love, if it had been well employed; but "envy is mere unmixed and genuine evil." If only on the basis of a higher, more demanding pride, envy can be resisted if we wish "to maintain the *dignity* of a human being." Yet, as Johnson's misgivings about the Stoics show, to overturn one form of pride by means of another, and then stop at that point, is not a final or satisfactory solution. Its value is only as a last resource or as an aid or inciter which should then be quickly supplemented with other more lasting aids. But we are not to disregard any help provided the means we use does not take over and create worse complications. "The cure for the greatest part of human miseries is not radical, but palliative."

V

Yet there is always the charitable tug back to recall that "the cold malignity of envy"—the nearest approach to "pure and unmixed evil"—is projected from our own "secret discontent." Johnson reminds us how adolescents, because of their uncertainty about themselves, are ready to regard everyone who approaches them as "an admirer or a spy," confident that every motion or word is remembered. So with those professions that, in any external reward they offer, seem to depend solely on "reputation." Johnson speculates how easily men of genius and learning could control the world if only they joined together, especially since the anti-intellectualism of the public is always present to stimulate them into making such a union. But the friendship of scholars—except among the most generous—is often like that of celebrated "beauties"; "as both depend for happiness on the regard of others, on that of which *the value arises merely from comparison,* they are both exposed to perpetual jealousies, and both incessantly employed in schemes to intercept the praises of each other." Hence scholars, for example, often end owing little to their colleagues "but the *contagion* of diligence," and "a resolution to write, because the rest are writing." The merchant is fortunate in being able to judge his success by income, and the physician by cures, but mere "reputation" is too uncertain and fluid a measurement of success to give any rest or satisfaction: it can never be securely held to a fixed standard, especially among scholars and writers where the reputation desired is intellectual, arising "solely from their *understanding,*" and can hardly be sensed, as Johnson says, except as is involves direct comparison with others.

Much of the argument—fortunately not all—that we self-righteously seem to base on principle really arises from the automatic impulse of human nature to ward off another's threat to our opinion of ourselves. The pathetic tenuousness of our own self-confidence is shown by our quickness to defend not only what we think we believe, but what we may have said casually or argued for only because we had previously lacked anything else to say at the moment. Hence a dispute on a subject, "regarded with careless indifference" a moment before, "is continued by the desire of conquest, till *vanity kindles into rage,* and opposition rankles into enmity." And yet a personal reassurance, a more open and generous exchange of personal esteem, would at once collapse these awkwardly colliding balloons. Hate, when it is not produced by the fear of obvious and direct threat, is the product of vanity colliding without such reassurance. And envy is the unsatisfied "hunger of imagination" as it seeks excuses and further motives for hate.

The purifying of the motives that otherwise create most of the evil and unhappiness of the world is one final theme of all Johnson's work. Not the least of his success is the concrete example of his own compassion, which sees the whole vast network of man's "stratagems of self-defense" for what it is—as a self-made prison, or web, built largely by projections, fears, or wants, in which the desire is not so much "to impose on others as on ourselves," and in which, as "helpless man" becomes enmeshed with it, his faculties begin to "serve only for his torment." The somber elevation already apparent in *The Vanity of Human Wishes* joins with a close empirical charity that never fails to rise above envy and extinguish it by clearly realizing that "there are none to be envied, and surely none can be much envied who are not pleased with themselves." And Johnson at once goes on to add:

> Such is our desire of *abstraction from ourselves,* that very few are satisfied with the quantity of stupefaction which the needs of the body force upon the mind. Alexander himself added intemperance to sleep, and solaced with . . . wine the sovereignty of the world; and almost every man has some art by which he steals his thoughts away from his present state.

The remark is almost a caricature of his thinking. For the word "stupefaction" at once puts the situation in a surprising, almost comic light. Yet there is also implicit the same charity—the same inability to remain closed to all the possible fears and hopes that can swerve the heart—that led him, as we have mentioned before, to turn on Mrs. Williams when, complaining of men drinking, she wondered "what pleasure men can take in making beasts of themselves": "*I* wonder, Madam, that you have not penetration enough to see the strong inducement to this excess; for he who makes a *beast* of himself, gets rid of *the pain of being a man.*"

VI

When you feel that your own gaiety, said Imlac to Rasselas,

> is counterfeit, it may justly lead you to suspect that of your companions is not sincere. Envy is commonly reciprocal. We are long before we are convinced that happiness is never to be found, and each believes it possessed by others, to keep alive the hope of obtaining it for himself.

The injunction is not one of despair but an injunction for the use of the heart. It is a plea for the cleansing of illusion through compassion, and through the outward reach to sympathetic understanding: an understanding that demands both range of mind and sincerity of feeling, and can never become complete with either alone. In his own practice, exactly this use of the heart is what gives base and reassurance to his thought. Considering how frequently such subjects as envy and hostility recur, it is tempting to turn for explanation to his own long struggle. But it appears that they were something he had to face in others more than himself. The further we go into Johnson's life, the plainer it seems that his aggressive struggle and sense of rivalry had pitched itself so sincerely on the desire for understanding, that it completely avoided the pitfalls of personal jealousy. The success is a tribute to the ability of awareness, however fitfully or aggressively obtained at first, to act formatively, when it is sincerely desired, on one's own experience. Unquestionably, the unhappy youth, caught in the bleak little school at Market-Bosworth, must have felt a sort of general envy of others; and there may have been occasions when it became sharper in the twenty years that followed. Moreover, although Johnson's habit of "talking for victory" indicates a desire to clarify, to achieve greater certitude, it also discloses a keen sense of rivalry. Indeed, the idea of asserting "superiority" dodges about and appears in the most unpredictable and amusing ways. Boswell teased him to study the Scottish dialect in the pastoral, *The Gentle Shepherd,* by Allan Ramsay, and offered to help him do so: "No, Sir, I won't learn it, *you shall retain your superiority by my not knowing it.*" "Do not," he once said to Mrs. Thrale, indulge in *"the superiority* of inattention . . ." We may also feel that here is a certain compensation, or bending over backward, in Johnson's strong Tory regard for social rank. Certainly he disliked those who project their political and social envy so that they wish to "level *down* as far as themselves; but they cannot bear levelling *up* to themselves." But it is healthful to recall that there are different ways of compensating, and that they vary in the final result and value. It is as possible to be governed or controlled by compensation as by simpler and cruder motives. But it is also possible to use compensation rather than be used by it—to use it as an aid or a temporary stabilizer, and then in turn to correct or modify it. Johnson might feel it sane and healthful to give a nobleman his due, and yet take issue with others who laughed when Oliver Goldsmith complained of being snubbed by Lord Camden, and state, "Dr. Goldsmith is in the right. A nobleman ought to have made up to such a man as Goldsmith; and I think it is much against Lord Camden that he neglected him."

There is a state, in other words, in which pride, however dangerous, has not yet passed into envy, and there is a largeness of perception that can prevent its doing so. No matter how rough his replies, as Reynolds and others stressed, there was never anything that could be called "little or mean" about him. As compared with Swift, there is something childlike, perhaps humanly reassuring, about even Johnson's most extreme outbursts of pride. Mr. W. B. C. Watkins has cited one of the more marked instances of Johnson's defensive pride that at once links him with and separates him from Swift. We may think of Swift's entry in the *Journal to Stella*, when he talks of sitting next to Lady Godolphin, and trying to talk to her: "but she would not give me one look or say a word to me . . . *She is a fool for her pains, and I'll pull her down.*" While Johnson was writing the "Life of Pope," Boswell spoke to Lord Marchmont, who had known Pope. He officiously made an appointment for Johnson without his permission ("tomorrow at one o'clock") and then bustled off to tell the news to Johnson, who was out at Streatham. Johnson, surprised, taken off-guard, astonished Boswell by suddenly saying:

> "*I shall not be in town to-morrow. I don't care to know about Pope.*"
> MRS. THRALE: (surprised as I was, and a little angry.) "I
> suppose, Sir, Mr. Boswell thought, that as you are to write Pope's
> Life, you would wish to know about him." JOHNSON. "Wish!
> why yes. If it *rained knowledge* I'd hold out my hand; but I would
> not give myself the trouble to go in quest of it." There was no
> arguing with him at the moment. Some time afterwards he said,
> "*Lord Marchmont will call on me, and then I shall call on Lord
> Marchmont.*"

The innocence of the opening statement is increased when we remember not only that it was Boswell who had made the appointment, but that Johnson— restive in his conscience—later called on Lord Marchmont, talked with him, and said afterward, "I would rather have given twenty pounds than not have come."

Remembering the struggle to excel, which had become rooted in Johnson's behavior, it is moving to see him, as he grows older, increasingly urging the need for "good humor." He turns to the first demand of the human heart: "*it is always necessary to be loved, but not always necessary to be reverenced.*" "Good humor," which he defines as "*a habit of being pleased*" will draw people to us when more positive and difficult virtues will not. Without it "learning and bravery can only confer that superiority which swells the heart of the lion in the desert, when he roars without reply, and ravages without resistance." Consequently, despite illness and the liabilities of his own temperament, he struggled, as we have noted in the first chapter, to develop a habitual "willingness to be pleased," and experienced a high, almost diverting satisfaction on those rare occasions when he could feel that the habit had been acquired. For example, he once turned to Boswell as they were riding in a carriage, stating

> "It is wonderful, Sir, how rare a quality good humour is in life. We meet with very few good humoured men" . . . *Then, shaking his head and stretching himself at his ease in the coach, and smiling with much complacency,* he turned to me and said, "I look upon *myself* as a good humoured fellow."

This valuing of "good humour" is impressive because it is unillusioned but still active and formative. The moral essays, taken as a unit, contain an almost frightening analysis of the reasons why "good humour" appeals to the human ego. There is, for example, the little portrait in *Idler,* No. 83, of the man liked by all, whose only problem, when his acquaintances are present and arguing, is "how to be of two contrary opinions at once," but who has learned the "art of distributing his attention and his smiles in such a manner, that each thinks him of his own party." *Rambler,* No. 188, takes up the reason why the telling of stories is so popular. For one thing, everyone has "some real or imaginary connexion with a celebrated character, some desire to advance or oppose a rising name." But ultimately it is because stories are heard "without envy"; for they imply no "intellectual qualities above the common rate. To be acquainted with facts not yet echoed by plebian mouths, may happen to one man as well as to another." But stories wear themselves out; an inexhaustible stock is impossible to attain. Yet "such is the kindness of mankind to all, except those who aspire to real merit and rational dignity," that everyone can find some way of exciting benevolence "if he is not *envied.*" And the irony that Johnson was always trying to check in himself sharply switches to the "good-natured man,"—whose benevolence largely proceeds from "indolence" and lack of commitment, who follows the stream of talk wherever it leads, bears jokes without retaliation, and "retires rejoicing at his own importance"—down to the "modest man . . . whose only power of giving pleasure is not to interrupt it," and whose silence his companions interpret as "proceeding not from inability to speak, but willingness to hear." In short, Johnson recognizes with trenchant clarity that "good humour" appeals to men by not "*condemning* them to vigilance and caution," to insecurity and doubt of their worth.

Yet, seeing all this, Johnson at the same time saw more deeply, returning to the ultimate need, in all individual development, of open receptivity, of the capacity for *"being pleased."* With a certain personal desperation, perhaps, there is the reminder that, if the passive or opportunistic can appear to be pleased, then it is also possible for the intelligent to be genuinely pleased. It is not only a matter of being loved or accepted—though this is of primary importance to the human heart. It is ultimately that awareness, knowledge of things as they are, and therefore development, result from a largeness of response touched and led by generosity and sympathy. Surely, as he said to Mrs. Thrale, "delicacy" of taste—which so many seemed eager to show by negative reactions—does not consist in *"impossibility to be pleased."* And he ended by feeling that perhaps argument itself was not so valuable after all; that it aroused too many differences, or perhaps stemmed from defenses equally impure. Perhaps more was to be said for the quiet "interchange" of opinions. Considering Johnson's life and habits of sixty years this final admission was one of the greatest tributes to his capacity to revise himself. The success was not complete, of course. But the old man who, dying, cried out for *"new* topicks of merriment, or *new* incitements to curiosity"—who had written to Boswell a few months before, "Be well when you are not ill, and *pleased* when you are not angry"—is still the opposite of the old man in *Rasselas* to whom "the world has lost its novelty," and who feels that "nothing is now of much importance; for I cannot extend my interest beyond myself." It is safe to assume that there would have been differences in earlier years too. The first would have been in the quality of sincerity which in Johnson not only included the sense of sharing life with others but involved an inability to think or feel otherwise.

VII

The uninhibited Boswell once amused his fellow-spectators during a dull play by lowing like a cow. But he, like almost everyone else, seems to have been puzzled by the quick unpredictability and variety of Johnson's sense of comedy. All of Johnson's friends agreed with Mrs. Thrale that "No man loved laughing better, and his vein of humor was rich, and apparently inexhaustible." But what seemed to strike them were just two aspects of it. One was his imaginative play of wit. The other was his surprising delight— virtually forgotten after the nineteenth century began—in farce and playfulness that made him, as the Irish playwright Arthur Murphy said, "incomparable at buffoonery," and an "admirable mimic" despite his "inflexible" appearance. Certainly a part of the constant delight, as at least two of his friends implied, lay in the contrast of this ready mimicry with the "inflexible features," and also with the large brooding majesty of Johnson's face in repose. Even the dour Sir John Hawkins thought that "In the talent of humour there hardly ever was his equal, except perhaps among the old comedians, such as Tarleton, and a few others mentioned by Cibber"; and Hawkins goes on to add how this side of Johnson "disconcerted" grave people, like the scholar, William Warburton. Also, it is plain, from a contemporary account, that some of the antics that the rather prim Miss Reynolds interpreted and passed on to posterity as mere neurotic explosions— such as suddenly turning and seating himself on the back of his chair—have a different context from the one she suggests. They are outbursts of a "childish playfulness," quite on a par with his imitation of the kangaroo in Scotland, or the morning when he surprised Boswell by imitating Lady Macdonald, "leaning forward with a hand on each cheek and her mouth open."

By sheer infection, this active exuberance could be caught and shared by others. But there are occasions when, instead of acting it out, Johnson seems to stand aside, almost as a passive spectator. Then it is that, in place of mimicry and playfulness, we have simply the "immoderate laughter" that so puzzled his friends. This quick leap of the comic sense into a dimension that they could not reach appears to result when the enormous pressure in Johnson's effort at self-control and self-direction momentarily suspends the excuse he is usually finding for human motives, and instead the shams and self-deception in human nature are suddenly seen, as in slow motion or a still picture, with terrible clarity, and with something of the uncanny and huge mockery of Swift. One such instance is told by Boswell, who was at a loss to account for it, but thought it made an interesting contrast to what "might be expected from the author of 'the Rambler.' " Forcing himself out into company, though he "continued to be very ill," Johnson visited the eminent lawyer, Robert—later Sir Robert—Chambers at the Temple. He seemed to feel better as the conversation grew more animated. The talk turned on male succession in noble families, which Johnson defended with enthusiasm, and it then switched to the will of Johnson's friend, Bennet Langton, which had been drawn up that day by Chambers, and which left Langton's estate to his sisters—whom Johnson called "three *dowdies*"—in preference to the nearest male cousin. Then the account continues:

> I have known him at times exceedingly diverted at what seemed to others a very small sport. *He now laughed immoderately, without any reason that we could perceive,* at our friend's making his will; called him the *testator,* and added, "I daresay, he thinks he has done a mighty thing. He won't stay till he gets home to his seat in the country . . . he'll call up the landlord of the first inn on

the road; and, *after a suitable preface upon mortality and the uncertainty of life,* will tell him that *he* should not delay making his will; and here, Sir, will he say, is *my* will, which I have just made, with the assistance of one of the ablest lawyers in the kingdom . . . (*laughing all the time*). He believes he has made this will; but he did not make it: you, Chambers, made it for him. I trust you had more conscience than to make him say, 'being of sound understanding;' ha, ha, ha! . . . *I'd have his will turned into verse, like a ballad."*

In this playful manner did he run on . . . Mr. Chambers . . . seemed impatient till he got rid of us. Johnson could not stop his merriment, but continued it all the way till we got without the Temple-gate. He then burst into such a fit of *laughter, that he appeared to be almost in a convulsion;* and, in order to support himself, laid hold of one of the posts . . . and sent forth peals so loud, that in the silence of the night his voice seemed to resound from Temple-bar to Fleet-ditch.

It is all there, though the context is rather grim and extreme. The long habit of meeting vanity and self-deception by immediately piercing through them now lunges out almost automatically, under the pressure of illness and accumulated past effort. Also, Johnson's life-long struggle against the mere idea of death is suddenly stirred awake by the thought of the death of a close friend. Here both the obsession and recoil from death are instinctively controlled by focusing on one related aspect, the making of a will, plucking it out into the bright air of comedy, and then pushing it, as with a giant's hand, farther ("laughing all the time"), as he piles one image on another. Here is the picture of Langton "filling the *vacuities* of life," "*disburdening* the day," momentarily feeling more alive and significant as "the *testator,*" gratified at his magisterial power to bestow or deny, and doubtless imagining to himself the waves of gratitude or dismay he will have caused by this "mighty thing." Then, we have Langton, impressed with his own act, speaking gravely, in stock terms, about "mortality and the uncertainty of life" (one thinks of the ominous line about self-deception in *The Vanity of Human Wishes,* "The secret *ambush* of a *specious prayer*"), and advising others to follow his example. The whole sense of the meaningless and "incessant competition for superiority"—which will satisfy itself with the most trivial advantages—is also brought into play here. There is the picture of Langton "invigorating" his own new significance still more by mentioning, to the open-mouthed innkeeper, that his own will has now been drawn up "with the *assistance* of one of the ablest lawyers in the kingdom" ("everyone has a real or imaginary connexion with a celebrated character"). Pushing still farther, we have the merry Langton—now sobered and enlarged in his new role as "*testator*"—fast feeling it was he himself who has made this document ("but he did not make it: *you*, Chambers, made it *for* him").

Behind it all is the vast, fatigued sense of *The Vanity of Human Wishes*, of the flurry, the ultimate waste and triviality of hypocrisy and self-deception throughout every part of life. Only, at this moment, Johnson's almost endless capacity for charity seems partly suspended. Instead, the realization condenses itself into the final, puzzling tag: "I'd have his will turned into *verse*, like a ballad." It is like the spritely, macabre lines in ballad-meter, made up on the spur of the moment, that Johnson cried out to the young daughter of the Thrales as she deliberated solemnly with a friend about a new gown and hat that she was to wear to an assembly:

> Wear the gown, and wear the hat,
> Snatch thy pleasures while they last;
> *Hadst thou nine lives like a cat,*
> *Soon those nine lives would be past.*

When the young Fanny Burney, now a frequent visitor at the Thrales' house at Streatham, brought out her novel, *Evelina*, her main interest for some months seems to have been in recording the constant flattery that the fashionable and intellectual showered on it, and their persuasions that she should now devote her satirical power to *dramatic* comedy. So suffocating and persistent does this flattery become in reading her diary, especially that which she quotes from Johnson, who so rarely "read books *through*," that we feel a sense of relief in finding him admit to John Opie the painter—when asked whether he really thought *Evelina* so good: "I never read it through at all, *though I don't wish this to be known*." Finally, one morning after breakfast, occurs a scene when all at once the whole superstructure of pointless flattery and the polite protestations with which we are all led to "fill the day" and "vivify importance" are viewed as a dramatic comedy; and a comedy in which Johnson sees himself as clearly as anyone else could—"disburdening the day" in his own way, bandying flattery with the young authoress, grotesque and lonely, fretful at being left when the women went to a ball, and insisting on going with them, ill and deaf as he was, rather than stay alone. But Fanny Burney's only comment is, "How little did I expect from . . . this great and dreaded lord of English literature, a turn for burlesque humour." But it is not burlesque only. Behind it, as Mr. Watkins said, is "a more devastating laughter of intellect from a man who saw through all pretense and hypocrisy, even his own, with a terrible clarity." After breakfast at Streatham, the talk again flowed "copiously," said Fanny, urging her to "produce a comedy." While Mrs. Thrale was in the midst of her "flattering persuasions," the two women suddenly noticed that Johnson,

> see-sawing in his chair, began laughing to himself so heartily as to almost shake his seat as well as his sides. We stopped . . . hoping he would reveal the subject of his mirth; but he enjoyed it inwardly, without heeding our curiosity,—till at last he said he had been struck with a notion that "Miss Burney would begin her dramatic career by writing a piece called *Streatham."*
>
> He paused, and laughed yet more cordially, and *then suddenly commanded a pomposity* to his countenance and his voice, and added, "Yes! *Streatham—a Farce!"*

VIII

That Johnson is so far from being a comic writer is a fact of some significance. For most of what makes up the comic sense is abundantly present. To begin with, there are the strong accumulated pressures of which Freud speaks, built up throughout a lifetime of precarious effort. Mr. Watkins, in quoting Boswell's account of Langton's will, with its bewildered description of Johnson's violent and prolonged laughter, aptly appends the great lines from *King Lear:* "O! how this mother"—this welter and surge of feeling—

> swells up toward my heart;
> *Hysterica passio!* down, thou *climbing* sorrow!
> Thy element's *below!*

But the subjective need for outlet is only one element; for it is met and matched at the same time by the perceptive intelligence, by the close notice of detail and the immediate ability to generalize, which are necessary to make the comic sense into something more than a mere outlet for pressure. There is also a third element, which is particularly relevant in considering Johnson. It involves his own intimate and honest participation.

We cannot deal with morbid and destructive fears and impulses, as he told Boswell, simply by suppressing them ("to think them down is madness"). Part of the relief we find in comedy is that, instead of blocking feelings that disturb us, it joins with them, and allows them to propel themselves by their own momentum while it steers them around into a new context. Even mere mimicry can serve as a way of deflecting our reactions or getting them under some kind of control. Hence the tendency of people to mimic those whom they resent or fear, or to enjoy watching them mimicked by others. Reduction through caricature is, in fact, one of the common means by which fear or resentment can be turned into something less threatening and more manageable. Unquestionably the temptation for Johnson to use ridicule in this way was strong. His inability to yield to the temptation is one of the fascinating things about him. His habitual ways of meeting threat or pressure of any kind involve the courage of direct encounter, and the attempt to bring a fuller knowledge to bear.

But mimicry can also serve less malicious purposes, where what we are instinctively trying to control is not so much the threat of others as the pressure of our own desires, or our dissatisfaction with something in ourselves. Here we may simply burlesque what we are feeling, if we are histrionically inclined. Or, more commonly, we enjoy watching, in the expressions or actions of others, an exaggerated counterpart to what we are feeling, put on another stage, and made harmless beneath a comic light. Seeing it in this outside context, embodied in what Santayana calls a "correlative object," we can then view it with more detachment. And there is the further relief, of course, in discovering that we have companionship. The great comic characters in literature affect us in exactly this way. They do—only more openly—(as Johnson said of Don Quixote and his daydreams) what most of us are half afraid we do anyway, or else what we should like to do if we only dared. This use of comedy, kept generous and therapeutic as long as one's own participation is acknowledged, is always present in Johnson. It lends the sharp notice that only direct personal acquaintance can give, while remaining honest about itself. What Sir John Hawkins said about Johnson's gift for innocent mimicry—that despite his bad sight and inflexible features he could "discriminate" with the nicest exactness the character of those whom it concerned, in a way rivaled only by the "old comedians"—also applies to the humor that lurks in the moral essays, and breaks out in the satiric portraits scattered through them. For the exactness and fidelity with which Johnson senses motives, blows them up, and then punctures them after edging them into the absurd are largely based on his own self-perception; but they persuade because the admission of his own participation is so honestly implicit. The obsessive desire for "change of place"; the dreams of primitive romantic love, mocked in the little Eskimo Idyll he wrote for the *Rambler,* while years later Bishop Percy could still find him avidly reading "romances of chivalry"; the appetite for fame—the newly published author steeling himself to bear adverse comments on the book no one has ever noticed, while those who have arrived, or think they have, are seen as now "oppressed by their own reputation"—in almost every aspect of the "hunger of imagination which preys incesssantly upon life," and which is "always breaking away from the present moment," Johnson's latent sense of the comic involves a self-burlesque.

Even in the episode of Langton's will, the direct sharing is present, though less obvious. The picture of Langton as now "the *testator*" plucks up, from the ill and fatigued Johnson, and burlesques all the self-conscious weight of statement that he himself brings to bear, whether in the legal briefs he dictates to Boswell, or in the great opening paragraphs of the *Preface to Shakespeare* with their finality of phrase and their conscious sense of being bequeathed to posterity. As for Langton giving the inn-keeper a "suitable preface upon mortality and the uncertainty of life," what writer has composed more of them than the author of *The Vanity of Human Wishes*? And no one was more aware of this than Johnson himself, who begins a letter to the *Rambler* (No. 109) by saying "Though you seem to have taken a view sufficiently extensive of the miseries of life . . . you have not yet exhausted the whole stock of human infelicity." He then goes on to picture the author of the *Rambler,* delighted at receiving this letter, locking the door, and sitting down to "enjoy a new calamity without disturbance." There is self-perception also as he cuts through pretense in human institutions, even those he strenuously defends with his informed and vital conservatism. Certainly his Tory sympathies were not a whim. They were based on real reasons. But he was still able to see these reasons for what they were—as tentative, uncertain, perhaps groping, always incomplete. He could disarmingly admit that he thought he had certain merit "in being zealous for subordination and the honours of birth; for I can hardly tell who was my grandfather," and at the same time he could reproach the elder Pitt for "feudal gabble." It is significant that the background to the incident of Langton's will was Johnson's defense of male succession, his dismissal of the women who were to receive the estate as "three *dowdies,*" and his spirited talk about keeping up noble families. As he plunges into the subject, the perception of himself and the whole scene immediately triggers the explosive laughter that follows—the irritable, ailing Johnson, so "zealous" for the "honours of birth," when he could "hardly tell who was my grandfather," bringing out his stock shibboleths, and using strong talk out of all proportion to the subject, as he sits there in the Temple, with the prim, professional Chambers and the open-eyed Boswell. It is like the incident, years before, when he visited

Plymouth with Sir Joshua Reynolds. A new, rival town, "Dock-Yard" (now Devonport), was being built two miles off, and was petitioning to use the water-supply of Plymouth:

> Johnson, affecting to entertain the passions of the place, was violent in opposition: and *half-laughing at himself* for his pretended zeal . . . exclaimed, "No, no! I am against the *dockers:* I am a Plymouth man. Rogues! Let them die of thirst. They shall not have a drop!"

And at the beginning of the long cascade of laughter about Langton's will we can see something of the self-burlesque we find three months later when, on the tour through Scotland, he strutted grotesquely about with a Scottish warbonnet on, or when MacLeod of Skye playfully offered to give Johnson the little island of Isay, on condition Johnson would live there one month a year. Johnson grew increasingly merry: "I have seen him please himself with little things, even with mere ideas . . . He talked a great deal of this island—how he would build a house, how he would *fortify* it." And then, immediately seeing himself as he really was, and delighting in the title, *Island Isay,* which he said he would assume, he went on, telling

> how he would have cannon . . . how he would sally out and *take* the Isle of Muck; and *then he laughed with a glee that was astonishing, and could hardly leave off.* I have seen him do so at a small matter that struck him, and was a sport to no one else. Langton told me that one night at the Club he did so while the company were all grave around him; only Garrick in his smart manner addressed him, "Mighty pleasant, sir; mighty pleasant, sir"

This self-participation of Johnson provides relief not so much by blunting the effect of ridicule as in diffusing its effect through general sharing. The writer or comedian who includes himself in comic exposure, who himself shoulders much of the weight of its impact, makes less of a demand. We ourselves are less on the defensive, and are readier to follow the contagion of example. The rather fatiguing effect of what is easily the most intricate and brilliant satire in literature, Swift's *Tale of a Tub,* may be partly explained in this light. Ultimately its audience consists of critics or other writers; it is a scholar's or writer's satire; and few scholars or writers have really found it very laughable. In the last of its many levels, it may be satirizing satire, including itself. But Swift—who supposedly laughed only twice in his life, once when he read Fielding's *Tom Thumb,* and another time in watching a juggler—is present, if at all, only as a lynx-eyed and sardonic observer, who holds all the cards. Comic relief, like any other, involves repose and reassurance as well as release. For mere release, by itself, cannot last very long.

Bergson has a point, however, in saying comedy rests on a "momentary anesthesia of the heart." Concern, if it is too avid, can blot out the comic sense, replacing it either with mere earnestness or else with a sympathetic identification that is too intense to permit laughter. And in Johnson the participation is so strong that burlesque is only a temporary thing. He seems instinctively to realize that, if we dwell too long on the incongruity between reality and appearance, between human motives and the pretense, the exuberance will soon pass. In its place will be a state of mind essentially destructive—a state the opposite of a "willingness to *be pleased*"—which will begin to rationalize and project its discontent, by the rate of neglected pride and the languishment of unsatisfied desire." What Johnson says is true enough. But his instinctive recoil from Swift—and partly because he was in some ways temperamentally akin—was strong enough to warp his whole estimate of Swift's work. This is rare for Johnson. Despite casual statements about other writers, torn out of context and repeated by Victorian critics, we now believe that Johnson is really unfair, in his total judgment, to only one author, Swift. The reaction to Swift illustrates why Johnson could never be a comic writer in the strict sense of the word. He had an "aversion," said Mrs. Thrale, "to general satire" of any sort. So honest and experiencing a nature was too much aware of the force of circumstances which comedy—almost by definition, in so far as it is a "momentary anesthesia of the heart"—must disregard when it unclothes and exposes hypocrisy and self-delusion.

Still, the compassion of Johnson does not so much destroy the comic sense as fill it out, for the moment, in a richer form, and then afterward gather it back into sympathetic understanding. Nothing so much distinguishes him from the greatest of satirists as his own immediate sympathy for anything from which his intellect tears away the veil, and his endearing willingness not only to acknowledge that he shares in it but actually to plunge in, voluntarily, and increase it. The object is never a "you" alone, but a "*we*," as in the little imaginary playlet, *Streatham—a Farce.* Resolving repeatedly to rise in the morning, despairing of his own lack of will in failing to do so, he could still, when friends dropped in during the morning, sense the grotesque contrast between his own cluttered room and a royal levee in a palace chamber; and the laughter that followed could include the comedy of self-awareness. This was the Johnson whose nights, as he approached seventy, were "full of misery," and yet, when Boswell stopped by before he was up, called him to his bedside, crying out "in the gaiety of youth," to Francis Barber, "Frank, go and get coffee, and let us *breakfast in splendour.*" And there is the little scene during the tour through Scotland, when he is told one morning that a friend has received a pension. Sitting bolt upright in bed, a knotted handkerchief crowning his head, he clapped his hands at this regal news, and—using "a peculiar exclamation of his when he rejoices"—cried out happily, "O brave *we!*"

W. K. WIMSATT

In Praise of Rasselas:
Four Notes (Converging)

AFTERTHOUGHTS IN *RASSELAS*

Johnson most likely began to write *Rasselas* not long after Saturday, 13 January, 1759, when he seems first to have heard of his mother's serious illness. A week later, on Saturday, 20 January, he wrote to the publisher William Strahan that he would deliver the book to him on Monday night, and that the title would be "The Choice of Life/or/The History of . . . Prince of Abisinnia." The several learned editors of *Rasselas* have, accordingly, not been inclined to take literally Johnson's later statement to Reynolds, as reported by Boswell, that he not only wrote *Rasselas* "in the evenings of one week," but "sent it to the press in portions as it was written." In portions, as it was corrected during days subsequent to Monday, 22 January, perhaps. It is not difficult to imagine revisions and afterthoughts even during the original week of rapid composition. One of the most obvious internal suggestions of such afterthought, or at least of a certain absent-mindedness during the course of writing, appears in the development of the character of the lady Pekuah. We hear of her first, momentarily, in the escape from the happy valley (chapter XV). "The princess was followed only by a single favourite, who did not know whither she was going . . . The princess and her maid turned their eyes toward every part, and, seeing nothing to bound their prospect, considered themselves as in danger of being lost in a dreary vacuity. They stopped and trembled." A second very brief allusion occurs in the next chapter (XVI), as they arrive at Cairo. "The princess . . . for some days, continued in her chamber, where she was served by her favourite

From *Imagined Worlds: Essays on English Novels and Novelists in Honour of John Butt*. © 1968 by Methuen & Co.

as in the palace of the valley." Thereafter, for fourteen chapters (XVII–XXX), or during the whole first period at Cairo, including the trip to the cataract of the Nile to visit the hermit, we miss this personage altogether, until in chapter XXXI, at the great Pyramid, she reappears abruptly: "the favourite of the princess, looking into the cavity, stepped back and trembled. 'Pekuah, said the princess, of what art thou afraid?' " In the first edition, this was the first introduction of the lady's name. For the second edition, Johnson went back and inserted this name after the word "favourite" in the sentence quoted above from chapter XVI. We remember that Pekuah, through her terror of the gloomy inside of the pyramid, remains outside and in chapter XXXIII is kidnapped by a band of Arab horsemen and becomes the central object of attention during six succeeding chapters (to XXXIX). She reappears thereafter, to the end of the story, in every family conversation (chapters XLIV, XLV, XLVII, XLIX); and in chapter XLVI, her interest in the stars, acquired while she was a prisoner of the Arab chief, is exploited when the ladies invade and civilize the mad astronomer. Once he had conferred a few colours upon this lady, Johnson found her a convenient enough addition to his *dramatis personae.* It is possible that, having in chapters XV and XVI, provided for her presence, he then forgot her, or even deliberately left her out of sight, for seventeen chapters. But it seems at least possible—to me it seems more likely—that he first conceived of the lady Pekuah as his travellers stood at the entrance of the Pyramid, and he bethought himself of Arab horsemen on the horizon and the opportunity to give his story an impetus towards action which at that juncture it badly needed. In that case, he went back (nothing could be simpler) and inserted the allusions to a "favourite" in chapters XV and XVI, and in the second edition the name Pekuah in chapter XVI.

As Geoffrey Tillotson has already observed, Johnson throughout *Rasselas* is preoccupied with the passage of time and pays close attention to the number of days, months, and years which measure out his story. At the age of twenty-six, for example, when he first becomes restless in his confinement, Rasselas lets twenty months slip away in day-dreaming, then awakes and estimates with chagrin that, since the active life of man, between infancy and senility, amounts to no more than forty years, he has just allowed a twenty-fourth part of his life to run to waste ($12 \times 40 = 480 \div 20 = 24$). In contrast to such numerical nicety, the following curious sequence occurs in chapters XIX, XX, and XXI. Rasselas and his friends hear of a hermit, famous for sanctity, who lives near the "lowest cataract of the Nile." They set out to visit him but stop during the "heat" of the [first] day at the tents of some shepherds, whose barbarous conversation proves disgusting to the princess (chapter XIX). Presumably they do not linger for the afternoon or spend the night with these shepherds. But: "On the *next day* [the italics are mine] they continued their journey," says the first sentence of chapter XX. Again they stop during the "heat" of the day, but this time at the "stately palace" of a very prosperous gentleman. He entreats them to stay. They do. And the "next day" he entreats them again. The "continued," in fact, "a few days longer, and then went forward to find the hermit." Then the next chapter (XXI) begins: "They came on the third day, by the direction of the peasants, to the hermit's cell." By the direction of the peasants? Some might argue that this means simply "*the* peasants" of that region. But this kind of slipshod phrasing is not like Johnson. It appears to me all but certain that "peasants" is one of Johnson's occasional quiet or pronominal "elegant variations." He means the "shepherds" with whom they stopped at midday during chapter XIX. After that, and "on the third day" after setting out, they came to the hermit's cell. It seems to me very likely that the episode of the prosperous country gentleman is something which occurred to Johnson at some time after he had written the sequence about the shepherds and the hermit (chapters XIX, XXI), and that, wishing to get it in, he wrote it in where he could, but without noticing a slight derangement of the details of the itinerary. The stop with the shepherds is a brief episode which does not sidetrack the journey to the hermit. Chapter XX, on the downfall of a prosperous country gentleman, is an extended intrusion into that journey. *Raaselas* is in a sense a travel story, but it is not on the whole a picaresque story.

The third example of narrative absent-mindedness which I wish to notice does, however, give us another exception to that rule. Chapter XL (immediately after the narrative of Pekuah's captivity with the Arab), begins: "They returned to Cairo . . . none of them went much abroad. The prince . . . one day declared to Imlac, that he intended to devote himself to science, and pass the rest of his days in literary solitude. 'Before you make your final choice, answered Imlac, you ought to examine its hazards . . . I have just left the observatory of one of the most learned astronomers in the world.' " For the space of five chapters (XL, XLI, XLII, XLIII, XLIV) Imlac continues a non-stop lecture upon the mad delusion by which the astronomer believes himself possessed of the power to control the seasons, bringing rain or sunshine to any part of the world as his conscience dictates. We discover that not only Rasselas but Nekayah and Pekuah are present during the whole conversation (chapters XLII and XLIV). Then chapter XLV breaks into this sequence as follows: "The evening was now far past, and they rose to return home. As they walked along the bank of the Nile, delighted with the beams of the moon quivering on the water, they saw at a small distance an old man." But this does not really make sense. If we look back through the involvements of Imlac's long discourse on the mad astronomer, to the beginning of chapter XL, we remember that they are already at home and have been during the whole episode. (Looking back yet farther, a long way back, to chapter XXV, one might recall that during the first period at Cairo the prince and princess "commonly met in the evening in a private summer-house on the bank of the Nile." But this summer-house either was on the grounds of the main house rented and magnificently furnished in chapter XVI, or it was not. If not, if it was away from home, nothing in chapters XL–XLIV intimates that they have now gone there.) The episode of the mad astronomer has not been concluded. After chapter XLV, "They discourse with an old man," the long and dramatically important chapter XLVI immediately resumes the story of the astronomer, telling how he is visited by the ladies, Nekayah and Pekuah, and under the softening influence of feminine conversation is gradually cured of his delirious fantasy. Chapter XLV, devoted to the old man, a characteristically and passionately Johnsonian projection of the bitterness of old age, is a stark intrusion into the sequence about the astronomer. In its absent-minded opening, it seems to me another of Johnson's afterthoughts, so important that it had to go somewhere. Where else would seem better when the other episodes were already in sequence?

"STRUCTURE"

I have been urging genetic inferences and have not meant to imply that the actual inconsistencies which I observe (with the possible exception of Pekuah's long absence from the stage) are in any sense aesthetic deficiencies. They do, however, appear to me as complements of and accents upon a much larger and more clearly observable character of the whole story— what I would describe as its highly episodic, and hence very lumpy or bumpy, structure. One recent critic of *Rasselas,* Professor Kolb, has said that it is arranged in two main parts, one in the happy valley, one after the escape. Another critic, Professor Hilles, has discerned three main parts:

1. in the valley, chapters I–XIV;
2. the escape and a period of relatively detached and orderly *observation* at and near Cairo, chapters XV–XXX;
3. beginning with the abduction of Pekuah and the grief of Nekayah, a period of greater personal *involvement* and, at the end, of more somber experience, chapters XXXIII–XLIX.

In the chapters following the episode of Pekuah's abduction (if I may expand this theme a little), the mad astronomer is not merely observed, but converted from his delirium and received into the family; even the bitter old man comes home with them for a brief conversation. A climax of experience and reflection is reached in the antepenultimate chapters, with the visit to the Catacombs, Imlac's argument for the immortality of the soul, and Nekayah's conclusion: "To me . . . the choice of life is become less important; I hope hereafter to think only on the choice of eternity."

Nevertheless, I believe that the forty-nine chapters of the tale fall even more readily into another and more piecemeal pattern—more readily because with more aesthetic immediacy, more clearly segmented colouring. Thus:

1. chapters I–VI, the *unrest* of Rasselas in the valley, climaxed by the attempt at flying;
2. chapters VII–XV, the *story* of Imlac (surely too long in proportion to the whole book) and the implausible *escape* by tunnelling through the mountain;
3. chapters XVI–XXII, the first period at Cairo, *exploratory,* varicoloured, embracing the visit to the hermit;
4. chapters XXIII–XXIX, an extended *conversation,* on public and private life, on marriage and celibacy, between Rasselas and Nekayah;
5. chapters XXX–XXXIX, *adventures:* the Pyramids, abduction and recovery of Pekuah;
6. chapters XL–XLIX, return to Cairo and more *somber* experiences: the mad astronomer, the bitter old man, the Catacombs, the end.

In each of these six segments, certain subdivisions can of course be seen. The first period in Cairo is notable for the rapid succession of separately sought-out episodes. The relentlessly continued conversation between the prince and his sister (chapters XXIII–XXIX) occupies the middle of the whole story as a prolonged central stasis or dead center. The sequence in which Pekuah is the focus of attention (chapters XXXI–XXXIX) is notable for the relative continuity of the adventure story. The visit to the Pyramids which begins this part, or ends the preceding, seems like a heavy punctuation mark (the accent of antiquity and the tomb), and this indeed is echoed in a second and similar punctuation, the visit to the Catacombs, which signals the end of the whole. The second period at Cairo, though it has fewer incidents than the first, is a sort of counterpart to the first, echoing its

structure across the interval of the long conversation and the long adventure.
Inside one episode in each Cairo period, a shorter and abruptly introduced
intercalary episode, as we have seen, stands out like a special bump or knob
in the grain of the story. The embittered and malignant old man looks out
from his knot-hole or niche back across the chapters to the fearful and ruined
country gentleman. But it is difficult to say just what is accomplished for
the whole pattern by features of this sort. It is difficult, on the whole, to
speak of the "structure" of *Rasselas* in a sense anything like that in which
one speaks of the structure of a play by Shakespeare or of a novel by Fielding
or Jane Austen. *Rasselas* has the kind of structure which satisfies, more or
less, its modest requirements as a quasi-dramatic narrative—not the causal
progression, the beginning, middle, and end of the Aristotelian "whole,"
but a structure of accumulation, something like that of a series of laboratory
reports, or a series of chapters on animals sighted or taken, on a hunt across
the veldt with gun or camera. "Eye Nature's walks, shoot Folly as it flies,
And catch the Manners living as they rise."

Both Professor Kolb and, with less emphasis, Professor Hilles point
out that the story, and especially the section dealing with the first period
at Cairo, organizes a series of parallels and oppositions of human states and
moral ideas: "prince and princess, male and female," wise Imlac . . . naïve
prince," "normal life . . . the happy valley," "urban life . . . rural," "epicurean . . . stoic," "shepherd, landlord, and hermit," "great and . . .
humble," "youth and age, celibacy and matrimony . . . past and present."
There is nothing wrong with this kind of analysis. This kind of order, in
some degree, may well be one of the requisites for the successful telling of
such a tale. On the other hand, some such order is needed too in a moral
essay or treatise, and maybe there it is needed even more. (It fits the conversation of the prince and his sister even better than their explorations.)
We do not contrive a story for the sake of getting this kind of order, but
perhaps the contrary, for the sake of relieving the threat of its rigors.

THE STREAKS OF THE TULIP

To put the matter conventionally and moderately, it is a paradox that
a man who had Johnson's preference for both the homely and the abstract
should undertake an oriental tale at all. Or better, it is a strangely fit
incongruity that this tale, which both tries and refuses to be oriental, should
contain as one of its most memorable exhibits a discourse on the art of poetry
in which occurs the following sequence of assertions:

1. "I could never describe what I had not seen . . . I ranged mountains and deserts for images and resemblances, and pictured upon my mind every tree of the forest and flower of the valley."
2. "The business of a poet . . . is to examine, not the individual, but the species; to remark general properties and large appearances: he does not number the streaks of the tulip."
3. "He must be acquainted likewise with all the modes of life . . . and trace the changes of the human mind as they are modified by various institutions and accidental influences of climate and custom."

The local colour of *Rasselas,* the "oriental imagery" to the "charms" of which Boswell alludes, is not luxuriant. It is even very thin, and we may at moments wish it were thicker. It has a curiously deductive and even conjectural character—like the effort of a man who has read long ago a book of eastern travels for the purpose of translation; perhaps too has dipped into another book or two in the more recent past.

The most conspicuous colour consists simply in the proper names of places, persons, and offices. We are "oriented" at the outset (chapter I) by the names "Abissinia," "Egypt," and "Amhara." Soon we follow Imlac (chapters VIII–XII) from "Goiama," near the "fountain of the Nile," by way of "the shore of the red sea," to "Surat," and to "Agra, the capital of Indostan," city of the "great Mogul," and thence to "Persia," "Arabia," "Syria," "Palestine," "many regions of Asia," "Egypt," "Cairo," and "Suez"—the latter names pre-establishing for us the route which will be followed by the fugitives from the valley a few chapters hence. Later, the sequence of adventure chapters (XXX–XXXIX) gives us "old Egyptians," the "Pyramids" (over and over), a "troop of Arabs," "Turkish horsemen," the "Bassa" at Cairo, the "borders of Nubia," "the monastery of St. Anthony," "the deserts of Upper-Egypt," the "Arab's fortress" on an "island of the Nile . . . under the tropick."

"How easily shall we then trace the Nile through all his passage," says the aeronautical artist back in chapter VI. This is the first of altogether fifteen allusions by name to that great geographical feature and symbol. The escapees from the happy valley behold "the Nile, yet a narrow current, wandering beneath them." The hermit of chapter XXI lives "near the lowest cataract of the Nile." The "annual overflow" or "inundation" of the Nile is a leitmotif of chapters XLI–XLV, dealing with both the mad weather-maker

[margin handwritten notes: "15 allusions to the Nile"; "the hermit lives at the lowest cataract of the Nile"]

and the sad old man. ("I rest against a tree, and consider, that in the same
shade I once disputed upon the annual overflow of the Nile with a friend
who is now silent in the grave.") In chapter XLIX, the Conclusion, a final
"inundation of the Nile" confines the prince and his friends to reflection at
home (as, long since, in the happy valley, Rasselas and Imlac had been
brought together in "domestick amusements" forced upon them by an "inundation" from the lake). "No man," says the wise and aphoristic Nekayah,
concluding an earlier chapter of conversation (XXIX), "can, at the same
time, fill his cup from the source and from the mouth of the Nile." But
Johnson has come close to doing just this.

Another vehicle of exoticism may be identified here and there in a
certain courtly, ceremonious, and archaic flourish of words—what Professor
Hilles has called "the Grand Style," an aspect of the sublime. This occurs
a few times in the author's own voice, as in the opening of the first chapter:
"Ye who listen with credulity to the whispers of fancy . . . attend." More
often it is from the mouths of the characters—no doubt what the country
gentleman of chapter XX detected as the "eloquence of Imlac . . . and the
lofty courtesy of the princess." (It is Miltonic—like "Daughter of God and
Man, immortal Eve.") As Rasselas saw the animals by moonlight, " 'Ye,'
said he, 'are happy . . . nor do I, ye gentle beings, envy your felicity.' "
(chapter II). " 'Dear princess', said Rasselas, 'you fall into the common error
of exaggeratory declamation.' " (chapter XXVIII). " 'My dear Pekuah,' said
the princess . . . 'Remember that you are companion of the princess of
Abissinia.' " (chapter XXXI). "Whoever thou art, that . . . imaginest happiness in royal magnificence, and dreamest . . . perpetual gratifications,
survey the pyramids, and confess thy folly!" (chapter XXXII). Here Imlac
echoes the rhythm of the narrator in the first sentence of the book. "Illustrious
lady," said even the Arab outlaw, "my fortune is better than I had presumed
to hope." "Lady," said he, "you are to consider yourself as soverign." (chapter
XXXVIII, XXXIX). Probably the most full-blown instance in the book
returns us, characteristically, to geography and to the mighty river. In
chapter XXV, "The princess and her brother commonly met in the evening
in a private summer-house on the bank of the Nile . . . As they were sitting
together, the princess cast her eyes upon the river that flowed before her."
And:

> "Answer," said she, "great father of waters, thou that rollest thy
> floods through eighty nations, to the invocations of the daughter
> of thy native king. Tell me if thou waterest, through all thy

course, a single habitation from which thou dost not hear the murmurs of complaint?"

Certain other details of local colour are much less distinctive. At the start (chapter I) we are treated to "mountains," "rivulets," a "lake," "fish of every species," water falling "from precipice to precipice," "the banks of the brooks . . . diversified with flowers," "beasts of prey," "flocks and herds," "beasts of chase frisking in the lawns." We hear also of a "palace" with "squares or courts," "arches of massy stone," "upper stories," "private galleries," "subterranean passages," "columns," and "unsuspected cavities" closed with "marble." Such terms, so frequent throughout the work, whenever the argument seems to call for some evocation of physical decor, work as local colour mainly or only in conjunction with the proper names of places and persons which we have seen. It seems scarcely extreme to say that these combinations make the kind of local colour a schoolboy might supply. When I was in the eighth grade, we studied geography (which that year was Africa), and we had to write an imaginary journey through Egypt. I can still remember, approximately, one sentence of my composition—because it struck me at the time as so neatly yet richly executed. "Turning a bend in the Nile, we came in sight of the giant Assouan Dam."

Certain other descriptive details are indeed more specially exotic. These, however, are scarce. I attempt the following approximately exhaustive list. In the "torrid zone" of chapter I, we find the "monkey" and the "elephant." At the start of Imlac's travels in chapter VIII, we have "camels" and "bales" of goods. In chapter IX and again in XII, we have a "caravan," and in chapter X the "mosque of Mecca." In chapter XVIII, at Cairo, a "spacious building," with "open doors," housing a "school of declamation, in which professors read lectures," seems in spite of its vagueness, much like a part of the ancient Alexandrian world. The shepherds in chapter XIX live in "tents." At the estate of the prosperous country gentleman in chapter XX, "youths and virgins" are "dancing in the grove" near a "stately palace." In XXI, the hermit's "cell" is a "cavern" beneath "palm-trees." In XXX, as we begin to think of the Pyramids, we hear of "fragments of temples" and "choked aqueducts." In XXXII appear "galleries" and "vaults of marble"; in XXXIII, "dark labyrinths." The travel in the desert (chapters XXXI– XXXIX) gives us "tents" (nine times), "camels" (three), "ounces of gold" (three), "deserts" and "the desert," a "monastery," a "refectory," and a "prior"; in XXXVIII appear "carpets," "finer carpets," Pekuah's "upper vest" (with "embroidery"), "the lance," "the sword," "palaces," "temples," "granite," "porphyry"; in XXXIX, "the tropick," a "couch," "turrets," two special plums: "crocodiles" and "river-horses," "needlework," "silken flowers," and another plum: the "seraglio." In the final expedition, to the catacombs (XLVII–XLVIII), we have a "guard of horsemen," "sepulchral caves," a "labyrinth of subterraneous passages," "embalming" and "embalmed" bodies, "caverns."

A few ingenous manipulations of this slender exotic store, cunning jointures of it with the Johnsonian philosophic and plastic staple, stand out. In chapter I, just as I become mildly annoyed at "beasts of chase frisking in the lawns" and "the sprightly kid . . . bounding on the rocks," I am moderately diverted by "the subtle monkey frolicking in the trees, and the solemn elephant reposing in the shade." (No matter whether elephants would really be found in that mountain fastness). By a somewhat different sort of conjunction, it seems to me, Johnson creates a moment of interesting local colour in chapter XXXIX, as Pekuah looks out on the "winding" river from her island prison: "The crocodiles and river-horses are common in this unpeopled region . . . For some time I expected to see mermaids and tritons, which, as Imlac has told me, the European travellers have stationed in the Nile." And here let us quote too that moment of pregnant phrasing from chapter XXX: "The most pompous monument of Egyptian greatness, and one of the most bulky works of manual industry . . . are the pyramids." And from chapter XXXVIII, the Arab's observation to the lady Pekuah that

> buildings are always best preserved in places little frequented, and difficult of access: for, when once a country declines from its primitive splendour, the more inhabitants are left, the quicker ruin will be made. Walls supply stones more easily than quarries, and palaces and temples will be demolished to make stables of granite, and cottages of porphyry.

By a slight extension of the idea of the exotic, perhaps we can bring in such learned words from the realm of *Mathematical Magick* as Johnson borrowed from his archaic dictionary source of that title, or from other "philosophic" sources, and worked into chapter VI, the story of an attempt at the art of flying: "the tardy conveyance of ships and chariots," "the swifter migration of wings," "the pendent spectator," "volant animals," "the folding continuity of the bat's wings." And with these we come close to yet a wider category of somewhat notable descriptive phrases—all those, I should say, which, without including any word in any way exotic or bizarre, yet by some special energy of compression are likely to strike our attention or force on us the feeling that the description has "texture." In chapter I, the lake

is "frequented by every fowl whom nature has taught to dip the wing in
water . . . every blast shook spices from the rocks, and every month dropped
fruits upon the ground. All animals that bite the grass, or brouse the shrub
. . . wandered in this extensive circuit." Such phrases as these may be looked
on as Johnsonian substitutes for local colour.

A recent observer from the vantage point of Saudi-Arabia has expounded
the extreme unrealism of the journey made by the princely party of fugitives,
by ups and downs, through the nearly impassable tropical forests of the
Abyssinian plateau, and then down the steep seven or eight thousand feet
from the eastern escarpment to the narrow coastal plain and the port where
they stayed several months. (This was probably Masawa, a typical Red Sea
port, a "horrible place," lying under relentless sun, in saturation humidity.)
No less dimly realized seem their "quick and prosperous" coastal voyage [of
twenty or thirty days] in a primitive sailing dhow, their slow trip by camel
caravan under the desert stars to Cairo, and finally what must have been the
astonished arrival of this party of Coptic Christians amid the teeming contrasts of a vast Islamic city.

Johnson, we know, had long enjoyed some awareness of the Abyssinian
locale, for as a young man he had written and published (1735) a translation
from a French version of the seventeenth-century Portuguese Jesuit Father
Jerome Lobo's *Voyage to Abyssinia.* Of recent years, the scholarship of sources
has been urging Johnson's debt to other writers on Abyssinia. Lobo, it is
clear, could not have been his only source, for Lobo said the prison of the
princess was a rocky and "barren summit." But the paradise on the Abyssinian hill was a commonplace—"where Abassin kings their issue guard,
Mount Amara—by some supposed True Paradise, under the Ethiop line."
One of the reasons why Johnson was interested in Lobo's *Voyage* was that
the Jesuit missionary and diplomat himself was more interested in human
character and mores, the hardships and vicissitudes of the human adventure,
than in exotic or fantastic colourations. Thus, Lobo reports of the crocodiles
(which Pekuah saw from the Arab's island fortress): "Neither I nor any with
whom I have convers'd about the *Crocodile,* have ever seen him Weep, and
therefore I take the Liberty of ranking all that hath been told us of his Tears,
amongst the Fables which are only proper to amuse Children." And Johnson,
in a Preface to Lobo which Boswell by quoting has made the best-known
part of the book:

THE *Portugese* Traveller, contrary to the general Vein of his Countrymen, has amused his Reader with no Romantick Absurdities
or Incredible Fictions . . . HE appears by his modest and un-

affected Narration to have described Things as he saw them, to have copied Nature from the Life, and to have consulted his Senses not his Imagination; He meets with no *Basilisks* that destroy with their Eyes, his *Crocodiles* devour their Prey without Tears, and his *Cataracts* fall from the Rock without Deafening the Neighbouring Inhabitants.

Samuel Johnson—both Johnson the man and Johnson the translator of Lobo and the narrator of *Rasselas*—no doubt believes that even the local colours, the geography, the flora, the fauna, the architecture, and the costumes, of exotic places are far less exotic than is commonly reported. Beyond doubt, he believes that human living and human nature in Amhara or in Cairo are far less exotic than is commonly supposed, are indeed essentially the same as in London.

> THE Reader . . . will discover, what will always be discover'd by a diligent and impartial Enquirer, that wherever Human Nature is to be found, there is a mixture of Vice and Virtue, a contest of Passion and Reason.

General human nature is of course Johnson's theme—vice and virtue, passion and reason. Why not then generalized local colour? The deliberate simplification, even complacent ignorance about the actual colours of life in the supposed locale of Johnson's story, is a kind of counterpart and symbol of the general human truth he would be getting at.

A CHORUS OF SAGES

Various critical questions might be asked about *Rasselas,* but surely the main question must always be: What are we to make of the fact that the obvious element of morality is cast in the shape of an oriental tale? Or, what are we to make of the fact that the equally obvious oriental tale is invested with so much morality? The problem, or the task, of a writer who would tell a moral tale is, of course, to get the story and the morality together. He will have to do better than give us a close juxtaposition or rapid alternation of plot and sermon (programme and commercial plug), or a set of essays in a curiously wrought frame, a series of *Ramblers* inserted in a version of the *Arabian Nights*. "We do not read *Rasselas* for the story," says Professor Hilles. "We read it for a view of life that is presented majestically in long sweeping phrases." But he immediately adds: "Diction, rhythms, character and plot are all of a piece." So that he really has a warmer affection for the story (character and plot) than, for instance, Professor Kolb, who, while implying some distress at those critics who "have been content to praise, the wisdom and ignore the narrative," at the same time (and on the same page) concludes "that the tale is not the principle which best explains . . . the book . . . the problem of happiness rather than the element of 'story' emerges . . . as the determinant by reference to which questions about the book's structure may be most adequately answered." The structure is "didactic." And this seems to imply somehow that we can call it a "narrative," but not a "tale" or a "story."

In the second section of this essay, I have already given up the "structure" of *Rasselas* so far as that idea pretends to any Aristotelian or organistic and dramatic implications. But then a story does not have to have *much* structure in order to be a story. It is a story if it has any characters and places at all, and if the characters do any talking at all and move about a little, from one place (or one state) to another. The story of *Rasselas* as such, a certain movement of certain persons in certain places—loosely constructed, vaguely characterized, largely undramatic or half-heartedly dramatic as it may be, unfictional fabric of a fiction that it is—has, nevertheless, some kind of imaginative bearing on the moral ideas. This is not an original thesis. "The eastern background," says Professor Kolb, "provides . . . the aura of strange and distant lands where human happiness is commonly thought to be complete and lasting; . . . reminding us of the superficial likenesses and essential differences between *Rasselas* and ordinary oriental tales with their happy-ever-after conclusions." "The judgement of human life," says Professor Leyburn, "would leave a very different impression if it were presented stripped of such aesthetic distance as the regions of the Nile provide." Oriental decor had been used in Augustan England for stories of adventure and fantasy (*Arabian Nights* and *Persian Tales*). It had well-established didactic uses too—as in *Spectator* and *Rambler* visions and apologues. An oriental spokesman could be used to throw a strange and skeptical perspective on Western mores (Montesquieu's *Persian Letters*, Goldsmith's *Chinese Letters*— just after *Rasselas*). The peculiar twist of Johnson's *Rasselas* is that he uses a sort of nominally or minimally exotic tale for the purpose of displaying the most homely human materials and of asserting a workaday perspective upon them. The philosophy of *Rasselas* (Johnson's resistance to eighteenth-century "optimism") might readily enough become our theme now, but I am pushing, not the philosophy but the literary actualization of it, trying to improve the view that it is important for Johnson's anti-rationalist and conservative purpose that he *should* have a story, of sorts, and foreign scene.

The Johnsonian substitutes for local colour, we have said, are abstractive, at moments "philosophic," and all but invisible. They may, for that very reason, have a broader spread than we have so far mentioned. It was Johnson himself who observed of Sir Thomas Browne that he "poured a multitude of exotick words," and Johnson's friends Boswell and Arthur Murphy who thought that Browne was a main source for Johnson's own "Anglo-Latian" peculiarities. "How he differed so widely from such elegant models [the Augustans] is a problem not to be solved, unless it be true that he took an early tincture from the writers of the last century, particularly Sir Thomas Browne." Twenty-five years ago I ventured the opinion that Browne "deserves the name 'exotick' which Johnson applies to him," but that this name would sit "curiously on Johnson himself." "Where Browne uses remote terms to make us think of remote things"—Pharaoh, mummy, golden calf, scorpion, and salamander—"Johnson 'familiarizes.' " That much is still true. But, on the other hand, I will now undertake to argue that Johnson's whole way of moral writing, what we may call the *Rambler* style, is a form of moderate exoticism which did not find its ideal setting until he wrote *Rasselas.* During the course of producing his 208 *Ramblers,* Johnson tried out a number of domestic settings of voices for the Rambler mood: the country housewife and her kitchen (No. 51), Mr. Frolick the Londoner in the country (No. 61), Quisquilius the curio-collector (Nos. 82–83), Nugaculus the gossip (No. 103), Mrs. Busy (No. 138), Captator the legacy-hunter (Nos. 197–198). But in all such instances, the more dramatic he makes the treatment, the more the peculiar Rambleresque pomp of phrasing thins out. This happens even in the exotic setting of the Greenland idyll of Anningait and Ajut (Nos. 186–187). Perhaps it happens too with the several oriental tales, including that of the Emperor Seged of Ethiopia (Nos. 204–205). Yet with the Emperor Seged, Johnson was verging on the discovery of a curiously heightened affinity between story and philosophic idiom. Perhaps the *Rambler* had been all along a series of oriental apologues without the plot and local colour?—the Rambler himself a kind of Abyssinian sage without the name and the overt ethnic colouration? It was a strange language, that language of the Rambler in his own persona. Who really talked that way? Not Dryden or Addison, or Lord Chesterfield. Not really Johnson himself, except perhaps in the moments of his conversation when he was being the consciously pompous self-parodist or when Mrs. Thrale and Burney had come into the library at Streatham to "make" him "speak" a *Rambler.*

The part of *Rasselas* which we remember best and carry away with us for allusion and quotation—the portable part—is beyond question the aphoristic moralism, the lugubrious orotundity. "We do not read *Rasselas* for the story." "Human life is everywhere a state in which much is to be endured, and little to be enjoyed." Who says this? Imlac, Rasselas, Nekayah, the Stoic philosopher, the hermit, the Arab, the mad astronomer, the old man? Any one of these, at the right moment, might say it. Actually, of course, we remember it is Imlac, near the end of his narrative of his own life (chapter XI)—the same Imlac who later, seated in one of the "most spacious chambers" of the great Pyramid, discourses so eloquently, in a vein of inverse romantic vision: "It seems to have been erected only in compliance with that hunger of imagination which preys incessantly upon life, and must be always appeased by some employment . . . I consider this mighty structure as a monument of the insufficiency of human enjoyments." (chapter XXXII). The same Imlac, who when the prince looks on a fissure in the rocks as a "good omen" of escape from the valley, replies—almost like a wound-up automaton, a speaking toy-philosopher: "If you are pleased with prognosticks of good, you will be terrified likewise with tokens of evil . . . Whatever facilitates our work is more than an omen, it is a cause of success . . . Many things difficult to design prove easy to performance."

"Marriage has many pains, but celibacy has no pleasures." Who says this? Any one of several characters might say it. Actually the speaker is the maiden princess Nekayah, in the course (chapter XXVI) of that lengthy and soon quarrelsome conversation with her brother about such profound issues: public and private life, youth and age, celibacy or marriage. The same princess who a few pages later, in the accents of a proto-Screwtape, "reckons" for us "the various forms of connubial infelicity . . . the rude collisions of contrary desire . . . the obstinate contests of disagreeable virtues, where both are supported by consciousness of good intention" (chapter XXVIII). The same princess whom we have already heard, seated in the summer-house by the bank of the Nile, utter her apostrophe to that mighty "father of waters" who rolls his "floods through eighty nations."

The courtly and ceremonious discourse which we have already noticed as a kind of local colour is only the most obvious instance of a lofty and reflective idiom which plausibly pervades nearly the whole of this oriental tale. (The notion of an oriental sage, philosopher, poet, emperor, prince, is an easy one for us to entertain. Who ever heard of an oriental buffoon or ninny?) The *Rambler* idiom, Johnson's own idiom, if we like, an expansion of homely human wisdom into the large perspective of Latinate philosophic diction, is projected across time and space, straight from London and Fleet Street, to cover appropriately, with a veil of the delicately exotic, scenes which we know, by a more than willing suspension of disbelief are enacted at places along the Nile from Amhara to Cairo.

The notion of *Rasselas* as a "comedy" (Johnson's "greatest comic work") has been urged by two recent writers. A third, Professor Hilles again, thinks that they "overstress" the "comic element." Probably they do overstress it. Professor Tracy sees a "comic" (perhaps, rather, a "satirical") reduction of man's fatuousness, shrewd laughter at the prince's chronic failure of common sense, demolition of the poet Imlac's "grandiloquent . . . rapture." Professor Whitley finds "pure comedy of ideas" in the episodes of the first period at Cairo, "comedy of emotion and behaviour," and "deflated oriental romance," in Pekuah's abduction, "dark comedy" in the later chapters about the mad astronomer and the catacombs. Probably we are on safer ground if we are content to say, with Professor Hilles, simply that the attitude prevailing in the story is not, as so often said, "pessimistic," not morose, not cynical, not even satirical; it is rather, gently "ironic" and "realistic." The "smile of the author is a sad smile." Yes—though one may need to insist that it *is* a smile. With Professor Hilles, we must differ from certain critics who have supposed that a "tragic sense of life . . . informs it." It appears to me next to impossible that anyone should be moved either to tears or to shudders at any part of *Rasselas*. "In a short time the second Bassa was deposed. The Sultan [at Constantinople], that had advanced him, was murdered by the Janisaries." But that was, if not a long time ago, yet very far in another country. (The chapter, XVIII, where the Stoic philosopher mourning the death of his daughter is put in a position of nearly laughable contrast to his declamation of the preceding day is perhaps the only part of the whole book that verges on the uncomfortable.) "In a year the wings were finished and, on a morning appointed, the maker appeared furnished for flight on a little promontory: he waved his pinions a while to gather air, then leaped from his stand, and in an instant dropped into the lake." There we have the characteristic motion of the story as action—the immediate and inevitable plunge, so inevitable and so confidently foreseen as to warrant not the smallest flourish or comment. " 'I . . . resolve to return into the world tomorrow' . . . He dug up a considerable treasure which he had hid among the rocks, and accompanied them to the city, on which, as he approached it, he gazed with rapture." (chapter XXI). At many moments the comic smile of the narrator is turned directly on one or another of his characters. " 'But surely, interposed the prince . . . Whenever I shall seek a wife, it shall be my first question, whether she be willing to be led by reason?' " (chapter XXIX). More often, however, or in general, the smile of this narrator envelops in a less direct way, in a more reticent parodic spirit, the whole of his own Abyssinian tale. He is very close to the endlessly meditative and controversial nature of each of his personae. What does the narrator think of his own "Tale" when he gives his chapters titles such as these: "The prince continues to grieve and muse," "A dissertation on the art of flying," "Imlac's history continued. A dissertation upon poetry," "Disquisition upon greatness," "Rasselas and Nekayah continue their conversation," "The dangerous prevalence of imagination," "The conclusion, in which nothing is concluded"?

In real life, Johnson sometimes indulged in a complacent self-consciousness and amusement at his own inflations. His moments of self-parody are celebrated. In his essays too, *Ramblers* and *Idlers,* a sort of shackled playfulness often parodies the solemn parade. A shadow of grimace accents some restrained contrast between gravity of diction and homeliness or meanness of sentiment. In *Rasselas,* the Johnsonian speaker has translated himself into a realm of sober fantasy where the grim smile, the sad smile, the wan smile, can be more or less constant. Probably it was some feeling like this about the tale that prompted Voltaire to say that its philosophy was *aimable.* Indeed there are profoundly reflective and even solemn moments—and they occur increasingly in the later chapters—at the Pyramids, in the conversation about the astronomer's madness, in the confrontation with the savagely embittered old man, and finally at the Catacombs, in the contemplation of death and immortality. But the last seems to me the only place where it may be impossible to find a smile. Here the initially dominant tone is metaphysical sobriety ("as thought is, such is the power that thinks; a power impassive and indiscerptible"), and this deepens at the end of theological solemnity ("The whole assembly stood a while silent and collected . . . 'To me,' said the princess, 'the choice of life is become less important: I hope hereafter to think only on the choice of eternity' "). But this is an exceptional moment, not the ground tone of the book and not its conclusion. The conclusion, in which nothing is concluded, reverts to the basic plan.

It is not possible to smile sympathetically at nothingness without a degree of participation. Johnson's way of laughter is not the high-comedy way of the wit and his butts, but a quieter way of partly encumbered rehearsal and laboured formulation. Martin Price has deftly alluded to the "gently preposterous oriental setting" of Johnson's tale, "the self-mocking formality of its dialogue, the balance and antithesis of characters as well as dialogue, and the circularity of its total structure." All this is the *imagination* of Johnson's quasi-oriental and ceremonious no-tale—"the wine of absurdity," or absurdity mitigated only in its own rich self-contemplation. In our day, Albert Camus has explained absurdity in Kantian terms as "the division between the mind that desires and the world that disappoints." Johnson's *Rasselas* has much in common with modern versions of the absurd—with a *Godot* or a *Watt.* One main difference, which may disguise the parallel for us, is that the modern versions of the descent take place at a level which is, to start with, subterranean, the very sub-cellar or zero level of modern man's three-century decline from the pinnacles of theology and metaphysics. Johnson's descendental exercise, with its saving theological clause in the Catacombs, takes place at a level still near the top of the metaphysical structure. It is of course all the richer for this. In the "endgame" played at the modern level, a nearly complete numbness and boredom is roused only as occasional stabs and jolts of obscenity reach a buried nerve. In the more spacious and better lighted areas available to Johnson, there was still eloquence—an eloquence profound and moving as it verges continually on a smiling absurdity.

PAUL FUSSELL

"The Anxious Employment
of a Periodical Writer"

It is now time to turn to Johnson's main writing enterprises—the *Rambler,* the *Dictionary, Rasselas,* and *The Lives of the Poets*—and to consider what they are and what their meaning is within the context of his paradoxical critical and moral equipment, First, the *Rambler.*

"I purpose to endeavor the entertainment of my countrymen by a short essay on Tuesday and Saturday": thus, with an appearance of security and even jauntiness, Johnson announced his plans for the *Rambler* in the first number, on Tuesday, March 20, 1750. Two years and 208 essays later, he looked back over his accomplishment and began the last of the *Ramblers* in the tone of a man sadly illuminated by experience. We hear now of "labors" and anxiety instead of "entertainment" and an easy brevity: "Time, which puts an end to all human pleasures and sorrows, has likewise concluded the labors of the Rambler. Having supported for two years the anxious employment of a periodical writer, and multiplied my essays to upwards of two hundred, I have now determined to desist."

Finding a title had been the first problem, and Reynolds recalls Johnson's report of the way he solved it: "What *must* be done, Sir, *will* be done. When I was to begin publishing that paper, I was at a loss how to name it. I sat down at night upon my bedside and resolved that I would not go to sleep till I had fixed its title. The *Rambler* seemed the best that occurred, and I took it." This must be one of the very few times that one of his "resolutions" came to anything. On this occasion he was perhaps assisted by recalling the title of Savage's poem *The Wanderer,* a work he admired

From *Samuel Johnson and the Life of Writing.* © 1971 by Paul Fussell. Harcourt Brace Jova-novich, 1971.

and often alluded to. And he was certainly assisted by recalling the title chosen in similar circumstances by two of his predecessors: the *Spectator*.

Once the title was settled, the next problem—an unremitting one— was to get down to work, which meant encountering for two years an irrevocable deadline twice a week. For a man so given to procrastination as Johnson, this experience must have been ghastly. Indeed, the twice-weekly crises would remind him in many ways of his twice-weekly examinations (every Thursday and Saturday) by his master Humphrey Hawkins at the Lichfield Grammar School. Or if writing the *Rambler* was not like going to school again, it was at least like presiding over one, and a depressing one at that: Boswell quotes from one of Johnson's notebooks, "I do not remember that since I left Oxford I ever rose early by mere choice, but once or twice at Edial, and two or three times for the *Rambler*." Writing regularly invited him to conceive of regularity as a theme for the *Rambler*. As he encountered his first and second deadlines every week, he was reminded of that week's Christian meaning, and often he devoted Saturday's essay to a Christian exhortation appropriate to the following day. And regular performance month in and month out excited a similar consciousness of the meaning of the Christian year. Robert Voitle has noticed "how much the tone of the *Ramblers* changes around Christmas and Easter. . . . [On these occasions] the *Ramblers* became grave largely because he feels that during these seasons his readers should also meditate on how pitifully weak man is and how little he can accomplish on his own."

Taken as a whole the papers of the *Rambler* are much too rich and complicated to be described easily. They range from the gay to the austere, from the whimsical to the solemn. It can be said, however, that one important object of the *Rambler* is to describe and recommend the psychological technique by which contentment is to be achieved, by which a degree of happiness is to be derived from an acceptance of unalterable circumstance. As Johnson puts it in No. 178, "The reigning error of mankind is that we [not *they*, notice] are not content with the conditions on which the goods of life are granted." Where Christian mechanisms are appropriate for securing content, Johnson invokes them; but almost as often the techniques he suggests derive from pagan commonplaces or from his understanding of his own experience, very closely scrutinized for real motive, or the experience of others he has observed closely. In the many papers devoted to psychological and moral problems, he tries to look at life purely, disregarding the adventitious ornaments and temporary details which give a delusive appearance of specialness or uniqueness to one place or one time. By focusing on the essential springs of human action, by analyzing human desires and their customarily ironic or otherwise unsatisfactory results, he takes us deep into the heart of human psychological experience. His topics are the universal human feelings, the same now as they ever have been and ever will be, of joy, guilt, shame, curiosity, boredom, excitement, frustration, satiety. What the *Rambler* provides is a virtual anatomy of the human emotional life. And there is an unforgettable tenderness in many of Johnson's inquiries; here is no rigorous anatomist like Swift. One of his recurrent topics is the torment of self-consciousness; another is the social desire to be liked; another is, as he designates it in No. 132, "the anxiety of irresolution"; and a favorite is the embarrassments occasioned by social awkwardness. The poles of Johnson's focus are individuals and society; and his topics come alive when he mediates between these poles, studying that point where the individual makes contact, sometimes satisfying, more often humiliating, with society.

As W. J. Bate has perceived, well over a fourth of the *Ramblers* deal in some way with the motive of envy as a primary disturber of the human peace and as the main social cause of discontent and self-imposed misery. In these papers he may have been mindful of Savage's treatment of this theme in *The Wanderer* (lines 353–410). Although the treatment of envy is generally somber and sermonesque, occasionally Johnson brings a severe levity to bear, and we get witty syntactical exhibitions comparable to Popian couplets: "Let it . . . be constantly remembered that whoever envies another confesses his superiority, and let those be reformed by their pride who have lost their virtue" (No. 183). An indication of the curious neglect of Johnson by what might be called the intellectual community is the fact that Professor Helmut Schoeck has recently managed to write 408 pages on *Envy: A Theory of Social Behavior* (London, 1969) without once alluding to Johnson or the *Rambler*.

But he is not always busy analyzing viciousness. Sometimes he turns to anatomize mere folly. As Bate says,

> Johnson seems to become most light-hearted and amusing . . .
> when he is discussing either marriage, the pursuit of wealth, or
> the hopes we place in retirement to country retreats. The ex-
> pectations we feel, in all three cases, also serve for Johnson as
> recurring symbols of the way in which the imagination, in com-
> mon and daily life, is always simplifying the endless desires of
> the heart into specific wants, and then finding them insufficient.

In other words, what he is doing in these gently satiric papers on the pathetic folly of most human wishes is discovering in domestic or low life the same self-destructive motive which, in *The Vanity of Human Wishes,* he has imputed to heroes and scholars and administrators and which, in *Rasselas,* he will disclose as animating the builders of the Pyramids. His ultimate topic, as he puts it in *Rasselas,* is "That hunger of imagination which preys incessantly upon life."

Something of the quality of the whole collection of essays is projected in *Rambler* 208, the paper where Johnson announces his determination to desist. In appearing to reveal the reason why he is quitting he behaves typically: that is, he behaves ironically and frustrates expectation by declining to offer a reason. "The reasons of this resolution," he says, "it is of little importance to declare, since justification is unnecessary when no objection is made." Launched now on the rhetoric of apparent self-pity, he conceals the reason for terminating within a sentence asserting that no reason is going to be vouchsafed: "I am far from supposing that the cessation of my performances will raise any inquiry, for I have never been much a favorite of the public, nor can I boast that, in the progress of my undertaking, I have been animated by the rewards of the liberal, the caresses of the Great, or the praises of the eminent." In announcing that in the role of the Rambler he has "never been much a favorite of the public," Johnson may be comparing his popularity with Addison's, for it is only in comparison with the *Spectator* that the *Rambler* will appear to have been neglected by readers. Although the print-order in London was 500 copies, provincial newspapers all over England picked up and reprinted the essays; and it has been estimated that "within a few days of the first printing, many, if not all, of the *Rambler* papers were being read by thousands of people who did not live in London." Some *Ramblers* even crossed the channel. In 1754 Johnson's friend Arthur Murphy, desperate for copy, came across an appealing Near Eastern morality tale in a French journal. He hastily appropriated and published it, translated, in *Gray's Inn Journal.* It proved to be *Rambler* 190. Johnson was amused.

If, as Johnson says, he cannot "boast" one wild kind of success, he is proud to claim a better sort of triumph, the result of his declining to confuse the momentary and trivial with the permanent and essential:

> If I have not been distinguished by the distributors of literary honors, I have seldom descended to the arts by which favor is obtained. I have seen the meteors of fashion rise and fall without any attempt to add a moment to their duration. I have never complied with temporary curiosity, nor enabled my readers to discuss the topic of the day. I have rarely exemplified my assertions by living characters; in my papers no man could look for censures of his enemies or praises of himself; and they only were

expected to peruse them whose passions left them leisure for abstracted truth, and whom virtue could please by its naked dignity.

It is this complicated sound of mingled failure and success, this subtle interweaving of humility and pride and self-pity, that gives *Rambler* 208 its distinction as an eminently characteristic piece of complex Johnsonian orchestration.

He was especially sensitive to the endings of things ("Time . . . puts an end to all human pleasures and sorrows"), not least literary projects and pieces of writing. The complex tone with which he invests the valedictory *Rambler* anticipates the great conclusion of the Preface to the *Dictionary* three years later. There shame and pride, self-pity and self-congratulation displace each other by turns to bring him to his final confession of foolish procrastination and subsequent misery. But in the Preface he has devised a complex prose world: the proclaimed misery and despair are belied stylistically in his final clause, which achieves a proud, self-sufficient harmony, balance, and rhythm (the final nine words constitute a line of iambic pentameter) suggesting a state of mind and soul quite different from the announced hopelessness: "I have protracted my work till most of those whom I wished to please [he is thinking especially of the dead Tetty] have sunk into the grave, and success and miscarriage are empty sounds: I therefore dismiss [the *Dictionary*] with frigid tranquillity, having little to fear or hope from censure or from praise." As usual, what Johnson's writing "means" is to be searched for where opposites and contradictions encounter each other. As usual, Johnson appears less an annunciator of "views and conclusions than a complicator of the apparent. If the positions asserted in the prose are noble, the means by which they become asserted are sly.

After the paragraph in *Rambler* 208 describing his ideal readers—and flattering them in the act of describing them—he descends to necessary housekeeping details, acknowledging the assistance of others for contributions to seven of the essays. But even here, pride and humility merge inextricably: "My obligations having not been frequent, my acknowledgments may be soon dispatched. I can restore to all my correspondents their productions with little diminution of the bulk of my volumes, though not without the loss of some pieces to which particular honors have been paid." What remains is entirely his own, he goes on to say, and he will neither apologize for it nor seek a patron to protect it: "Having hitherto attempted only the propagation of truth, I will not at last violate it by the confession of terrors which I do not feel; having labored to maintain the dignity of virtue, I will not now degrade it by the meanness of dedication." The parallelism of syntax here implies strongly that the violation of truth and the writing of dedications are close to synonymous: no matter that Johnson was in actual fact the greatest eighteenth-century writer of dedications.

Conscious as always of his own inappropriateness as a moral example and consequently aware of the necessity of a salutary duplicity, he next sets forth his theory of the moral mask under which he has been conducting the *Ramber*. He has expatiated before on this theme, in *Rambler* 14, where he equates the homely human weakness of "oriental monarchs" with the natural frailty of the moral writer considered as a man:

> It has long been the custom of oriental monarchs to hide them-
> selves in gardens and palaces, to avoid the conversation of man-
> kind, and to be known to their subjects only by their edicts. The
> same policy [defined by Johnson in the *Dictionary* in this sense
> as "stratagem"] is no less necessary to him that writes [didac-
> tically], than to him that governs; for men would not more
> patiently submit to be taught than commanded by one known
> to have the same follies and weaknesses with themselves.

And with himself clearly in mind, he goes on in *Rambler* 14: "It may be prudent for a writer who apprehends that he shall not enforce his own maxims by his domestic character to conceal his name that he may not injure them." So concealment is required, not merely as a cloak to cover the actual weak-nesses of author but also as a device of freedom. As he says in *Rambler* 208, quoting Castiglione—an author he never mentions without high praise— " 'A mask . . . confers a right of acting and speaking with less restraint, even when the writer happens to be known.' "

In the *Rambler* Johnson assumes many masks. The main one is that of the "Rambler" himself, the moral instructor who speaks with secure author-ity, entertaining no doubts about his right to instruct others. He is an elderly man who, unlike the actual forty-one-year-old Johnson, has long ago learned to command his passions by studying "the severest and most ab-stracted philosophy" (No. 18). But the roles played in the essays are not always so austere: Johnson clearly enjoys wearing the masks of the various letter-writers who send in their contributions: these fictive correspondents are male and female, young and empty as well as experienced and wise— maltreated servants, eccentric collectors, impatient heirs, awkward scholars embarrassed in fine society. By this gallery of masks Johnson constructs an image of a whole society deeply dipped in folly but capable of a step toward redemption through literary means, that is, through its capacity for re-gretting and confessing its follies in letters to the *Rambler*.

As Johnson continues in No. 208, we are reminded that the whole series of essays is inextricably bound up with his work on the *Dictionary*, from which it served as a twice-weekly respite, if that is the right word to describe a self-imposed disciplinary task. "Only a language experiment" is what Whitman was to call *Leaves of Grass,* and there is a sense in which this formulation describes the *Rambler* as well, despite its overt didacticism and piety. Johnson indicates that while producing the *Rambler* he has been conscious of something much more technical than moral virtue. "I have labored," he says, "to refine our language to grammatical purity, and to clear it from colloquial barbarisms, licentious idioms, and irregular combinations." And then a sentence which syntactically and rhythmically enacts beautifully what it is saying: "Something, perhaps, I have added to the elegance of its construction, and something to the harmony of its cadence." Immersed at the moment in the lexicographer's concern with accurate definition, he goes on to record his reliance on scientific ("philosophic") terminology to clarify the principles of human motivation and its results: "When common words were less pleasing to the ear or less distinct in their signification, I have familiarized the terms of philosophy by applying them to popular ideas, but have rarely admitted any word not authorized by former writers. . . ." The pressure of the continuing work on the *Dictionary* appears in many other places in the *Rambler*: in No. 125, for example, a disquisition on the text "Definitions are hazardous"; or in No. 143, we are told that "Descriptions . . . are definitions of a more lax and fanciful kind." But the most revealing signs of the impact on the *Rambler* of the too-slowly-advancing *Dictionary* are the frequent wry allusions to large, difficult tasks airily undertaken. These allusions are abstract, just as if Johnson were not, in fact, recognizing and deploring in each his own personal victimization by hope. He writes in No. 122: "Nothing is more subject to mistake and disappointment than anticipated judgment concerning the easiness or difficulty of any undertaking, whether we form our opinion from the performance of others, or from abstracted contemplation of the thing to be attempted." *Rambler* 127 considers the unsuspected impediments that can be counted on by the experienced to threaten and delay "great undertakings." And in No. 137, he seems engaged largely in an attempt to cheer himself up: formidable tasks, overwhelming in their magnitude, *can* be accomplished if they are undertaken in small parts. "Divide and conquer," he assures himself, "is a principle equally just in science [that is, learning] as in policy." In No. 145 he behaves as if he has just depressed himself by contriving the famous witty *Dictionary* definition of a lexicographer as "a harmless drudge"; for in this essay he breathes a sigh of sympathy for the pathetic, anonymous hacks of literature, for "the abridger, compiler, and translator," and exhorts all such to a mutual affection based on a grave mutual need: "The common interest of learning requires that her sons should cease from intestine hostilities, and, instead of sacrificing each other to malice and contempt, endeavor to avert persecution from the meanest of their fraternity."

The *Rambler* throughout seems impressed by a somberness deriving perhaps less from Johnson's general "personality" than from the implications of the specific professional trap in which he found himself during the early 1750's. Obsessed by his own contractual obligations, he instinctively made obligation—both divine and social—one of the central topics of the *Rambler*. It would not be going far wrong to say that the *Rambler* constitutes a translation into objective moral and psychological terms of much of the personal anguish Johnson felt in forcing himself to fulfill the *Dictionary* contract. In No. 207 he quotes "the malicious remark of the Greek epigrammatist [Palladas of Alexandria] on marriage"; "Its two days of happiness are the first and the last." Similarly with a large literary project, as Johnson was intensely aware: the only two moments when the heart leaps up are at the signing of the contract and the delivery of the manuscript—in between stretches a desert of boredom diversified only by occasional outcrops of self-contempt.

He concludes the retrospective *Rambler* 208 by classifying in ascending order of importance and dignity the four sorts of essays he has been writing for two years. Lowest in the hierarchy are the few papers aiming largely at "harmless merriment" with no very elevated moral intent, papers like Nos. 132, 194, and 195, which retail the narrative of a feckless tutor frustrated by the folly of his noble pupil. Next in Johnson's hierarchy, but still in a very unexalted position, are "the disquisitions of criticism, which . . . is only to be ranked among the subordinate and instrumental arts." He is thinking of essays like No. 4, on romance and novel as literary kinds; Nos. 36 and 37, on pastoral; or No. 60, on biography. Ranking above these because more broadly applicable in moral terms are papers dealing with what he calls "pictures of life: he is thinking of essays like No. 59, which depicts Suspirius, the lugubrious prophet of evil and disaster, or No. 200, which satirizes Prospero, the *nouveau riche* who receives his old friend only so that he can lord it over him. Johnson ranks these essays higher than the critical ones simply because life is more important than literature. And in these "pictures of life" resemblance (that is, "Nature") is essential. Talking about the danger of deviating too far toward burlesque in monitory character-sketches, he warns that "as they deviate farther from reality, they become less useful, because their lessons will fail of application. The mind of the reader [notice his rhetorical focus] is carried away from the contemplation of his own manners; he finds in himself no likeness to the phantom before him; and though he laughs or rages, is not reformed."

It is efficiency of moral rhetoric, then, that determines Johnson's own hierarchy of *Rambler* papers, and in the highest position he ranks "the essays professedly serious," which he earnestly hopes "will be found exactly conformable to the precepts of Christianity, without any accommodation to the licentiousness and levity of the present age." An example of this sort of paper would be No. 32, on Christian patience, or No. 185, on forgiveness. These differ from sermons only in the way they begin: they start not from some Biblical text but from some general proposition of psychology or ethics. Thus the opening of No. 185: "No vicious dispositions of the mind more obstinately resist both the counsels of philosophy and the injunctions of religion than those which are complicated with an opinion of dignity." Or No. 21: "Every man is prompted by the love of himself to imagine that he possesses some qualities superior either in kind or in degree to those which he sees allotted to the rest of the world; and, whatever apparent disadvantages he may suffer in the comparison with others, he has some invisible distinctions, some latent reserve of excellence, which he throws into the balance, and by which he generally fancies that it is turned in his favor." Or No. 14—and here we come very near to autobiography: "Among the many inconsistencies which folly produces or infirmity suffers in the human mind, there has often been observed a manifest and striking contrariety between the life of an author and his writings."

Having arrived by ascending steps to specify the only one of the four sorts of *Ramblers* of which he is genuinely proud—and implying by the way his faith in the superior moral efficacy of overt discursive instruction to even powerful fictional representation—he concludes the final *Rambler* with his moralist's mask intact to the end: "I shall never envy the honors which wit and learning obtain in any other cause if I can be numbered among the writers who have given ardor to virtue, and confidence to truth." And just as he began work on the *Rambler,* by inscribing a prayer, so he ends it, translating a passage from Dionysius' *Periegesis:*

> Celestial powers, that piety regard:
> From you my labors wait their last reward.

Why is writing the periodical essay such *anxious* employment, even if one is not, at the same time, slogging slowly ahead on an enormous dictionary? Johnson offers one answer to the question in the middle of this final *Rambler*. Despite his later insistence in conversation that "A man may write at any time if he will set himself doggedly to it," he reveals here that he knows that compositional occasions are never faced and resolved so simply. Even the well-conducted will does not—as perhaps "schematically" it should—urge the writer smoothly to the writing table and prompt him to the immediate and fruitful exercise of memory, intelligence, and expression. As Johnson admits:

> He that condemns himself to compose on a stated day will often bring to his task an attention dissipated, a memory embarrassed, an imagination overwhelmed, a mind distracted with anxieties, a body languishing with disease: He will labor on a barren topic till it is too late to change it; or, in the ardor of invention, diffuse his thoughts into wild exhuberance which the pressing hour of publication cannot suffer judgment to examine or reduce.

When he asserted the contrary in 1773, saying that a man may write at any time if he will merely set himself doggedly to it, he was in Edinburgh, suspicious of his company and ready to contradict all their utterances. "Somebody," says Boswell, "talked of happy moments for composition; and how a man can write at one time and not another." "Nay," said Johnson—and he continued that day saying Nay, deprecating the locals' romantic view of Scottish independence, condemning the dirtiness of Scottish churches, belittling Scottish learning as well as the literary achievement of Swift, denying the authenticity of Ossian's poetry, ridiculing Lord Monboddo's hope that the orangutan might be taught to speak English, and even denying the force of theatrical illusion. Such is the importance of context and genre in deducing what we may still be tempted to call Johnson's "real" views.

If in *Rambler* 208 the vision of composing "on a stated day" resembles a nightmare of anxiety, quite a different image of enforced composition surfaces in *Rambler* 184, written less than three months before. Here it all sounds dreadfully easy, even mechanical:

> The writer of essays escapes many embarrassments to which a large book would have exposed him: he seldom harasses his reason with long trains of consequences, dims his eyes with the perusal of antiquated volumes, or burdens his memory with great accumulations of preparatory knowledge. A careless glance upon a favorite author, or transient survey of the varieties of life, is sufficient to supply the first hint or seminal idea, which, enlarged by the gradual accretion of matter stored in the mind, is by the warmth of fancy easily expanded into flowers, and sometimes ripened into fruit.

It sounds even farcical: we are reminded of Holofernes, in *Love's Labor's Lost,* accounting for his talent in extemporaneous composition:

> This is a gift that I have, simple, simple; a foolish extravagant spirit, full of forms, figures, shapes, objects, ideas, apprehensions, motions, revolutions. These are begot in the ventricle of memory, nourished in the womb of *pia mater,* and delivered upon the mellowing of occasion. But the gift is good in those in which it is acute, and I am thankful for it.

To both the speaker in *Rambler* 184 and Holofernes, it is an image of a seed sprouting indomitably under even a rather careless—or at least automatic—nurture that depicts the compositional process. Is this Johnson's real view? What, then, do we make of what he says in *Rambler* 208?

The answer is that it all depends upon context and rhetorical purpose. The object in *Rambler* 208 is to take a sentimental farewell and to generate sympathy for the Rambler, who has been toiling for two years solely in our interests. The object in *Rambler* 184 is to discourse on the domination of chance (rather than "schemes") in human affairs; and the image of the natural growth of an essay like a plant is there in the service of this larger idea, the idea which brings the Rambler finally to the pious but not entirely logical conclusion that "nothing in reality is governed by chance, but . . . the universe is under the perpetual superintendance of Him who created it; . . . our being is in the hands of Omnipotent Goodness, by Whom what appears casual to us is directed for ends ultimately kind and merciful."

One of Boswell's great handicaps in understanding Johnson as a writer is his naïveté about literary contexts such as these and about the ascendancy of rhetoric in Johnson's literary behavior. The popular simplification of Johnson as an odd wise man who is most interesting because he "says" witty and outrageously dogmatic things upon all occasions derives largely from Boswell's deficiency in literary sophistication, his lack of interest in what belongs to a given genre or literary moment. If Boswell is a great biographer, he is an appalling critic. And what makes him a great biographer, his devotion to "truth," to the unambiguously demonstrable and documentable, is one of the things that disables him as a critic. He thinks that a statement means simply what it says. And so do many later interpreters of Johnson's writings and conversation. The weakness of an otherwise excellent book like Joseph Wood Krutch's *Samuel Johnson* is its lumping together as if of equal weight and force and "reality" various Johnsonian utterances, whether barked out in the heat of conversational passion, where Johnson often said things merely to annoy people he didn't at the moment approve of, or embodied with various kinds of care in quite other contexts—prayers, dedications, moral essays, letters of various "kinds," poems of various genres, or fictions and allegories operating within very strict conventions. A statement about poetry embedded in the *Life of Cowley* is a statement of a very different weight and density from a statement about poetry put into the mouth of Imlac in *Rasselas*. And even in recognizing this we must go still further: the function and meaning of both statements will depend on this operation within the specific dynamics of the passages in which they are lodged. All this seems obvious enough once we articulate it: the problem is to keep it obvious when we find ourselves caught up in the act of reading Johnson or listening to him via Boswell's reproduction of his remarks.

Self-condemned to write upon a stated day whether ready or not, Johnson found himself in a recurring compositional predicament which turned out to determine the *ad hoc* structure of most of the *Rambler* essays as well as a great part of their substance. As we will see, many of them complicate their presumed topics surprisingly by setting out in one direction and then turning, oddly, in another. The anxiety-ridden compositional circumstances in which the *Ramblers* got written were inappropriate for the registration of any dogmatic certainties, or even for the achievement of a very seamless consistency. And in subject as in method they bear the mark of the way they were composed. The bulk of them are either openly or covertly about the insufficiency of preconcerted "schemes" or plans to deal with the actual occasions of life. The "outline" is the compositional analogue of schemes and plans: it proposes an easy articulation, but the number of times a writer has been betrayed by one is a measure of his experience and maturity. Schemes, plans, and outlines all prove ironically deficient, defeated always by the surprising and unpleasant actualities of *ah hoc*.

One pre-concerted scheme with which Johnson was living while producing the *Rambler* was the result of commercial necessity. The papers were advertised in advance by the publication in newspapers of their epigraphic mottoes, the equivalent of indicating their subjects in advance. Johnson had to supply these mottoes considerably beforehand. As publication day approached, he was thus obliged to flesh out something like a predetermined scheme. No wonder the bulk of the *Ramblers* glance either at anxiety or at the irony and pathos of the flagging will ridden by a consciousness of predetermined schemes.

There are numerous witnesses of the way Johnson wrote the *Ramblers*. All agree that twice a week he left the hated job until the very last moment (often until late on the night before publication), and then, and only then, forced himself to write compulsively, rapidly, and conclusively. What he says later of Dryden describes himself perfectly:

Of labor, notwithstanding the multiplicity of his productions, there is sufficient reason to suspect that he was not a lover. To write [like Pope, for example] *con amore,* with fondness for the employment, with perpetual touches and retouches, with unwillingness to take leave of his own idea, and an unwearied pursuit of unattainable perfection, was, I think, no part of his character.

Johnson's way of writing was so little *con amore* that he seldom even looked over what he had just written before handing the sheets to the waiting printer's boy; and sometimes he found himself so close to his deadline that the boy was running the firm sheet to the compositor while Johnson was agonizing over the remainder, holding in memory as well as he could what he had already irrevocably committed to the press. Boswell says: "He told us 'almost all his *Ramblers* were written just as they were wanted for the press; and that he sent a certain portion of the copy of an essay, and wrote the remainder while the former part of it was printing. When it was wanted, and he had fairly sat down to it, he was sure it would be done.' " According to another observer, the Rev. Mr. Parker, "Mrs. Gastrell was on a visit at Mr. Hervey's, in London, at the time that Johnson was writing the *Rambler;* the printer's boy would often come after him to their house, and wait while he wrote off a paper for the press in a room full of company." And Mrs. Thrale testifies that "the fine *Rambler* on the subject of procrastination [No. 134] was hastily composed . . . in Sir Joshua Reynolds's parlor, while the boy waited to carry it to press."

Indeed, in this *Rambler* 134, Johnson becomes his own witness to the ironic dynamics of his accustomed compositional process, and does so by exposing as usual the ironic distance between "schemes"—here, "this dream of study"—and actualities—"a summons from the press"; the distance is like that in the letter to Chesterfield between "that dream of hope" and "no act of assistance":

> I sat yesterday morning employed in deliberating on which among the various subjects that occurred to my imagination I should bestow the paper of today. After a short effort of meditation by which nothing was determined, I grew every moment more irresolute, my ideas wandered from the first intention, and I rather wished to think, than thought, upon any settled subject; till at last I was awakened from this dream of study by a summons from the press; the time was come for which I had been thus negligently proposing to provide, and however dubious or sluggish, I was now necessitated to write.

It is like going on stage without having learned one's lines. What arises is guilt: "I could not forbear to reproach myself for having so long neglected what was unavoidably to be done, and of which every moment's idleness increased the difficulty." But he now has found his topic, generalized from his own pathetic, farcical experience of delay followed by frantic composition: "Thus life is languished away in the gloom of anxiety, and consumed in collecting resolutions which the next morning dissipates; in forming purposes which we scarcely hope to keep, and reconciling ourselves to our own cowardice by excuses which, while we admit them, we know to be absurd."

This sort of pathological irresolution he now proceeds to objectify in a number of "characters": one man hesitates to choose until a rival takes all; another delays to choose until "some accident intercepts his journey"; another sees too far ahead—his lively imagination "extends to remote consequences," with the result that "he is entangled in his own scheme, and bewildered in the perplexity of various intentions"; another employs the neurotic technique of perfectionism to sanction doing nothing. Johnson ends *Rambler* 134 in quite a different mode from the one in which he began it: if he starts with ironic confessions of irresolution, by the time he has devised and contemplated all these human examples he enables himself to end it on a fairly resolute note: "The certainty that life cannot be long, and the probability that it will be much shorter than nature allows, ought to awaken every man to the active prosecution of whatever he is desirous to perform." But even here the imagery of dreams and waking, the recourse to *ought to,* and even the embarrassed prolixity with which the sentence ends reminds us of what he is really writing about: unsatisfactory, backsliding human beings, the author included. Instead of certainty or any sort of dogmatism, what we find in *Rambler* 134 is pathos, doubt, and the essential incertitude inseparable, we should notice, from the process of extemporaneous composition. Where the simple Boswell, lusting for unambiguous guidance, saw the Johnson of the *Rambler* only as "majestic teacher of moral and religious wisdom," more sophisticated readers will perceive that the *Rambler* papers are dynamic enterprises in which real doubts and uncertainties are constantly at war with the mere appearance of order and faith.

What we find in *Rambler* 134 we find throughout the series—Johnson, caught short at deadline time, is working things out *ad hoc* from page to page. His situation is quite different from the traditional image accepted, for example, by F. E. Halliday, who writes, "The matter was all in his head, neatly arranged, and it was merely a question of transcription." This view ignores the very many *Ramblers* in which Johnson finds that he must virtually retract in the final paragraphs what he has set forth with every appearance of confidence early on. Even if the first sheet has not already gone to the compositor, Johnson is too impatient of labor to go back and begin again when a contradiction presents itself. Frequently he will not even expunge the evidence of a contradiction by revising. Instead, he plunges on, writing rapidly and hating to write: "What *must* be done, . . . *will* be done." Where he cannot resolve inconsistencies, he ignores them; where he cannot ignore them, he embraces them. All this is to say that the psychological dynamics of his compositional predicament give him his essential critical method, in the *Rambler* as well as in *The Lives of the Poets*.

Johnson's conduct of *Rambler* 23 exemplifies what I am saying. Here his topic is the appropriate amount of advice a writer should solicit from critics and friends. As we should expect, Johnson's position on this matter is one of obstinate self-sufficiency. As he says,

> Whoever is so doubtful of his own abilities as to encourage the remarks of others will find himself every day embarrassed with new difficulties, and will harass his mind in vain with the hopeless labor of uniting heterogeneous ideas [contributed by a multitude of critics], digesting independent hints, and collecting into one point the several rays of borrowed light, emitted often with contrary directions.

Better for the writer to keep his own counsel and to do in his own way what must be done, knowing that, like any work of man, what he writes will always be capable of improvement, but at the same time knowing that what he writes must finally be concluded and uttered, imperfect through it will certainly be.

Johnson goes on developing this idea, and as he arrives at his seventh paragraph he remembers an observation by the Younger Pliny that he thinks might be useful to his purpose, the observation that the speaker should "not so much . . . select the strongest arguments which his cause admits, as . . . employ all which his imagination can afford: for, in pleading, those reasons are of most value which will most affect the judges; and the judges . . . will be always most touched with that which they had before conceived." By the time Johnson perceives where this point is taking him—to the position that the utterer should closely adapt what he says to the expectations of the audience, of which critics constitute an important segment—it is too late to expunge it. What he does is simply let it stand and audaciously change direction instead. He begins the next paragraph: "But, though the rule of Pliny be judiciously laid down, it is not applicable to the writer's cause." This is typical: Johnson embarks on one direction of argument, but sees that it is inapplicable; instead of returning and striking it out, he lets it stand and extricates himself later on as well as he can.

A similar act is visible in *Rambler* 139, where he criticizes *Samson*

Agonistes. But here the technique we can call "the involuntary 'turn' " occurs within a single sentence. He has begun the essay by citing Aristotle's perception that the events of the most affecting tragedies are causally connected. He goes on to say that Aristotle's observation applies rather to plot than to stylistic "decorations" like meter, diction, and metaphors; as he says, "This precept is to be understood in its rigor only with respect to great and essential events, and cannot be extended in the same force to minuter circumstances and arbitrary decorations"—he gets this far when he begins to subject what he has said to the strictest logic, asking himself, "But wouldn't even the 'decorations' be better the more organically they're connected with everything else in the work?" Perceiving now what logic requires of "decorations," he proceeds thus: "—which yet are more happy as they contribute more to the main design." He goes on to present the reasons which have urged this odd reversal: "For it is always a proof of extensive thought and accurate circumspection to promote various purposes by the same act, and the idea of ornament admits use, though it seems to exclude necessity." This "turn" is especially interesting, for it shows Johnson first lazily embracing one of the critical clichés of his age, the assumption that substance and style are readily separable, and then bravely perceiving that the cliché won't really do. But what is pre-eminently Johnsonian about this performance is that he allows the first part of the sentence simply to stand: it is not hard, indeed, to imagine it written at the bottom of a sheet just snatched away by the printer's boy.

To the attentive reader of the *Rambler,* these *buts* and *yets* become something like its very substance. Consider No. 151. Here his topic is the several ages of man and the general uniformity of desires in infancy, youth, age, and senility. By the time he arrives at his final paragraph, he perceives what he may have been implying: that man in his uniformity is essentially a mechanical, determined creature with very little real control over his successive follies. Aware only at the end of the essay of the confidence he may innocently have supplied to determinism, he proceeds to take it all back:

> I have in this view of life considered men as actuated [he still can't rid himself entirely of the quasi-mechanical and passive imagery in which he's been conducting the essay] only by natural desires, and yielding to their own inclination, without regard to superior principles, by which the force of external events may be counteracted, and the temporary prevalence of passions restrained. Nature will indeed always operate, human desires will

be always ranging; but these motions [that is, impulses], though very powerful, are not resistless; nature may be regulated, and desires governed; and to contend with the predominance of successive passions, to be endangered first by one affection, and then by another, is the condition upon which we are to pass our time, the time of our preparation for that state which shall put an end to experiment, to disappointment, and to change.

Thus he returns, and with great skill, to the position and tone appropriate to "The Rambler"; but he can do so here only by tacking on a conclusion which follows not at all from the premises.

This is what he does again in No. 184, another essay coming dangerously close to an impious determinism and relativism. He writes: "It is not commonly observed how much even of actions considered as particularly subject to choice is to be attributed to accident, or some cause out of our own power, by whatever name it be distinguished." He proceeds through the whole essay to present one example after another of "the dominion of chance." And again, by the time he is ready to write the last paragraph, he sees where he has been led: instead of canceling what he has written, he executes one of his "turns," and suggests now that what he has been saying is virtual nonsense consisting of "unideal sounds." He now insists that

> nothing can afford any rational tranquillity but the conviction that . . . nothing in reality is governed by chance, but that the universe is under the perpetual superintendance of Him who created it; that our being is in the hands of Omnipotent Goodness, by whom what appears casual to us is directed for ends ultimately kind and merciful; and that nothing can finally hurt him who debars not himself from the divine favor.

This is lame, having the effect of substituting one determinism for another; and the lameness seems to betray itself in the wooden rhetoric ("debars not himself"). But no matter: the essay must be finished, and yet it must not finish in anything that might comfort determinism or irresponsibility. Besides, tomorrow is Sunday—this is a Saturday essay—and a pious ending will not come amiss. If a jack is seen, a spit will be presumed—maybe the reader won't notice that the final paragraph is attached rather than integral.

Terrible temptations, Johnson knew, await the author who is near the end of a work. When in the *Preface to Shakespeare* he observes that Shakespeare must often have tired of the latter parts of the plays and hustled willy-nilly to a conclusion, he knew sympathetically the experience he was describing. As he says in *Rambler* 207:

In some of the noblest compositions of wit, the conclusion falls
below the vigor and spirit of the first books; and as a genius is
not to be degraded by the imputation of human failings, the
cause of this declension is commonly sought in the structure of
the work, and plausible reasons are given why in the defective
part less ornament was necessary, or less could be admitted.

But Johnson, knowing himself, knows better:

But perhaps the author would have confessed that his fancy was
tired and his perseverance broken; that he knew his design to be
unfinished, but that, when he saw the end so near, he could no
longer refuse to be at rest.

It is not only with the most serious moral topics that Johnson performs
the act of public mind-changing that we have been looking at. Sometimes
his second thoughts are elicited by lighter matter. *Rambler* 177, for example,
is devoted almost wholly to an odd letter from one Vivaculus, odd because
the letter begins with unconscious self-satire of its writer's austistic complacency and then shifts to ridicule a gang of virtuosos comprising three
idiot book collectors and a coin collector whose felicity is complete because
his collection of halfpence is. "Every one of these virtuosos," says the suddenly
wise Vivaculus, "looked on all his associates as wretches of depraved taste
and narrow notions. Their conversation was, therefore, fretful and waspish,
their behavior brutal, their merriment bluntly sarcastic, and their seriousness
gloomy and suspicious." Johnson thus devotes more than nine-tenths of his
space to mounting a standard eighteenth-century attack on grubbers of the
silly or the remote. But with a final paragraph to go—a little over one
hundred words—he bethinks himself, considers what he's done, and, to the
surprise of the reader, concludes this way:

It is natural to feel grief or indignation when anything necessary
or useful is wantonly wasted or negligently destroyed; and therefore my correspondent cannot be blamed for looking with uneasiness on the waste of life. Leisure and curiosity might soon make
great advances in useful knowledge were they not diverted by
minute emulation and laborious trifles.

And now the "turn":

It may, however, somewhat mollify his anger [which has clearly
been Johnson's as well] to reflect that perhaps none of the assembly
which he describes was capable of any nobler employment, and

that he who does his best, however little, is always to be distinguished from him who does nothing.

And finally the "conclusion," which a careful reader will perceive to be at
variance with the tendency of the bulk of the essay:

> Whatever busies the mind without corrupting it has at least this
> use, that it rescues the day from idleness, and he that is never
> idle will not often be vicious.

Johnson's treatment of Vivaculus's satire has its counterpart in the
crucial relation between two *Ramblers,* Nos. 82 and 83. No. 82 consists of
a ridiculous letter from Quisquilius (cf. Latin *quisquiliae,* rubbish), "long
. . . known," by his own account, "as the most laborious and zealous virtuoso
that the present age has had the honor of producing." He has ill-spent a
lifetime and a fortune accumulating stones, mosses, shells, hornet-stings,
butterflies, grubs and insects, "the longest blade of grass upon record," an
albino mole, various shabby antique fragments, and innumerable historical
relics chosen with an audacious disregard of their meaning. But he has
overextended himself and is now the victim of his creditors. His whole letter
constitutes a comic self-exposure of an energetic man who has brought
disaster on himself wholly by his silliness and egotism. And Johnson leaves
it at that.

But in Tuesday's paper he is entertaining serious second thoughts about
what he has done on Saturday. He begins *Rambler* 83: "The publication of
the letter in my last paper has naturally led me to the consideration of thirst
after curiosities, which often draws contempt and ridicule upon itself." He
goes on:

> There are, indeed, many subjects of study which seem but re-
> motely allied to useful knowledge and of little importance to
> happiness or virtue.

And then, as if thinking of himself last Saturday:

> Nor is it easy to forbear some sallies of merriment or expressions
> of pity when we see a man wrinkled with attention and emaciated
> with solicitude in the investigation of questions of which, without
> visible inconvenience, the world may expire in ignorance.

But now, the crucial *yet*:

> Yet it is dangerous to discourage well-intended labors or innocent
> curiosity; for he who is employed in searches which by any de-

duction of consequences tend to the benefit of life is surely laud-
able in comparison of those who spend their time in counteracting
happiness and filling the world with wrong and danger, confusion
and remorse.

And again, the obsessive theme of idleness:

No man can perform so little as not to have reason to congratulate
himself on his merits when he beholds the multitudes that live
in total idleness and have never yet endeavored to be useful.

He concludes with an elaborate justification of just such activities as his
previous paper has been at pains to deride.

The crucial *yet* performs its humane work not only in the *Rambler*: in
the *Idler* as well it operates as a brake upon dogmatism. *Idler* 66 is a good
example. It begins by lamenting very plausibly the losses of classical literary
texts (like the missing plays of Sophocles and Euripides) occasioned by the
destruction of ancient libraries. But halfway through (at the beginning of
his second sheet of manuscript?) he takes quite a new direction: "Such are
the thoughts that rise in every student when his curiosity is eluded and his
searches are frustrated; yet it may perhaps be doubted whether our complaints
are not sometimes inconsiderate, and whether we do not image more evil
than we feel." And he proceeds to offer every reason he can think of why
we should be satisfied that we have enough classical literature already.

Another *Idler* pivoting on the interesting *yet* is No. 85. Here the subject,
always good for a few hundred words in weekly journalism, is the lamentable
"multiplication of books." During the first half of the essay we get the
impression that Johnson deplores—as we would expect—the gross flux of
shallow compilations, encyclopedias, digests, and other productions of those
"who have no other task than to lay two books before them, out of which
they compile a third." As we read, we are led to embrace Johnson's apparent
view that this is a racket practiced on the half-educated and lazy by the
slick and cynical:

It is observed [by Tacitus] that "a corrupt society has many laws";
I know not whether it is not equally true that "an ignorant age
has many books." When the treasures of ancient knowledge lie
unexamined, and original authors are neglected and forgotten,
compilers and plagiaries are encouraged, who give us again what
we had before and grow great by setting before us what our own
sloth had hidden from our view.

So far, so good. But, Johnson realizes, this is too simple: some good is produced even by intentions which the moral dogmatist would have to brand as unambiguously evil. Johnson thus executes his "turn":

> Yet are not even these writers to be indiscriminately censured and rejected. Truth, like beauty, varies its fashions, and is best recommended by various dresses to different minds; and he that recalls the attention of mankind to any part of learning which time has left behind it may be truly said to advance the literature of his own age.

This barrister-like defense presented, Johnson is still not satisfied. He goes on worrying the question, and before he arrives at the end of the essay he gives us one more *yet* and two more *buts,* and terminates in something very close to naked indecision. He concludes, significantly, by telling us not what he has decided about the question he has introduced but what Callimachus might thing:

> But such is the present state of our literature that the ancient sage who thought "a great book a great evil" would now think the multitude of books a multitude of evils. He would consider a bulky writer who engrossed a year, and a swarm of pamphleteers who stole each an hour, as equal wasters of human life, and would make no other difference between them than between a beast of prey and a flight of locusts.

The final attitude and image would recommend themselves to our memories as "typically Johnsonian" if we did not notice how shy, tentative, and essentially uncommitted the rhetoric here really is, supported by "He would consider" rather than "It is true." Its method betrays an uncertainty about how the essay should be ended, an uncertainty registering Johnson's genuine puzzlement over the (conventional) "two sides" of the question.

One of the best known of all Johnson's periodical papers is *Rambler* 200. Most of it is taken up with a brilliant and memorable letter from "Asper (cf. Latin *asper,* harsh, rough) expositing the insufferably snobbish behavior of his former friend Prospero. All contemporaries agree that in Prospero Johnson had in mind the sensationally successful David Garrick, once his own pupil in the doomed school at Edial and his companion on his ragged passage to London. "We set out in the world together," says Asper, "and for a long time mutually assisted each other in our exigencies, as either happened to have money or influence beyond his immediate necessities."

But Asper is awakened from this dream of reciprocated beneficence by paying a call which the newly rich Prospero has insisted upon. Asper finds now that Prospero's wish to be visited arises "not from any desire to communicate his happiness, but to enjoy his superiority":

> When I told my name at the door, the footman went to see if his master was at home, and by the tardiness of his return gave me reason to suspect that time was taken to deliberate. He then informed me that Prospero desired my company, and showed the staircase carefully secured by mats from the pollution of my feet. The best apartments were ostentatiously set open that I might have a distant view of the magnificence which I was not permitted to approach; and my old friend, receiving me with all the insolence of condescension at the top of the stairs, conducted me to a back room, where he told me he always breakfasted when he had not great company.

From this inauspicious beginning, the visit goes from bad to worse as Prospero's house-pride takes over completely. Asper is cunningly denied contact with fine carpets, upholstery, tea, and china at the same time that he is made aware of their suitability for finer guests than he. He finally departs in a fury "without any intention of seeing [Prospero] again, unless some misfortune should restore his understanding."

At the end of Asper's letter, we feel that his sense of injury is entirely justified, wich is to say that we naturally identify Asper with Johnson. But to our surprise, Johnson follows Asper's letter with two paragraphs in which a very different attitude presides. This attitude can be described as that of "The Rambler":

> Though I am not wholly insensible of the provocations which my correspondent has received, I cannot altogether commend the keenness of his resentment, nor encourage him to persist in his resolution of breaking off all commerce with his old acquaintance.

And the voice of moderation goes on to observe that performances like Prosper's, while undoubtedly offensive, issue rather from stupidity and folly than outright malice. Besides, the wise man will learn to bear, friends being always desirable but always imperfect:

> He that too much refines his delicacy will always endanger his quiet. Of those with whom nature and virtue oblige us to converse, some are ignorant of the art of pleasing, and offend when

they design to caress; some are negligent, and gratify themselves without regard for the quiet of another; some, perhaps, are malicious, and feel no greater satisfaction in prosperity than that of raising envy and trampling inferiority. But whatever be the motive of insult, it is always best to overlook it, for folly scarcely can deserve resentment, and malice is punished by neglect.

We could say of *Rambler* 200 that its dynamics are really those of a dialogue: one of Johnson's modes and styles speaks first, and then another is permitted its say. But however we choose to express it, the whole paper makes clear that, as usual, Johnson is apportioning his loyalty between equally attractive attitudes rather than occupying "positions"—very like "schemes," after all— or enunciating "views." The final "official" reprehension of Asper's annoyance does nothing to diminish the attractiveness of his rhetoric and the charm of his narration: those things stick in the mind in dynamic opposition to the cooler second thoughts of the "conclusion"—a conclusion which, not being a logical one, is a conclusion in which nothing is concluded. Johnson is equally committed to both parts of the essay, whose essence is the drama generated by the two parts as they operate to play out the action of "judiciousness" or "honest second thoughts." And as before, it is the *ad hoc* method, the natural attendant of Johnson's neurotic writing habits, that makes oppositions and contraries of this sort offer themselves so naturally to him. What a given *Rambler* tends to be about is the act of Johnson, *agonistes,* making up his mind as he writes.

Johnson's practice in the *Rambler* seems to reveal his prime quality of mind: an instinctive skepticism, no matter what he finds himself saying, of "systems" and unambiguous positions. To his mind, answers are generally determined by the context of the questions that elicit them. That is, genre, occasion, and human rhetorical purpose are the main determinants of truth. It follows that universally applicable or extreme positions—especially those not colored by a meaningful concrete context—are generally wrong. Boswell says: "I mentioned to him a friend of mine [George Dempster] who was formerly gloomy from low spirits, and much distressed by the fear of death, but was now uniformly placid, and contemplated his dissolution without any perturbation." Johnson's reply suggests his suspicion of "uniform" opinions: "Sir, . . . this is only a disordered imagination taking a different turn."

Even his "opinion" of the ventilation of Scottish houses, set forth in *A Journey to the Western Island,* complicates itself as he writes it down. The trouble with windows in Scotland is that, because the sashes are not equipped with weights, "He that would have his window open must hold it with his hand." The result is foul air: "The incommodiousness of the Scotch windows keeps them very closely shut . . . and even in houses well built and elegantly furnished, a stranger may be sometimes forgiven if he allows himself to wish for fresher air." But in the very act of writing this, Johnson is visited by shame and uneasiness: hasn't he been too picayune? What does it matter, after all? What he writes next might be written by a critic of his work disappointed to find a writer capable of better things descanting like a school administrator about windows and ventilation: "These dimunitive observations seem to take away something from the dignity of writing. . . ." For this reason, he confesses, they are "never communicated but with hesitation [although we note that little hesitation has been visible in the criticism of Scottish ventilation] and a little fear of abasement and contempt." A sort of resolution of the uncertainty is finally arrived at in the next sentence, where Johnson concludes the little playlet his prose has been enacting: the playet sets in opposition four ideas (Scottish windows; trivial criticisms), and as before it is the humane *but* that brings us to what offers itself as a resolution.

> But it must be remembered that life consists not of a series of illustrious actions or elegant enjoyments; the greater part of our time passes in compliance with necessities, in the performance of daily duties, in the removal of small inconveniences, in the procurement of petty pleasures; and we are well or ill at ease as the main stream of life glides on smoothly or is ruffled by small obstacles and frequent interruption.

So much for the logical justification. But there seems to lurk still a sense that he really has compromised dignity by noticing fetid air. How else are we to account for the noble, elevated, "Rambler" passage which follows immediately than to see it as Johnson's attempt to efface the undignified passage he has written (and chosen to let stand) two paragraphs back?

> The true state of every nation is the state of common life. The manners of a people are not to be found in the schools of learning, or the palaces of greatness, where the national character is obscured or obliterated by travel or instruction, by philosophy or vanity; nor is public happiness to be estimated by the assemblies of the gay or the banquets of the rich. The great mass of nations is neither rich nor gay: they whose aggregate constitutes the people are found in the streets, and the villages, in the shops and farms; and from them collectively considered must the mea-

sures of general prosperity be taken. As they approach to delicacy
a nation is refined; as their conveniences are multiplied, a nation,
at least a commercial nation, must be denominated wealthy.

We can almost hear one of the voices within Johnson telling him, "Say
something dignified and unqualified, something with the appearance of
certitude and noble usefulness, to cancel the effect of that window business."
The writer that Johnson is sometimes mistaken for would literally have
crossed out the window business; the writer that Johnson is lets it stand
and then anxiously justifies it.

The *ad hoc* method of composition suits Johnson for more reasons than
his mere hatred of revising and rewriting. He observes in *Adventurer* 107:
"We have less reason to be surprised or offended when we find others differ
from us in opinion, because we very often differ from ourselves." Differing
from himself is one of Johnson's activities that has not always been sufficiently
appreciated. Boswell's genius in bottling and peddling the Johnsonian ether
sometimes gives the impression that the mighty sage operates from a body
of principles firmly held and fearlessly applied. But as the method of the
Rambler suggests, the fact is quite different. Johnson's "thought" is not a
great fixed structure, as we might be led to assume from, say, the tables
listing his "likes" and "dislikes" at the end of Krutch's *Samuel Johnson*. It
is rather a varying, dynamic mélange of reactions recognizing hardly any
fixed principles except an adherence to empiricism and a skepticism about
the certainties embraced and promulgated by other people. It is this likewise
that makes compilations like J. E. Brown's *The Critical Opinions of Samuel
Johnson*, for all their air of reasonableness, so useless, for Johnson's criticism
operates only within living contexts of actions, reactions, and generic purposes. If you remove the contexts, you misrepresent the criticism. If we
want to find out what Johnson is doing, we must, finally, read him.

And reading him brings to light all kinds of interesting contradictions.
Everyone who has read the *Lives of the Poets* knows that Johnson "disliked"
pastoral peotry. And yet in *Adventurer* 92, as well as in two *Ramblers* (Nos.
36 and 37), he discusses pastoral poetry with no denigration whatever.
Indeed, in *Rambler* 36 he specifically awards pastoral the honor of pleasing
many and pleasing long: "It is generally pleasing," he says, "because it
entertains the mind with representations of scenes familiar to almost every
imagination, and of which all can equally judge whether they are well
described." Pastoral, just like the plays of Shakespeare, gives "universal
pleasure." How do we account for the fact that the views expressed in the
Rambler quite contradict the views expressed in the *Lives of the Poets*? Simply

by understanding that when one has the task of writing 1500 words on pastoral for a general audience, one does not proceed by suggesting that the topic is too contemptible to be written about.

Readers of the *Lives* and the *Preface to Shakespeare* know likewise that Johnson's ultimate critical criterion for judging writings is the skeptical one of "length of duration and continuance of esteem." But as he suggests in *Adventurer* 138, even this criterion, apparently so logical and bed-rock, won't do: "Whoever has remarked the fate of books must have found it governed by other causes than general consent arising from general conviction. If a new performance happens not to fall into the hands of some, who have courage to tell and authority to propagate their opinion, it often remains long in obscurity, and perhaps perishes unknown and unexamined."

Again, readers of the *Lives* as well as eavesdroppers on Johnson's conversation will know that one of his favorite targets of scorn is the notion that weather or climate affect a writer's literary production. In the *Life of Milton* we are assured that "The author that thinks himself weather-bound . . . is only idle or exhausted." And in the *Life of Gray,* Gray's idea that "he could not write but at certain times" is stigmatized as "a fantastic foppery, to which my kindness for a man of learning and virtue wishes him to have been superior." *Idler* 11 also insists that any connection between seasons and literary fecundity is sheer nonsense. What, then, should be our reaction when, turning to *Rambler* 80, we hear a voice earnestly telling us that "To the men of study and imagination the winter is generally the chief time of labor. Gloom and silence produce composure of mind and concentration ideas."? The answer is that Johnson's context determines his position. His purpose in *Rambler* 80—written on December 22, 1750—is to justify a severe winter. He goes about this task—a part of his general work of offering techniques of contentment—by marshaling all the arguments he can find on behalf of the idea that the constant change of seasons is really a benefit to man. He descends even to arguments like this: "Winter brings natural inducements to jollity and conversation." His object is to justify the ways of God to man. To argue that men of letters derive particular benefits from winter is to advance another plausible reason for not repining. The rhetorical purpose determines what Johnson says.

In his preface to Lobo's *Voyage to Abyssinia* we have already encountered his skepticism about the reports of travelers. We know that he is almost pathologically skeptical about extraordinary narratives. But if we look at *Idler* 87, we find him warning against just this sort of skepticism and subjecting it to a probing moral analysis: "It is always easier to deny than to inquire. To refuse credit confers for a moment an appearance of superiority, which every little mind is tempted to assume when it may be gained so cheaply as by withdrawing attention from evidence and declining the fatigue of comparing probabilities." In short, "Many relations of travelers have been slighted as fabulous till more frequent voyages have confirmed their veracity." The difference between these two positions is that the purpose of the preface to Lobo is to recommend the book to purchasers and readers as a novelty, while the purpose of *Idler* 87 is to induce the reader to accept the hardly credible myth of the Amazons so that Johnson can make a point about the essential equality of the sexes.

There could hardly be a better example of the point that in Johnson as in other writers the genre determines the message than the relation between a passing in *The Vanity of Human Wishes,* on the one hand, and *Rambler* 202, on the other, works written no more than three years apart. One of the great moments in the poem is the depiction of the foot traveler whose very poverty secures him from assaults:

> The needy traveler, serene and gay,
> Walks the wild heath, and sings his toil away.
> Does envy seize thee [i.e., dear reader]? crush th' upbraiding joy,
> Increase his riches and his peace destroy;
> Now fears in dire vicissitude invade,
> The rustling brake alarms, and quiv'ring shade,
> Nor light nor darkness brings his pain relief,
> One shows the plunder, and one hides the thief.

What the passage is saying is that poverty itself ironically confers benefits, and that a wise man would be cautious about wishing for riches. Yet in *Rambler* 202 he vigorously denies this "point" and subjects the general "poetic" and pastoral conception of poverty to a skeptical inquiry so searching that it is hard to believe that he is not mindful of his own lines in the poem:

> Whoever studies either the poets or philosophers will find such an account of the condition expressed by [the term *poverty*] as his experience or observation will not easily discover to be true. Instead of the meanness, distress, complaint, anxiety, and dependence which have hitherto been combined in his ideas of poverty, he will read of content, innocence, and cheerfulness, of health and safety, tranquillity and freedom.

At this point he can hardly help recollecting his own words, "sings his toil away." And as if actually alluding to his poor and therefore happy traveler, he subjects this cliché to his irony: "It is the great privilege of poverty [we are told] to be . . . secure without a guard." The distinction to be kept in mind when we encounter literary behavior like this is between what is appropriate to a poetic satire "imitating" a Roman original—the happy because needy traveler is already present in Juvenal's Tenth—and what is appropriate to a moral essay taking place within a homely, domestic environment. The voice of the poetic satirist is not and must not be the voice of the prose moralist: if the voices become indistinguishable, each form becomes implausible—neither can effect its special kind of illusion.

The Vanity of Human Wishes is, after all, about the folly of human wishes. And yet in *Rambler* 66, written only a year after the poem, we find Johnson performing as if he were subjecting nothing to ridicule so much as his own poem:

> The folly of human wishes has always been a standing subject of mirth and declamation, and has been ridiculed and lamented from age to age, till perhaps the fruitless repetition of complaints and censures may be justly numbered among the subjects of censure and complaint.

This is precisely the sort of thing we must expect from a man who, extraordinarily gifted for the genre, writes scores of brilliant dedications for others and still, in the *Dictionary,* defines a dedication as "A servile address to a patron" and a dedicator as "One who inscribes his work to a patron with compliment and servility." We must likewise expect infinite complication from a man who, hating writing, revising, and retouching as almost no other author ever has and becoming, hence, one of the hastiest of all of them, declares that "Hasty compositions, however they please at first by flowery luxuriance, and spread in the sunshine of temporary favor, can seldom endure the change of seasons, but perish at the first blast of criticism, or frost of neglect" (*Rambler* 169). We are dealing with the man who delighted to conduct experimental, "scientific" inquiries with chemicals, orange-peels, and the growth-rate of his own fingernails, and who was at the same time reprehending such inquiries—in *Rambler* 24, for example—as tending to displace man's genuine business, the scrutiny of his moral nature and obligations. Johnson is the man who feels a natural suspicion of literary criticism and who ends by writing the *Lives of the Poets,* in large part devoted to exhibiting "the characters of authors." But just such books he is at pains to denigrate in *Rambler* 93:

> There are few books on which more time is spent by young students than on treatises which deliver the characters of authors;

nor any which oftener deceive the expectation of the reader or
fill his mind with more opinions which the progress of his studies
and the increase of his knowledge oblige him to resign.

For all his skill at literary impersonations, no one is quicker to expose and
reject personal or social duplicity. Everyone recalls the delightful *Adventurer*
84 censuring the outrageous dissimulations practiced on each other by a
group of stagecoach passengers. "Every man hates falsehood," Johnson asserts
in *Rambler* 20, an essay devoted to exposing whimsically the literary masks
incompetently assumed by many writers of letters to the Rambler. And in
Rambler 79 we find this most distinguished wearer of literary masks concluding that "Whoever commits a fraud is guilty not only of the particular
injury to him whom he deceives, but of the diminution of that confidence
which constitutes not only the ease but the existence of society." These words
are written by the hand that sixteen years later was to write for Robert
Chambers the law lectures that were to pass as his.

In his personal as well as literary behavior Johnson is equally capable
of astonishing anyone who conceives that a degree of consistency belongs to
the rational human character. Actually, for all his pretenses to know where
he is, Johnson is adrift. Far from being an eighteenth-century man of reason,
he is playing by ear. He wants to make up his mind, but he knows he
hasn't. His awareness of his plight is in large part what the *Prayers and
Meditations* are about. The tension in him is between the pull, on the one
hand, toward an appearance of certainty and firmness of will, and the drift,
on the other, toward absurdity and imprudence. Without entirely knowing
it, Boswell registers the poles of this opposition. For example:

> He said, "I am very unwilling to read the manuscripts of authors,
> and give them my opinion. If the authors who apply to me have
> money, I bid them boldly print without a name [that is, anon-
> ymously]; if they have written in order to get money, I tell them
> to go to the booksellers, and make the best bargain they can."
> BOSWELL. "But, Sir, if a bookseller should bring you a man-
> uscript to look at?" JOHNSON. "Why, Sir, I would desire the
> bookseller to take it away."

And Johnson's firm, well-considered reasons for this disinclination to read
manuscripts are both moral and social. "Nobody has a right," he tells Miss
Reynolds, "to put another under such a difficulty that he must either hurt
the person by telling the truth, or hurt himself by telling what is not true."

And yet—and yet: "There was," says Boswell, "perhaps no man who more frequently yielded to the solicitations even of very obscure authors, to read their manuscripts, or more liberally assisted them with advice and correction." A bit of the index to the Hill-Powell edition of Boswell's *Life* makes a pleasant emblem of Johnson's mental posture:

> Roman Catholicism . . . Johnson . . . respects it, ii, 105; attacks it, iii, 407.

"*Video meliora proboque,*" says Ovid, "*deteriora sequor*": I see and approve the better course, but follow the worse. Johnson's version of this confession is his perception that "No man practices as well as he writes." He explains, with recourse once again to the all-important *yet*: "I have, all my life long, been lying [abed] till noon. Yet I tell all young men, and tell them with great sincerity, that nobody who does not rise early will ever do any good." Being even more human than most, a moral writer places himself *ipso facto* in an ironical, if not overtly comical, situation, and it is from this situation that he must write. In *Idler* 27 Johnson considers the value of the exhortation underlying any moralist's advice, even the advice of the most sacred guides: "Know thyself":

> This counsel has been often given with serious dignity, and often received with appearance of conviction; but as very few can search deep into their own minds without meeting what they wish to hide from themselves, scarce any man persists in cultivating such disagreeable acquaintance, but draws the veil again between his eyes and his heart, leaves his passions and appetites as he found them, and advises others to look into themselves.

The "majestic teacher of moral wisdom" would be the first to appreciate the inscription written by Mark Twain when he presented a set of his books to the young Winston Churchill: "To do good is noble; to teach others to do good is nobler, and no trouble."

LEOPOLD DAMROSCH, JR.

The Vanity of Human Wishes

Among Johnson's noncritical works the two which have continued to enjoy the greatest esteem are *The Vanity of Human Wishes* and *Rasselas.* The first is a formal "imitation" of a classical satire and the second is rich in gently satirical effects, but both are often described as having an affinity with tragedy. In my view *Rasselas,* despite its inconclusive conclusion and its exposure of the perpetual frustration of human desires, succeeds in resolving tragic, comic, and satiric elements into a perspective of harmony and detachment. And although to many readers it may seem darker than this, its tragic elements are finally too tenuous and ambiguous to repay extended treatment here.

The case is quite different with *The Vanity of Human Wishes,* in which Johnson achieves what Ian Jack (adapting a phrase of Dryden's) has called "tragical satire." The poem has been the subject of so many excellent critical discussions that a comprehensive analysis here would be neither necessary nor useful. My purpose is a more limited one to investigate what is meant by the tragic quality which critics have consistently found in it, and to try to see what relation this quality may have to the satiric elements which it also contains.

The Vanity of Human Wishes is offered as an imitation of the tenth satire of Juvenal, in the specialized sense of "imitation" as it is defined in the *Dictionary:* "A method of translating looser than paraphrase, in which modern examples and illustrations are used for ancient, or domestick for foreign." The poet, then, will show his skill in adapting suitable modern instances

From *Samuel Johnson and the Tragic Sense.* © 1979 by Princeton University Press.

to the argument of his model. Johnson does not imply any significant alteration of tone and implication: that would detract from the success of the imitation, "which pleases when the thoughts are unexpectedly applicable and the parallels lucky" (*Life of Pope*). The greatest difficulty of the imitator will be in preserving fidelity to the original:

> The man of learning may be sometimes surprised and delighted
> by an unexpected parallel; but the comparison requires knowledge
> of the original, which will likewise often detect strained appli-
> cations. Between Roman images and English manners there will
> be an irreconcileable dissimilitude, and the work will be generally
> uncouth and party-coloured; neither original nor translated, nei-
> ther ancient nor modern.
>
> (*Life of Pope*)

Juvenal's tenth satire had already been translated by Dryden, whose version was reasonably faithful to the literal sense of the original but seemed open to criticism for its prevailing tone. This poem, in particular, was considered sufficiently solemn to serve as a magazine of materials for preachers. Thus Johnson's opinion of Dryden's version, and his decision to enter into competition with it, are based on well-accepted assumptions.

> The general character of this translation will be given when it is
> said to preserve the wit, but to want the dignity of the original.
> The peculiarity of Juvenal is a mixture of gaiety and stateliness,
> of pointed sentences, and declamatory grandeur. . . . It is there-
> fore perhaps possible to give a better representation of that great
> satirist, even in those parts which Dryden himself has translated,
> some passages excepted, which will never be excelled.
>
> (*Life of Dryden*)

Let us pause, then, to see what we can surmise about Johnson's conception of his task. He had to furnish modern instances in place of Roman ones, while preserving a fairly strict fidelity to their effect in the original; and he had to capture the tone of his model, which comprised two quite different aspects, wit and grandeur. To Juvenal he applies the term "that great satirist," and we are certainly not led to suppose that the poem, though declamatory and weighty, is anything other than a satire. He intended, we may suppose, to "imitate" that quality in Juvenal which has been called "a vehement and burning passion, like the 'saeva indignatio' of Swift."

Yet the difference between his poem and Juvenal's is so striking, particularly in this matter of tone, that it has led a series of modern critics to deny its satiric intention. The Roman poet mercilessly exposes the result of intemperate desire and belittles his subjects with cruel caricature. Johnson, on the contrary, shows a deep sympathy for the common fate of man, and quite early in the poem suggests a radical divergence from Juvenal's attitude. Democritus, according to the original, "laughs at all the Vulgar Cares and Fears; / At their vain Triumphs, and their vainer Tears" (Dryden's version, 79–80). In the same passage in Johnson the emphasis is wholly different: "All aid the farce, and all thy mirth maintain, / Whose joys are causeless, or whose griefs are vain" (67–68). There would seem to be an implied exception of genuine suffering, which is not "vain" and is therefore not included in the "farce." And later in the poem there are two passages of more or less autobiographical content, the descriptions of the scholar and of innocent old age, that illustrate the point.

The neoclassical writers who called Juvenal "tragical" were principally alluding to the technical matter of his elevated style, or in Dennis's words "the violent Emotions and vehement Style of Tragedy." But a number of modern critics have found tragedy, in its metaphysical sense, in *The Vanity of Human Wishes,* in consonance with Walter Scott's remark that its "deep and pathetic morality . . . has often extracted tears from those whose eyes wander dry over pages professedly sentimental." From various excellent discussions of this kind, that of Mary Lascelles may be chosen as exemplary. Her conclusion is that Juvenal employs a satiric irony to expose the distance between our pretensions and our powers, while Johnson regards the human condition with a deeper kind of tragic irony. Thus, "Johnson's response to the man who plays high and loses all is the Shakespearean—that is, the tragic—response"; and again, "The awe and pity with which Johnson contemplates the spectacle of human unfulfilment makes of *The Vanity of Human Wishes* a great tragic poem."

Miss Lascelles' position suggests the approach of what we may call the tragic school of interpreters, which has been to emphasize the portraits, especially those of Wolsey and Charles XII. In Juvenal the fall of Sejanus, for example, is full of circumstantial detail, which is intended to focus the reader's attention on the fickleness and hypocrisy of the people who first supported and then reviled him (as in Ben Jonson's *Sejanus*). Johnson presents his Wolsey with far greater dignity, and with only the briefest allusion to the hostility of the former sycophants (four lines, to Juvenal's twenty-five). The passage ends in a generalized allusion to Shakespeare's *Henry VIII,* with Wolsey seeking "the refuge of monastic rest" (118) and reproaching the broken faith of kings. It is very much like the outline of a tragedy.

This kind of interpretation compels us to recognize that parts of the poem, at least, are either not satiric at all, or satiric in a very peculiar way. The point is best illustrated in the often-noticed disparity between Juvenal's Hannibal and Johnson's Charles XII of Sweden. Johnson was well aware of the antiheroic convention in Augustan satire, as for example in Prior's ballad on the taking of Namur or Swift's satirical elegy on Marlborough; in a way he draws upon it in the terrible lines, "From Marlb'rough's eyes the streams of dotage flow, / And Swift expires a driv'ler and a show" (317–18), with the deep irony of compelling Swift and the man he hated to share the closed unity of a couplet, just as they have had to share the fate of man. But he is often interested in effects of a very different kind. Dryden renders Juvenal's account of Hannibal fairly literally in lines like these:

> A Sign-Post Dawber wou'd disdain to paint
> The one Ey'd Heroe on his Elephant. . . .
> Go, climb the rugged *Alps,* Ambitious Fool,
> To please the Boys, and be a Theme at School.
>   (254–55, 271–72)

The sarcasm is brutally unforgiving. For Johnson the subject aroused more solemn emotions.

> The death of great men is not always proportioned to the lustre
> of their lives. Hannibal, says Juvenal, did not perish by a javelin
> or a sword; the slaughters of Cannae were revenged by a ring.
> The death of Pope was imputed by some of his friends to a silver
> saucepan, in which it was his delight to heat potted lampreys.
>   (*Life of Pope*)

Johnson perceives the ironies in the situation, but in Pope's case his reference is mild and humane, with its pleasant use of the phrase "it was his delight." And he transformed Juvenal's Hannibal into the great portrait of Charles XII of Sweden.

> His fall was destin'd to a barren strand,
> A petty fortress, and a dubious hand;
> He left the name, at which the world grew pale,
> To point a moral, or adorn a tale.
>   (219–22)

It is Johnson, not schoolboys, whose moral is pointed and whose tale is adorned.

Further analysis of the passage would demonstrate that Charles, though he exhibits definite limitations of vision and perhaps even of humanity, is heroic in the sense that figures in Augustan satire seldom are. He is an overreacher, he is deluded, but he is certainly not ignoble. But can we go further, and claim that he is genuinely tragic? Eliot remarked that "these thirty-two lines compose a paragraph which is, in itself, quite perfect in form: the rising curve of ambition, the sudden calamity, and the slow decline and degradation." The effect seems to be that of a miniature tragedy, and Johnson actually contemplated writing one on this subject.

Against such a view at least three objections can be raised. One is that the tragedy, if it exists at all, is only potentially present, since the story is not especially particularized. Johnson's characters are really emblematic figures, as indeed the transposition of Roman and modern examples would suggest; they are the agents or representatives of abstract forces that are larger than any individual however great. Thus we see Wolsey, "Law in his voice, and fortune in his hand" (100), and thus Charles XII, "Unconquer'd lord of pleasure and of pain" (196). What we have is more like the prospectus for a tragedy than the tragedy itself, and Charles is present mainly in order to support a thesis. Moreover, the shapely form which Eliot describes suggests something quite different from the quality of most political tragedies, which might be characterized in the words of Bacon's essay "Of Great Place": "The standing is slippery; and the regress is either a downfall, or at least an eclipse." For Johnson the rise and fall of great men seems a relatively slow and stately process, like the waxing and waning of the moon, or growth and decay. In tragedy it is perhaps more like mountain-climbing: immense skill expended in the face of ever-present danger, and the stroke of disaster coming like a sudden blow.

A related objection is that the simple *de casibus* exemplum, while it is fundamental to the idea of the tragic, is (considered simply in itself) an inadequate basis for tragedy as the artistic imitation of an action. Modern criticism would not care to accept as tragic all of the stories related by Chaucer's Monk, and in fact the type, depending on its treatment, need not be tragic at all. Humpty Dumpty is a *de casibus* figure. If the Charles XII passage is tragic, it must be so by virtue of its imaginative presentation, however brief (as I have argued in opposition to Joyce, or at any rate Stephen Dedalus [elsewhere]).

Finally, an even more fundamental objection may be advanced: that a tragic interpretation of Charles XII is a wilful misreading of Johnson's intention, which is satiric. Howard D. Weinbrot, approaching the poem from a formal analysis of Augustan satire, inverts the values of the tragic school and regards it as an assault on human pride. Thus Charles is seen as "super-human but inhuman," held up as an example to avoid, not to admire or sympathize with. Such a view is a useful corrective to the notion that we have any clear—much less any intimate—understanding of Charles' feelings, but it does not really disprove the possibility of tragic emotion. Many tragic heroes are inhuman in their greatness, arrive at a fate which is both appropriate and effected by their own actions, and do not necessarily "learn" from their fall.

A fully satiric treatment of Charles is implied in a brief allusion in the *Essay on Man:*

> Heroes are much the same, the point's agreed,
> From Macedonia's madman to the Swede;
> The whole strange purpose of their lives, to find
> Or make, an enemy of all mankind!
> Not one looks backward, onward still he goes,
> Yet ne'er looks forward farther than his nose.
>
> (IV. 219–24)

When Johnson quoted these lines from memory, Boswell objected to "Yet ne'er looks forward farther than his nose" as being low. Johnson replied, "Sir, it is intended to be low: it is satire. The expression is debased, to debase the character" (*Life*). And in *Adventurer* 99, where he defends "projectors" from the unthinking derision of the Augustan satirists, he describes Charles XII as one of those true projectors whose ambitions should be regarded with revulsion.

> I cannot conceive, why he that has burnt cities, and wasted nations, and filled the world with horror and desolation, should be more kindly regarded by mankind, than he that died in the rudiments of wickedness; why he that accomplished mischief should be glorious, and he that only endeavoured it should be criminal: I would wish Caesar and Catiline, Xerxes and Alexander, Charles and Peter, huddled together in obscurity or detestation.

For whatever reason, he did not choose, four years earlier, to present Charles in this light in *The Vanity of Human Wishes.*

But considerations like these should not lead us to suppose that the poem is altogether remote from satire. One may imagine that Johnson knew he was ignoring much of Juvenal's sarcastic acerbity, and that he was transforming passages of vivid (not to say grotesque) particularity into something much more solemn and general. But it is quite another matter to believe that he intended the poem to be essentially unsatiric, or, what is more important, that it would actually convey that impression to us if we were not reading selectively. It is clear that the tragic school, from Scott to Miss Lascelles, have been responding to something that really exists in *The Vanity of Human Wishes*. But in so doing they have not given full weight to another equally real aspect, which led Joseph Warton to write, "The imitations of Horace by Pope, and of Juvenal by Johnson, are preferable to their originals in the appositeness of their examples and in the poignancy of their ridicule." For this one-sidedness of emphasis the comparison with Juvenal is partly to blame. The difference between Johnson's version and its model is so apparent that critics have been inclined to regard it as one of kind rather than degree. And their approach, emphasizing as it does the great set-piece portraits, is likely to neglect other passages which have considerable poetic merit and are essential to the structure of the poem.

Here, however, we must ask what kind of structure *The Vanity of Human Wishes* may reasonably be said to have. Early in the poem Johnson follows Juvenal quite closely, and appears to recommend the example of jesting Democritus. Later he departs a good deal from his source and for much of the time, at least, evokes a mood which has been called tragic. What, then, should we make of Democritus? One critic concludes that he has been "unsuitably" retained; another takes the somewhat desperate course of declaring *The Vanity* a failure, which abruptly drops its mocking program and attempts a treatment quite unsuited to its subject. But another possibility all but forces itself upon us: that Johnson has attempted to do more than one thing in this poem, to join both the satiric and the tragic modes in a larger whole.

To take this approach need not imply an especially high claim for the "unity" of the poem, or an assertion that it embodies some kind of symbolic *concordia discors*. Indeed, I shall urge that the terms of the argument explicitly deny the possibility of reconciling its discordant elements, except by escaping them entirely in the way proposed by the ending of the poem. If I am right, then Johnson is making a virtue of his tendency, which Geoffrey Tillotson has noticed, to conduct an argument rather erratically through a series of quite independent paragraphs. Or, looking at it in another way, Johnson obeys the principle of organization by accretion which Ralph Cohen finds in the Augustan mode: the verse paragraphs are carefully shaped within themselves, but assembled in the larger structure with an additive rather than an organic effect. In either case, one cannot claim too subtle an interrelation of parts. *The Vanity of Human Wishes*, even more than Juvenal's tenth satire, is a very miscellaneous poem. One could easily fabricate reasons to explain why Johnson expands one passage or contracts another, but perhaps it is wisest to assume that he has a right to be simply idiosyncratic in these matters. To take a relatively trivial example, there is no obvious reason why he should substitute modern parallels for all but one of Juvenal's portraits, retaining Xerxes (though adding "the bold Bavarian" as well). I am tempted to believe simply that the passage had a special imaginative fascination for him. We know that he alluded to it later, on two quite different occasions, and that a couplet from it was his favorite in all of his poetry.

Let us return, at this point, to the lines, "From Marlb'rough's eyes the streams of dotage flow, / And Swift expires a driv'ler and a show" (317–18). This couplet is the only direct reference to Juvenal's Swiftian disgust at the impotence of old age, which he mocks with a vehement obscenity that the Loeb translator feels obliged to omit and Dryden to render more witty and less explicit:

> The limber Nerve, in vain provok'd to rise,
> Inglorious from the Field of Battel flies:
> Poor Feeble Dotard, how cou'd he advance
> With his Blew-head-piece, and his broken Lance?
> (Dryden, 328–31; in Juvenal, 204–209)

Dryden if anything softens Juvenal's revulsion in the lines,

> The Skull and Forehead one Bald Barren plain;
> And Gums unarm'd to Mumble Meat in vain:
> Besides th' Eternal Drivel, that supplies
> The dropping Beard, from Nostrils, Mouth, and Eyes.
> (318–21)

To compare these lines with Johnson's treatment of old age may easily lead us to call his version tragic, but we should not forget that the prevailing tone of the passage is satiric as much as sympathetic. The lines inspired by Johnson's aged mother (291–310), in which Nature at last "bids afflicted worth retire to peace," have frequently been mentioned as if they were the entirety of the section. But in fact they are an expansion of Juvenal's brief reference to the sorrows of age *even when* it is not contemptible; and they are preceded by lines which correspond perfectly to Warton's opinion of the poignancy of Johnson's ridicule. The dotard loses the pleasures of the senses, and "shuns to know, / That life portracted is protracted woe" (257–58)— a sentence which is often quoted, and justly so, as a typically Johnsonian statement about the life of man. Thus far we may presume that Johnson intends a degree of sympathy; we all feel a kind of horror when we consider that "Time hovers o'er, impatient to destroy, / And shuts up all the passages of joy" (259–60). As he so often does, Johnson universalizes the condition by attributing it to a force, *Time,* to which we are all in bondage, and gives it point and immediacy by the brilliant stroke of personification: Time is *impatient* to destroy.

The old man, then, is tedious to himself, and with this we may easily sympathize. On the other hand, we must do justice to the epigrammatic skill with which Johnson depicts another aspect of his condition: he is tedious to others, and insofar as it is worth their while to humor him, he encourages moral debasement of a particularly despicable kind.

> But everlasting dictates croud his tongue,
> Perversely grave, or positively wrong.
> The still returning tale, and ling'ring jest,
> Perplex the fawning niece and pamper'd guest,
> While growing hopes scarce awe the gath'ring sneer,
> And scarce a legacy can bribe to hear;
> The watchful guests still hint the last offence,
> The daughter's petulance, the son's expence,
> Improve his heady rage with treach'rous skill,
> And mould his passions till they make his will.
>
> (273–82)

From the loathsome old man—loathsome morally, not just physically—the emphasis shifts to the predatory heirs, whose skill in fawning is "perplexed" by the rambling confusion of his stories and jests. He has become so appalling that even a legacy is barely reward enough for their attentions. And at last, tyrannical though he is, he becomes the victim and they the agents, as they "hint," "improve," and "mould" his feelings, until—with a neat pun— "they make his will.' Johnson has often been praised for the strength and vitality of his verbs, but his adjectives and participles as well show a peculiarly Augustan accuracy of implication. The tale is "still returning"—the listeners perceive with despair that, like fate, it looms once again into view; the jest is "ling'ring," as it stumbles laboriously through its familiar course. And the sycophants' role forbids them to deflect the tale and the jest; on the contrary, they are obliged to welcome them with every sign of delight.

Thus far, I have suggested that *The Vanity of Human Wishes* contains two predominant modes, those of satiric attack and tragic sympathy. Sometimes they alternate; sometimes they appear more intimately joined. But it is not necessary to claim that they are reconciled in any profound way, for, as I have intimated, Johnson denies the possibility of real reconciliation. The overtly religious conclusion to the poem does not emerge logically from it, but is supplied, as if from outside, as the only possible escape from its dilemmas. We have been given a series of impressions of human life, producing emotions which are varied and perhaps even contradictory. Just as in the final sentence of *Rasselas,* we are offered no means of finding stability amid the vicissitudes of life, but are advised instead to redirect our attention to "the choice of eternity" (*Rasselas,* ch. 47).

The radical difference between Juvenal's ending and Johnson's has often been noticed. The Roman poet recommends the Stoic posture which Johnson so often criticized as inhuman, and far from endorsing the efficacy of prayer, instructs his reader to concede as little as possible to the gods.

> Yet, not to rob the Priests of pious Gain,
> That Altars be not wholly built in vain;
> Forgive the Gods the rest, and stand confin'd
> To Health of Body, and Content of Mind:
> A Soul, that can securely Death defie,
> And count it Nature's Priviledge, to Dye.
>   (Dryden, 546–51)

Mens sana in corpore sano: this is the answer to both of the themes of Juvenal's satire, the vanity of ambition (for power, wealth, and so on), and the final disillusionment with life itself. Johnson would probably agree with the former ("the wisest justice on the banks of Trent," 124), but his answer to the latter is the reverse of Juvenal's: only "celestial wisdom," acting for a benevolent God, can make "the happiness she does not find" (367–68).

In this sense *The Vanity of Human Wishes* is not only didactic, but actually homiletic. If I were to guess at Johnson's conception of his relation to Juvenal, I would surmise that he wanted us to be struck by precisely this difference between the two poems. While admiring the aptness of his modern parallels and the weighty solemnity of his language, we will have noticed how much less mocking his version is, and how a tragic feeling keeps breaking in upon the satire, though never wholly displacing it. We know from Johnson's many discussions of Stoicism that he cannot have regarded Juvenal's answer as in any sense adequate, so that it deserves the criticism of the *Rambler:* "The folly of human wishes and persuits has always been a standing subject of mirth and declamation, and has been ridiculed and lamented from age to age; till perhaps the fruitless repetition of complaints and censures may be justly numbered among the subjects of censure and complaint" (*Rambler* 66). Mere censure, mere mirth and declamation, are "fruitless'; Johnson's method is to lead us through the stages of the Roman poet's argument, and then to show that religion reveals a conclusion of which

Juvenal had not the slightest intimation. Thus I suggest that he intended his Christian ending as a kind of tour de force, answering the despair of the classical poet with the truth of revelation, and making the happiness he could not find.

The title which Johnson gave his imitation suggests this correction of classical by means of Biblical wisdom. We are meant to think of Ecclesiastes, to which he often alluded in his sermons and periodical writings.

> The numerous miseries of human life have extorted in all ages an universal complaint. The wisest of men [Solomon] terminated all his experiments in search of happiness, by the mournful confession, that "all is vanity"; and the antient patriarchs lamented, that "the days of their pilgrimate were few and evil."
>
> (*Adventurer* 120)

To dwell upon the miseries of life would be useless, and indeed cruel, if it did not perform the essential service of distracting man from the illusory pleasures of this world and impelling him to fix his attention on eternity.

> Some have endeavoured to engage us in the contemplation of the evils of life for a very wise and good end. They have proposed, by laying before us the uncertainty of prosperity, the vanity of pleasure, and the inquietudes of power, the difficult attainment of most earthly blessings, and the short duration of them all, to divert our thoughts from the glittering follies and tempting delusions that surround us, to an inquiry after more certain and permanent felicity.
>
> (Sermon V, 1825)

In particular, this "inquiry" involves a redirection of two of man's most fundamental passions, those of hope and fear. In his sermon on the text, "I have seen all the works that are done under the sun; and behold, all is vanity and vexation of spirit" (Ecclesiastes 1 : 14), Johnson says that Solomon "had taken a survey of all the gradations of human life," just as *The Vanity of Human Wishes* begins with observation surveying mankind; and Solomon reached a similar conclusion, that "the history of mankind is little else than a narrative of designs which have failed, and hopes that have been disappointed" (Sermon 12, 1825). Before undertaking his "survey," Johnson asks,

> Then say how hope and fear, desire and hate,
> O'erspread with snares the clouded maze of fate,
> Where wav'ring man, betray'd by vent'rous pride,

> To tread the dreary paths without a guide,
> As treach'rous phantoms in the mist delude,
> Shuns fancied ills, or chases airy good.
>
> (5–10)

If man is indeed "without a guide"—Johnson takes for granted the inadequacy of Juvenal's *mens sana* in this regard—then the catalogue of human folly and misery must compel us to rise the question again, in even more pessimistic terms.

> Where then shall Hope and Fear their objects find?
> Must dull Suspence corrupt the stagnant mind?
> Must helpless man, in ignorance sedate,
> Roll darkling down the torrent of his fate?
>
> (343–46)

In the first published edition the final line read "Swim darkling down the current of his fate"; the revision forcibly enhances the idea of utter helplessness.

Hope and *Fear* are not the vague, indefinite terms that they have become today, but denote a view of the human condition that Johnson believes to be both psychologically and theologically true. First of all, these emotions are an inseparable part of life; as Imlac found, not even the Happy Valley could empower him to "bid farewell to hope and fear" (*Rasselas,* ch. 12). But more importantly, empiricist psychology defines them as a sort of double mainspring of human life. "Every man is conscious," Johnson writes in a sermon, "that he neither performs, nor forbears any thing upon any other motive than the prospect, either of an immediate gratification, or a distant reward" (Sermon 14). The answer to the vanity of human wishes, then, is to redirect these basic drives in the right way. "To live religiously, is to walk, not by sight, but by faith; to act in confidence of things unseen, in hope of future recompense, and in fear of future punishment" (Sermon 10). Thus Aspasia's eloquence briefly impels Irene to recognize the emptiness of "The glitt'ring vanities of empty greatness, / The hopes and fears, the joys and pains of life." Aspasia seizes the hint, and urges her friend, "Let nobler hopes and juster fears succeed" (*Irene,* II.i.6–9). Only in heaven will hope and fear cease to be necessary.

In effect, *The Vanity of Human Wishes* counsels a Boethian withdrawal from the inevitable disappointments and sorrows of the temporal world. It warns against subservience to "delusive Fortune" (75), and urges the lesson of the passage from Beothius which Johnson translated for the 1752 edition of the *Rambler* (repeating his use of the word "darkling"):

> O Thou whose pow'r o'er moving worlds presides,
> Whose voice created, and whose wisdom guides,
> On darkling man in pure effulgence shine,
> And chear the clouded mind with light divine.
> 'Tis thine alone to calm the pious breast
> With silent confidence and holy rest:
> From thee, great God, we spring, to thee we tend,
> Path, motive, guide, original, and end.
>
> (Motto to *Rambler* 7)

It is now time to draw back a little from the poem, and to ask whether it does in fact convey the impression which, if my argument is correct, Johnson intended that it should. Is Ian Jack right in seeing an "almost medieval" pessimism in the *contemptus mundi* tradition? Does the poem genuinely escape the tragic (and the satiric) by refusing to be bound by transitory hopes and fears, in the way that *Antony and Cleopatra*—to take an extra-religious example—seems to escape from the confines of tragedy?

> 'Tis paltry to be Caesar:
> Not being Fortune, he's but Fortune's knave,
> A minister of her will.
>
> (*Antony and Cleopatra*, V.ii.2–4)

These are questions which every reader must answer for himself. For my own part, I am inclined to think that even in this poem the moralist never quite suppresses the man. As Gray wrote in the lines which Johnson singled out for particular admiration,

> For who to dumb Forgetfulness a prey,
> This pleasing anxious being e'er resign'd,
> Left the warm precincts of the cheerful day,
> Nor cast one longing ling'ring look behind?

And, retreating still further from the poem, it is possible to distinguish between the meaning it is intended to enforce and the meaning we give it if we cannot share Johnson's religious premises. Like Pascal, he wins through to his knowledge of a higher truth by exposing the sickening inadequacy of any temporal truth; but for many readers today this is a conclusion which may be imaginatively understood but not shared. In this case, the main body of the poem may take on a different appearance, and become something much closer to tragedy than Johnson designed it to be. Nor is such an interpretation an anachronistic, twentieth-century misreading. To illustrate

my meaning I cannot do better than to quote the following passage from
F. M. Cornford's brilliant study of Thucydides' *History* as a tragic drama:

> Elpis had not to the Greek the associations which Christianity
> has given to "Hope"; she is not a virtue, but a dangerous passion.
> The future is dark and uncertain, and although rational foresight
> (*gnóme*) can see a little way into the gloom, Fortune, or Fate, or
> Providence, is an incalculable factor which at any moment may
> reverse the purposes and defeat the designs of man. Elpis is the
> passion which deludes man to count on the future as if he could
> perfectly control it; and thus she is a phase of infatuate pride, a
> temptress who besets prosperity.

Man in this sense is, we may say, condemned indeed to "tread the dreary
paths without a guide" (8), he is indeed the helpless victim of delusive
Fortune, but to know these things is not to be able to escape them.

Such reflections as these may help to explain why the "tragic" elements
of *The Vanity of Human Wishes* have so often been admired, and indeed
interpreted as setting the tone of the poem as a whole. But although it is
idle to ask that our aesthetic response be governed by the presumed intention
of the writer, it may yet be true that Johnson intended the poem to have
an effect that was neither tragic nor satirical, moving beyond both into a
larger and more comprehensive vision. It should be emphasized that no
absolute statement of value is intended in a phrase like "larger and more
comprehensive vision." A work which draws upon tragedy and satire at once
may lack the intensity and penetration of either kind at its best, and may
seem more discursive than imaginative. May it not also seem peculiarly
Johnsonian?

FRANK BRADY

The Strategies of Biography
and Some Eighteenth-Century Examples

The rudimentary state of biographical theory can be blamed on biography's anomalous status among literary forms. It is based on fact, and modern criticism hardly knows what to do with the factual. Our critical position presents a curious inversion of eighteenth-century literalism: "The value of every story depends on its being true. A story is a picture either of an individual or of human nature in general: if it be false, it is a picture of nothing." So Dr. Johnson, whose writings and conversation demonstrate how narrowly he interpreted "truth." But for the modern critic the only meaningful truth, in a *literary sense,* is the truth of the imagination. If the truthful is also "factual," if it claims to portray directly the world of present or past, it is cast into the literary limbo known as "descriptive or assertive writing." Imaginative literature must not be contaminated by anything more than incidental reference to historical experience, or it becomes suspected of such pernicious aims as trying to change our opinions or influence our behavior.

This argument from the necessity for "disinterest" provides one basis for the modern attitude toward the factual. Another assumption behind this attitude is that primarily factual material, like biography, is artistically unworkable, though an occasional life may inherently display that shapeliness, drama, or coherence characteristic of the best fiction. When fact and fiction are inescapably mixed, as in Shakespeare's history plays, critics ordinarily reduce the historical material to fictional status, which conveniently eliminates any possible theoretical problems posed by this combination. Yet

From *Literary Theory and Structure: Essays in Honor of William K. Wimsatt.* © 1973 by Yale University Press.

problems remain. Hugh Kenner remarks about *Robinson Crusoe:* "For to be told, poker-faced, that it is not the fabrication we would gladly accept, but the very thing that is normally fabricated—a memoir, a testimony—this somehow changes a book, even when we do not believe what we are being told about it." Yes, but how does it change a book? Consider, for example, the peculiarly unsettling effect of certain short stories by Borges, where fiction masquerades as fact.

Just a narrative device, the critic may comment, and in any case biography is safely factual. If it takes the form of a fictional reconstruction of the thoughts and actions of real persons, it is usually dismissed as a hybrid hardly worth despising. Biography indeed could be comfortably subsumed under history if it did not reveal some suspicious resemblances to the novel in plot, character, and setting. Also at its inception in the eighteenth century, the English novel was so intertwined with biography that the resemblances between these forms will not go away. In terms of plot, the fullscale (birth to death) biography belongs in the same class with its fictional counterpart, the "Life and Adventures of" or "History of" novel. The biographer still faces the same problems that confronted Defoe in *Moll Flanders* and Fielding in *Tom Jones*—and, incidentally, should be as ruthless as they are in skipping over uneventful periods in his hero's life. This birth-to-death plot structure may seem primitive, unless shaped with the sophistication of a Fielding or a Flaubert, but what the biography loses in smoothness and coherence may well be compensated for by its sense of actuality. For while fiction (poetry, drama) is superior to biography (history) in its intensive and generalizing properties, biography carries a greater feeling of authenticity than fiction. We grant to truth what we would refuse to imagination.

Novelists have exploited the fundamental plot resemblances between biography and fiction from the novel's beginning, but biographers with disastrous innocence have too often conceived of themselves as chroniclers. Chronicle is merely the basis of biography, the gathering of its material, not biography itself. Depending on his material, the biographer can assume some of the novelist's structural freedoms: he can emphasize the fictional or the thematic (as Northrop Frye defines these terms); or allegorically, portray the life as journey or battle; or experiment with the handling of time. Also he can shift point of view with less sense of strain than the novelist. Given the feeble lead of Mason's *Memoirs of Gray,* Boswell in the *Life of Johnson* achieves complex variations in perspective by mingling the first-person forms of the diarist (the subject seen by himself in the present) and the autobiographer (the subject seen by himself in retrospect) with third-person forms: the limited (the subject seen by contemporaries) and the quasi-omniscient (the subject seen by the biographer).

The handling of plot and point of view, two formal aspects of biography, make up part of the grander strategy every good biographer must settle upon in shaping his material. (In loose analogy, the novelist is to the biographer as the painter is to the sculptor: the painter can choose his materials freely, while the sculptor must be more conscious of the "resistance" of his material.) Since the biographer himself seems so often unaware that his work has either formal aspects or a general strategy, it is not surprising that the critic usually appears ignorant of any formal aspects in biography comparable to those he could at once specify in a novel or poem. As for larger questions of biographical strategy, they so seldom enter a critic's head that he can hardly believe that they exist. To account, then, for the merit of a biography the critic tends to generalize about historical accuracy, vividness, authenticity, and so forth. But good biographers have defined their subjects strategically for a long time.

In *Tom Jones,* Fielding insists on our participation in the artistic problems he faces. What do we call this thing he is writing? What materials can he properly use? How shall he handle questions of time and tone? What standards should be employed to judge it? In the *Lives of the Poets,* Johnson was also experimenting with new forms, but he leaves the reader to work out their rationales for himself. He had for precedent those various models so faithfully rehearsed by historians of biography: Plutarch's fusion of narrative, portrait, and commentary; Cavendish's extension of the *de casibus* tradition; Walton's secularized version of the saint's life; the Theophrastian sketch as revived in the seventeenth century; collections of ana and memorabilia from Xenophon to Ménage. None of these patterns suited his purpose. He had told Boswell on their Hebridean tour that "he did not know any literary man's life in England well-written. It should tell us his studies, his manner of life, the means by which he attained to excellence, his opinion of his own works, and such particulars." All these points he covered in his *Life of Pope,* the acknowledged paradigmatic example among the *Lives of the Poets,* but no single point directs our attention to the basic organizing principle of its long biographical section. Taken as a group, they do.

Modern study of the *Life of Pope* has stressed the extent to which Johnson is relying on and responding to previous biographers and critics of Pope, or remarked on such thematic concerns as "the vanity of human wishes." In his examination of the *Lives of the Poets,* Lawrence Lipking goes further to discuss perceptively various general ways of looking at the *Life of Pope,* but he seems puzzled by what may be called its "local structure": "Too much of it concerns local quarrels, and depends on references or on sequences of thought that are not specified, for it to possess the self-contained harmony of art."

Before discussing this local structure, one general comment: part of our difficulty with the *Life of Pope* as a whole lies in the critical expectations we bring to a study of Pope. For example, Johnson discusses the "Ode on St. Cecilia's Day" and the translation of the *Iliad* at length, while he brushes aside the Imitations of Horace. In an age which prized sublimity, which regarded the ode and the epic as the great poetic forms, this emphasis is natural. Likewise, Johnson's familiarity with Horace leads him to react to Pope's imitations with about the degree of attention we give to Pope's versions of Donne.

The larger problem posed by the *Life of Pope* derives from our sense that it is a great biography combined with a failure to see what holds together by far its longest part, the biographical section. As suggested earlier, the critic then takes refuge in such general attributes as the "air of authority, the energy of the expression, the seeming fairness, the clarity and arresting directness of its thought." Unquestionably these are important motives for our reaction to it, but they fail to consider any of the work's formal aspects, and in particular Johnson's basic organizing principle which also defines his strategy in dealing with Pope's life.

That organizing principle is a simple one which Mr. Lipking's reservations, just quoted, about the *Life of Pope* point straight toward. Why at the beginning, for instance, does Johnson make so much of Dennis's attack on the *Essay on Criticism?* Dennis's critique is a mixture of shrewdness, irritability, and dogmatism apparently of little interest to later readers. But this critique was the opening gun in the lifelong battle between Pope and many of his lesser contemporaries that was to culminate in the *Dunciad.* Johnson's organizing principle is that he is writing the life of a man whose "primary and principal purpose was to be a poet." Pope, he says, "considered poetry as the business of his life, and, however he might seem to lament his occupation, he followed it with constancy: to make verses was his first labour, and to mend them was his last." But Johnson's conception of the poet involves neither the Romantic interest in poetry as the outpouring of a noble soul nor the modern concentration on the poet's psychological makeup. In a typically eighteenth-century way, Johnson sees Pope as a poet in relation to other men, in his social context, in his *public* character.

If the opening section of the *Life of Pope* is read as a study of the poet in society, almost every detail falls into place. The various stories on which it centers—the cockfight for preeminence with Addison, the possible patronage of Halifax, even the "open war" with Hervey and attacks on the Ministry when Pope "forgot the prudence" with which he had earlier avoided politics—make the *Life of Pope* a judicial commentary on the public image of himself that Pope displays in the *Epistle to Arbuthnot* and elsewhere. For from the opening paragraphs in which Johnson contrasts his information about Pope's ancestry to Pope's assertions about it, Johnson plays his views of Pope as poet, thinker, and man against those of Pope's contemporaries and Pope's own. Johnson finds proper subjects for attack in the implied justification for suicide in the *Elegy to an Unfortunate Lady* and the simple-minded or misleading doctrines of the *Essay on Man* because the aim of poetry is to instruct by pleasing: the poet has an important role in society. (In this respect Johnson takes Pope more seriously than modern critics take Pound or Eliot or Yeats when they minimize or disregard the poet's political and social views.) Elsewhere Johnson concentrates on such "social" matters as literary collaboration, the poet's financial arrangements, and the letters which show Pope as he wished to appear to posterity.

Pope's character necessarily emerges in this biographical section as a product of Johnson's strategy in presenting him as a public figure. Sometimes using Dennis or Addison as a stalking horse, Johnson implies that Pope was affected, hypocritical, devious, snobbish, and vengeful. But he also gives due weight to Pope's filial piety, loyalty to his friends, and public charity. Pope as a man turns out to be a compound of virtues and vices, like the rest of us. Yet all these details reflect the poet's character in relation to other people, to his reputation, rather than in relation to himself. (Since almost every incident has literary significance, the account of Pope's narrow escape from an overturned coach stands out as an awkward exception.) Pope's sex life, sparse as it was by his own admission, would demand considerable scrutiny in any modern biography; apart from an indirect allusion to "an idle story" of Cibber's, Johnson never mentions it. Even Pope's long attachment to Martha Blount becomes linked to literary history, to Pope's relations with Allen and Warburton. Johnson's sense of the poet's role in society is so strong that he cannot bring himself to believe that Pope's expressed desire for solitude was sincere, though Johnson's own dependence on society obviously affects his judgment on this point. Interesting personal details Johnson reserves for the following character sketch, and even of those Johnson provides just enough to mark the "peculiarities" of Pope's private character and life.

On 20 April 1781, "somebody" remarked to Johnson that "the life of a mere literary man could not be very entertaining." Having just finished his *Life of Pope,* it is obvious why Johnson replied, "But it certainly may. . . . Why should the life of a literary man be less entertaining than the life of any other man? Are there not as interesting varieties in such a life? As *a literary life* it may be very entertaining." As well as the *Life of Pope,* the *Life of Dryden* and to a lesser extent several of the remaining *Lives of the Poets* are literary lives. In striking contrast to the simple but sufficient organizing principle used in these lives is the complex interweaving of patterns exhibited by the *Life of Savage*.

The basic problem to be resolved about the *Life of Savage* is its genre. Taken intentionalistically it is of course a biography, but factually it must be considered a very poor biography. Boswell's conclusion still holds about its *donnée,* that Savage was the illegitmate son of the Countess of Macclesfield: "The world must vibrate in a state of uncertainty as to what was the truth" (*Life*). Further, Johnson transposes two of the major events in Savage's life, his killing of Sinclair and consequent trial, and Tyrconnel's patronage of him; while many other of Johnson's "facts" are incorrect. Here we are on the borderline between fact and fiction with a vengeance, and the proper approach may well be to consider the *Life of Savage* a work of the imagination, taking it as a great short novel as Cyril Connolly did. But as a great short novel it is a most peculiar one, since its author was under the impression he was creating a factual work. In turn the reader vibrates in a state of uncertainty as to what is "factual" and what is not, an uncertainty compounded by Johnson's bewilderment in the face of the monstrous "facts" supplied him, and his attempt to reconcile them by the test of probability with the usual principles governing human motivation and conduct. In his discussion of Savage's life before they became acquainted and even later, Johnson seems at times to be going through the equivalent of a Rorschach test. Johnson's view of Pope is sharply differentiated from Pope's view of himself in the *Life of Pope;* in the *Life of Savage,* Savage is constantly refracted through Johnson's effort first to understand him and then to explain him to the reader. Yet, like the grin of the Cheshire Cat, Savage's own voice—in indirect conversation, in his speech at the trial, in poems, and in letters— erupts and fades throughout the story. The *Life of Savage* brings out with unusual clarity the three patterns inherent in any biography: the subject's view of himself, the biographer's view of the subject, and the reader's view of both subject and biographer.

It is apparent that the *Life of Savage* offers a glorious tangle of theoretical problems, which mainly will be avoided here. From the point of view of Johnson's central strategy as embodied in its basic structural patterns, the *Life of Savage* can be classified as a fictional work masquerading as fact, with an unreliable narrator who thinks he is reliable; in short, I will treat it as if it belonged to the same genre as *Moll Flanders*. (I am well aware that Johnson did not think of it in these terms, nor will the reader respond with the same "mental set" to both works.) When the two works are taken together, it becomes evident that the biography is more intricately ordered than the novel.

If, as Benjamin Boyce suggests, the *Life of Savage* finds some of its antecedents in "secret histories" or rogue stories—the underbrush of fiction—as well as in novels like *Roxana,* Johnson surely transcends them as he did the putative models for the *Life of Pope.* To make sense at all of Savage's life, Johnson had to organize it very tightly, and the initial organizing pattern, established in the opening sentence, centers on the terms *nature* and *fortune:* "It has been observed in all Ages, that the Advantages of Nature or of Fortune have contributed very little to the Promotion of Happiness."

"Nature" and "fortune" are the two assumed axes of the chart on which a man's life was commonly plotted in the eighteenth century. Nature resembles our term, heredity, with the distinction that nature emphasizes inherent disposition and abilities rather than what is given by genetic transmission. But fortune and our corresponding term, environment, are quite different. Environment suggests interaction, and often struggle, between the individual and his society. Fortune suggests, first, chance or vicissitude, a man's shifting place in this world as determined by Fortune's wheel. In this sense it evolves into one of Johnson's *Dictionary* definitions: "the good or evil that befalls man." By the eighteenth century, however, two further and overlapping definitions of fortune have become significant: "one's condition or standing in life," and "position as determined by wealth" (*OED*). Johnson blends the earlier and later meanings of fortune in the *Life of Savage.* As one of its overall patterns it shows "a turning of the Boethian wheel of Fortune," but this pattern when specified in the repeated use of "fortune," "misfortunes," "miseries," and so forth, usually takes on the later meanings of fortune.

Fortune and nature mesh in complicated ways, the complications arising because Johnson maintains two views of Savage in equilibrium. The first view is that Savage is a hero characterized by "intellectual Greatness," though heroic mainly in his suffering. Johnson establishes this view early: "The Heroes of literary as well as civil History have been very often no less remarkable for what they have suffered, than for what they have atchieved." In his heroic aspect, Savage's encounters with Fortune construct a *de casibus* pattern, of which the great early example in English biography is Cavendish's *Life of Wolsey.* But deluded and self-destructive as Savage is in Johnson's portrait, he is not the Micawberesque antihero that he has recently been taken for. There is nothing ironic in Johnson's description of Savage at the time he was writing his tragedy about Sir Thomas Overbury: "Out of this Story he formed a Tragedy, which, if the Circumstances in which he wrote it be considered, will afford at once an uncommon Proof of Strength of Genius, and Evenness of Mind, of a Serenity not to be ruffled, and an Imagination not to be suppressed."

Rising fortune enhances Savage's literary reputation and Johnson comments, "So powerful is Genius, when it is invested with the Glitter of Affluence; Men willingly pay to Fortune that Regard which they owe to Merit." When Savage loses Tyrconnel's favor, a different relationship between nature and fortune emerges: "As many more can discover, that a Man is richer than that he is wiser than themselves, Superiority of Understanding is not so readily acknowledged as that of Condition; nor is that Haughtiness, which the Consciousness of great Abilities incites, borne with the same Submission as the Tyranny of Wealth."

As the fortunes of Savage decline, Johnson's portrayal of him becomes increasingly somber. Yet with enough flaws to supply a half-dozen tragic heroes, Savage maintains "the same invincible Temper": "In his lowest State he wanted not Spirit to assert the natural Dignity of Wit, and was always ready to repress that Insolence which Superiority of Fortune incited, and to trample the Reputation which rose on any other Basis than that of Merit." More and more isolated from his society, even exiled into Wales, Savage still retains "the insurmountable Obstinacy of his Spirit"; he was, Johnson says, "a Lion in the Toils." In his independence, resentment, insolence, and self-delusion, there are some touches of Satan:

> that fixt mind
> And high disdain, from sence of injur'd merit . . .
> And study of revenge, immortal hate,
> And courage never to submit or yield.
> [*Paradise Lost,* I.97–98, 107–08]

But only touches. Johnson's central reaction to Savage as intellectual hero is to deplore the enormous waste of genius: "On a Bulk, in a Cellar, or in a Glass-house, among Thieves and Beggars, was to be found the author of the *Wanderer,* the Man of exalted Sentiments, extensive Views and curious Observations, the Man whose Remarks on Life might have assisted the Statesman, whose Ideas of Virtue might have enlightened the Moralist, whose Eloquence might have influenced Senates, and whose Delicacy might have polished Courts." This reflects Savage's view of himself, of course, as he expresses it in a letter from prison shortly before his death: "As to the World, I hope that I shall be endued by Heaven with that Presence of Mind, that serene Dignity in Misfortune, that constitutes the character of a true Nobleman."

The second view Johnson presents of Savage is the prudential one, taking "prudential" in Aristotle's sense as conducting oneself wisely in the world. This view has been too often discussed to need development here. In terms of prudence, the *Life of Savage* reads like a tragic version of *Tom Jones,* with intellectual greatness taking the place of instinctive benevolence as the hero's main attribute. Fortune waits on prudence in this world, or supposedly so: actually Tom never shows much prudence. Even so, Tom's cheerful benevolence leads naturally to his rescue by friends at the end of the novel, just as the deep solipsism lying under Savage's surface companionability inevitably provokes his friend's abandonment of him. What is remarkable about Johnson's two views of Savage's character is that they never fuse; they proceed side by side until they conclude in the double ending that has puzzled critics. The last paragraph comes down heavily on the necessity for prudence, while the three preceding ones eloquently reiterate that Savage had "a Genius truly poetical" and "a great Mind, irritated by perpetual Hardships." Of Savage as hero Johnson reminds us, "they are no proper Judges of his Conduct who have slumber'd away their Time on the Down of Plenty."

The unresolved tension between these two main structural patterns accounts, I think, for much of the interest generated by the *Life of Savage.* They are supplemented by a number of criss-crossing character, thematic, and verbal patterns: Savage as child in relation to his supposed mother and parental surrogates; the contrast between his theory and practice, between that "Knowledge of Life [which] was indeed his chief Attainment" and his inability to apply it in any proportion to his talent; the close connections between his life and his writings; even Johnson's use of maxims and legal metaphors. Underlying these patterns is Johnson's attempt to make psychological sense of the melodrama that marked Savage's life, complicated by his double attitude toward Savage's character: a recognition, often amounting to admiration, of Savage's independence of the world, and the realization that such independence can only be maintained at excessive cost. And, finally, there is the mystery of Savage himself, who emerges for the reader with the complex opacity that characterizes someone we have known well and long but really have never understood. Whatever he makes of Savage, each reader almost surely sees a different Savage than the one seen by subject or biographer.

The two main structural patterns of the *Life of Savage* lead in two different biographical directions. In the *Life of Johnson,* Boswell domesticates the heroic, one clue to his purpose being stated in the advertisement to the second edition: "It seems to me, in my moments of self-complacency, that this extensive biographical work, however inferior in its nature, may in one respect be assimilated to the ODYSSEY. Amidst a thousand entertaining and instructive episodes the Hero is never long out of sight; for they are all in some degree connected with him; and He, in the whole course of the History, is exhibited by the Author for the best advantage of his readers." Boswell then quotes two lines from Horace, given here in Francis's translation:

> To show what wisdom and what sense can do,
> The poet sets Ulysses in our view.

Boswell's central thematic purpose is to construct an epic, a moral epic of heroic proportions, in which a man with greater strengths and weaknesses than ordinary, struggles with the problems of daily life and overcomes them. The remote model for that epic is the *Odyssey* with its archetypal journey pattern, the *Life* substituting a journey in time for one in space. Boswell presents a definite ethical pattern in Johnson which is for "the best advantage of his readers," because Johnson deals on a large scale with the common problems of ordinary people. Of all the versions of epic produced in the eighteenth century—*The Rape of the Lock, The Dunciad, Tom Jones, The Decline and Fall of the Roman Empire,* even Blake's major prophecies—Boswell's remains the most immediate to our everyday concerns.

The other biographical direction suggested by the *Life of Savage* leads to Goldsmith's *Life of Nash,* that "inimitable mock heroic, conferring immortality on a marionette of supreme quality." Where Savage totally rejected the prudential, beau Nash followed the path of "prudence" to excess. Our final impression of Savage is of someone profoundly different from those around him; in Nash, Goldsmith says, "I attempt the character of one, who was just such a man as probably you or I may be, but with this difference, that he never performed an action which the world did not know, or ever formed a wish which he did not take pains to divulge." The mock-heroic form, however, indicates that Goldsmith's strategy is to take Nash at his face value. He was King of Bath; he gave his little province rules; "neither rank nor fortune shielded the refractory from his resentment." "Birth and fortune" replace nature and fortune as measuring sticks, because Nash was completely concerned with those surfaces of society called rank and fashion. Goldsmith treats Nash with the same blend of amusement and seriousness with which he surrounds the Reverend Charles Primrose. For though surfaces are the natural matter of comedy—think of *The School for Scandal* with its Surfaces, screen scene, disguises, portraits and character paintings—they are also where much of life goes on. Goldsmith seems close to a pun when he says, "The relations of great events may surprise indeed; they may be calculated to instruct those very few, who govern the million beneath, but the generality of mankind find the most real improvement from relations which are levelled to *the general surface of life;* which tell, not how men learned to conquer, but how they endeavoured to live . . ." (italics added). When Johnson defined politeness as "fictitious benevolence," he was recommending it as "of great consequence in society" (*Life*). Nash's mistake, of course, lay not in regulating the superficial manners and customs of society but in equating these manners with "manners" in the deeper sense, the whole span of social behavior. Surface becomes everything and Nash swells with importance: his full-length statue is placed between the busts of Newton and Pope; his funeral is pompously royal. But his life is increasingly empty, and all he leaves behind him are a small collection of books, some family pictures, and a few trifles that Goldsmith is careful to enumerate: "an etui mounted in gold . . . a silver terene . . . and some other things of no great value." Amiability mistook itself for greatness.

Against the prudential example—in a double sense—supplied in Nash, Goldsmith counterpoints an instance of "heroic" excess: the story of Miss Sylvia S———, whose romantic imprudence led to suicide. The same kind of counterpointing, but in a thorough and integrated fashion, characterizes Boswell's "Memoirs of Pascal Paoli." Boswell's main purpose was to compose a portrait, modeled on those of Sallust and Plutarch, of a classical hero. But essentially Boswell discovered a new biographical strategy: the biographer becomes the most important other character in his subject's biography. The "Memoirs of Pascal Paoli" revolves around a giant and a dwarf star, the mature Paoli and the naive Boswell, who exists to ask the innocent, revealing question, to evoke the grand response, to highlight the hero. In the process, Boswell exaggerates his own limitations: "Never was I so thoroughly sensible of my own defects as while I was in Corsica. I felt how small were my abilities and how little I knew." At most Boswell can playact the ruler, riding out on Paoli's own horse with his party of guards; real state and distinction, real power, rest in Paoli. Yet he is a human hero, kind to his young and ingenuous friend, and he displays both "great and amiable" virtues.

In the Benbridge portrait of Paoli, commissioned by Boswell, the background consists in some rather stylized rocks, trees, and hills, and Boswell treats his background, Corsica and the Corsicans, in much the same generalizing fashion: a rugged country inhabited by a brave, unspoiled, and rather primitive people, who throw Paoli's stern and active virtues into sharp relief. Boswell's tour with Johnson to the Hebrides offered the possibility of a more complex and exciting arrangement. Scotland becomes an active entity, initially set in ambivalent opposition to Johnson, their hostility well publicized. In this ready-made scenario, Boswell casts Johnson as John Bull, the "true-born Englishman." Boswell, as mediator, defends Scotland when necessary, but prefers the neutral, detached role of "a citizen of the world" (*Life*).

Even before the two leave Edinburgh, Boswell has set up this triangular plot, of which I shall cite one example. In the Records Room of Parliament House, the sight of the Treaty of Union between Scotland and England aroused Boswell's "*old Scottish* sentiments" about the loss of independence. Johnson, taking the bait, responded with one of the traditional sneers at the Scots, their failure to rescue Mary, Queen of Scots, from her English prison. Boswell then expands the scene dramatically:

> [JOHNSON.] ". . . and such a Queen too! as every man of any gallantry of spirit would have sacrificed his life for." Worthy *Mr. James Kerr, Keeper of the Records.* "Half our nation was bribed by English money."—JOHNSON. "Sir, that is no defence: that makes you worse." Good *Mr. Brown, Keeper of the Advocates Library.* "We had better say nothing about it."—BOSWELL. "You would have been glad, however, to have had us last war, sir, to fight your battles!"—JOHNSON. "We should have had you for the same price, though there had been no Union, as we might have had Swiss, or other troops. No, no, I shall agree to a separation. You have only to *go home.*"
>
> [*Life*]

Within this triangulation the narrative proceeds day by day, offering in its minute factuality the most resistant material imaginable to formal structuring. Johnson described its basis to Mrs. Thrale: "Boswell writes a regular journal of our travels, which, I think, contains as much of what I say and do, as of all other occurrences together—'For such a faithful Chronicler as Griffith.' " And later readers of Boswell's journal may be pardoned for thinking, like Johnson, of Boswell as essentially a faithful chronicler. In contrast, Johnson, in his *Journey to the Western Islands,* is constantly concerned with philosophical generalization about the flow of history. Even in acknowledging the "local effect" of Iona, Johnson characteristically rises beyond "sensation" in defining it: "Whatever withdraws us from the power of our senses; whatever makes the past, the distant, or the future predominate over the present, advances us in the dignity of thinking beings." But the *Tour to the Hebrides* is immersed in sensation, in the here and now. Reading the two works side by side can suggest that some eighteenth-century equivalents of Don Quixote and Sancho Panza are describing the same journey, and indeed the contrast between Johnson and Boswell within the *Tour* alone recalls some of the differences between Cervantes's great figures. (Also the *Tour,* like *Don Quixote* and many of its successors, includes an interpolated tale: the wanderings of Prince Charles Edward among the Hebrides, a grandly romantic counterpoint to Boswell's own main story.)

Based on the recurrent rhythm of daily experience, the journal is the only literary form that is truly open-ended, and any formal patterns it disclosed must be "accidental." Yet in the *Tour* this rhythm is not particularly insistent; our interest in what the travelers are saying and doing often overrides our sense of time and place. And, at the level of daily existence, the journal builds up a loose unity through the repetition of subjects (emigration, subordination, and so forth) and the links or comparisons among people, settings, and events. These might be considered as equivalent to thematic or symbolic patterns in a novel. But the *Tour* is given a more general shape by the contrast between expectation and experience, testifying to Johnson's dictum that "the use of travelling is to regulate imagination by reality, and instead of thinking how things may be, to see them as they are."

Generically the *Tour* is antiromance, and specifically it is an inversion of the usual Grand Tour account. The ordinary tourist on that expedition traveled back in time to the sources and monuments of Western culture, especially to the Rome of the first centuries, the golden age of civilization. To visit the semi-barbarous Scottish outlands tested an opposed vision of the past, which maintained that the primitive was superior to the civilized, that the groves of Eden might be approximated in the islands of the South Pacific or some other unspoiled region. (The primitive in this instance, of course, would take the form of a feudal or pastoral society.) Johnson, as might be expected, was skeptical that Nature's plan was anywhere near this simple or, if it was, that art did not improve upon it considerably. But it would be exciting to observe society in an earlier stage of culture. Boswell states their expectations, simply and naturally, as being to explore "a system of life almost totally different from what we had been accustomed to see" (*Life*).

The contrast between expectation and experience runs throughout the *Tour* as a strong, complicated patterning force. It may be helpful to recall a few landmarks: the debate beween Johnson and Lord Monboddo over the relative happiness of the London shopkeeper and the savage; the inspection of the old woman's hut near Loch Ness, which provides the first encounter with pastoral actuality; Johnson's vigorous lecture to Sir Alexander Macdonald on the behavior proper to a feudal chief; the travelers' enjoyment of the simple but civilized pleasures of Raasay and Dunvegan; the pursuit and destruction of Ossian; finally, the climactic visit to Iona, where Johnson and Boswell felt, if momentarily, in firm and exalted touched with the past. And the gradual realization that they had come too late to find the pure patriarchal society they anticipated. Perhaps it was just as well; by the time they returned to civilization they were prepared to laugh heartily "at the ravings of those absurd visionaries who have attempted to persuade us of the superior advantages of a *state of nature*" (*Life*).

All the while using himself as a mediating figure, in his journal as on their jaunt, Boswell keeps the *Tour* skillfully centered on Johnson. Boswell may be the only important biographer who has composed both a portrait (in the *Life*) and a narrative account (in the *Tour*) of the same subject. When he draws far back from his material, Boswell can speak of their jaunts as "the transit of Johnson over the Caledonian hemisphere" (*Life*): instead of the Johnson at rest that the *Life* mainly provides, here is Johnson in constant motion, resilient, patient, formidable, always himself. We tend to recall the *Tour* as a series of sharply defined episodes in which Johnson, "led" by Boswell, moves across a barren landscape densely populated with figures.

Two episodes deserve particular mention. Reduced to entertaining themselves one night, says Boswell, "I took the liberty to put a large blue bonnet on his head. His age, his size, and his bushy grey wig, with this covering on it, presented the image of a venerable *Sennachi* [Gaelic oral historian]; and, however unfavourable to the Lowland Scots, he seemed much pleased to assume the appearance of an ancient Caledonian" (*Life*). It was Johnson's most unexpected role, this transformation in which Boswell suggests the momentary reconciliation of opposites.

The other episode is the great unwritten scene in Boswell's journal, the quarrel between Johnson and Lord Auchinleck. Boswell must have reduced his account of this scene to safe generalities with the greatest of reluctance, for not only did it set his intellectual against his physical father but it provided a natural climax to the confrontation between Johnson and Scotland, here stoutly represented in its most Whiggish and Presbyterian aspects. What life gave to art with one hand, it took away with the other: custom and reverence prohibited Boswell from giving his narrative its proper denouement.

This interference of life with art also enters into the last and oddest of Boswell's biographical strategies—perhaps tactic, here—in the Tour: the use of the journal itself. At the heart of Boswell's journal lies a paradox. He presents each day's events and impressions in a totally unselfconscious way, a record of the normal flow of experience. At the same time, the journal is highly self-conscious, an account intended for Johnson, who read and occasionally corrected it. It was clearly preparation for the biography of Johnson Boswell meant to write. Johnson himself called it "a very exact picture of a portion of his life" (*Life*), and wished it twice as long as it was. And it raised his opinion of Boswell.

As the tour proceeded, the journal took on a shadow existence of its own that affected the relationship between the two men, as when Boswell continued an argument in it that Johnson then answered. Boswell even had the boldness to record some of Johnson's peculiarities, such as his not wearing a nightcap, or talking to himself and "uttering pious ejaculations," hoping that Johnson would explain them (*Life*). Johnson passed over these remarks without comment. Also the journal could get in the way. When Johnson complained at one point that they saw little of each other, Boswell blamed it on the need to post his journal. And once he confesses, "I did not exert myself to get Dr. Johnson to talk, that I might not have the labour of writing down his conversation" (*Life*). As well as *realizing* the present, the journal is shaping life itself. This blurring of life and art is a peculiarly Boswellian trait, but it suggests once again that the range and variety of strategies available to the biographer remain largely unexplored.

ROBERT H. BELL

Boswell's Notes toward a Supreme Fiction: From London Journal to Life of Johnson

Boswell's *London Journal, 1762–1763* reveals a great deal about the author's youthful struggles and tumultuous season in the city. As a vivid, intimate autobiographical record, the journal is unsurpassed; it is also a work of distinct literary artistry. Boswell affirms at the outset both his authenticity and artistic sensibility: "I shall here put down my thoughts on different subjects at different times, the whims that may seize me and the sallies of my luxuriant imagination. I shall mark the anecdotes and the stories that I hear . . . and the various adventures that I may have." He merely recounts what happens, as it happens ("the various adventures that I may have"), but he also renders his adventures in deliberately artful ways ("the sallies of my luxuriant imagination"). To what degree does Boswell achieve aesthetic distance and control over adventitious experience in the *London Journal?*

At the heart of this question is what Bertrand Bronson perceives as Boswell's "double consciousness," a simultaneous awareness of himself as both participant and observer. Some degree of distinction between the self then and now is inherent in all autobiographical narration. Naturally, Boswell's journal lacks the sustained telescopic perspective of Franklin's *Autobiography* or *The Education of Henry Adams;* yet Boswell's point of view, virtually on top of the experience, is certainly much more "many-minded" and reflective than we expect from any twenty-two-year-old involved in such heady activities as seducing an actress or conversing with Samuel Johnson. Boswell's usual practice was to record events a week or so after they occurred, sending them home to his friend John Johnston of Grange, so he was not

From *Modern Language Quarterly* 38, no. 2 (1977). © 1977 by University of Washington.

quite writing "to the moment," like Pamela, though he often pretends to do so, as Frederick Pottle notes in his introduction to the journal. In fact the observer, unlike the participant, has the benefit of knowing at least the immediate future; the result is a forward-straining narrative which is sometimes more like a novel than a diary. One must be careful to qualify this point: while the *London Journal* has abundant literary craft, it is hardly Boswell's *Portrait of the Artist as a Young Man*.

Most of the *London Journal,* unlike Joyce's novel, remains dependent upon what Johnson termed "stubborn and untractable nature." Circumstantial as it is, Boswell gives the journal a kind of rough-hewn shape in imagining himself on a voyage of self-discovery. The story begins with the "scene of . . . a son setting out from home for the wide world, thus introducing the familiar theme of a youth's growth from innocence to experience. The journal ends with an excursion with Johnson to Harwich from which Boswell embarks for legal training on the Continent. And he marks both the beginning and the end with an elaborate ritual. The denouement did indeed depend on Johnson's unexpected offer to " 'see thee go.' " But the story seems to have taken on a life of its own, progressing inevitably to the conclusion that this wayfarer has "been attaining a knowledge of the world" and has finally achieved "a less pleasurable but a more rational and lasting plan."

So there is a broad thrust to Boswell's argument, even though he is immersed in contingency. Boswell calls it a "consistent picture of a young fellow eagerly pushing through life," in pursuit of identity, happiness, self-fulfillment, purpose, and exciting adventures. The fact that Boswell did actually depart for London at the outset, and from Harwich at the end, should not obscure the general pattern he derives from such events. It is true that this "pattern" is a universal experience and not just a literary convention; but Boswell seems eager to pursue his growth as the stuff of a story. An autobiographer need not necessarily have lived a fascinating life, although it certainly may help; he need only be fascinated by the process of re-creating, as the word "life-story" itself suggests. "Very often," Boswell says, "we have more pleasure in reflecting on agreeable scenes that we have been in than we had from the scenes themselves."

Although he does not produce a "consistent picture," Boswell does intermittently depict his youthful naïveté and gradual development; at other moments he simply exposes his continuing lack of sophistication. In other words, the crucial distinction between participant and observer fluctuates and becomes blurred. The celebrated Louisa episode is exactly the kind of experience which should teach a young man the way of the world and more about himself; what Boswell presents is a series of self-consciously literary flourishes without coherent assessment or perspective. For example, how should we respond to the meditation, just before Louisa is introduced, devoted to "the delightful sex," his "present wonderful continence," and the "dignity of his sex"? Boswell casually informs us, "I have suffered severely from the loathsome distemper, and therefore shudder at the thoughts of running any risk of having it again." His whole conception of romance is dangerously callow and self-satisfied:

> Indeed, in my mind, there cannot be higher felicity on earth enjoyed by man than the participation of genuine reciprocal amorous affection with an amiable woman. There he has a full indulgence of all the delicate feelings and pleasures both of body and mind, while at the same time in this enchanting union he exults with a consciousness that he is the superior person. The dignity of his sex is kept up.

Boswell is delightfully preposterous here, but is he simply foolish or is he playing the fool for the sake of the story? One might plausibly argue that his fear of venereal disease and his confident masculine chauvinism *deliberately* characterize a young gallant headed for a fall. But I doubt it. Only if we insist on discovering subtle irony will Boswell's exaggerated raptures and self-delusions foreshadow an "ominous" denouement. As the story unfolds, we can in retrospect perceive an accidental irony which demonstrates Boswell's "double consciousness of himself." The narrative observer exposes his own extravagances and still loves what he reveals. Even if Boswell knew that he was fated to contract veneral disease—and at this point he did not—he remained incapable of seeing the connection between his character and his fate.

The distinction between a felicitous accidental irony and fully deliberate irony is apparent if we recall the wonderful episode in which Tom Jones gives full rein to his courtly idealism and romantic blither, only to forget his "vows of chastest constancy" the minute he can accompany Molly into the "thickest part of the grove" (Bk. 5, chap. 10). Both heroes have limited awareness and fixed responses; they invariably conclude that the best way to deal with temptation is to yield to it. And like Tom, Boswell can engage in the most frenzied wenching and remain imperviously romantic. But the difference between *Tom Jones* and the *London Journal* is crucial: Boswell does not have Fielding's wise narrator to point out all his foibles.

Fielding stages Tom's tryst to underscore the incongruity between romantic ideals and more basic needs. With his transcendent control and omniscient comprehension, Fielding reveals Tom enacting the role of a courtly lover with an utter lack of self-awareness or consistency. If Boswell is making a similar point about himself, he does so without Fielding's massive authority and leaves the question of judgment considerably less settled. Fielding instructs every reader exactly how to understand and assess everything he presents; Boswell is occasionally in error and frequently in doubt—and relies on the reader to put together, grasp, and cope with it all. The Boswell of the *London Journal* is thus a type of the unreliable narrator; he is not an utterly specious commentator, but he is surely an *inadequate* one.

The analogy is only partially valid, because Boswell as author does not regard his narrator as unreliable, in the way Conrad and Faulkner clearly qualify so many of their narrators. Nevertheless, the comparison invites an important conclusion: because the narrator of the *London Journal* is not wholly reliable, it is incumbent on us to examine how he renders and how well he understands his experience. The ritual sallies in which he displays his gallant colors, like an amorous peacock, depict him in the congenial role of courtly lover: "the god of pleasing anguish now seriously seized my breast. I felt the fine delirium of love." In his next dialogue he presses his suit too ardently: "Come, Sir, let us talk no more of that now." "No, Madam, I will not. It is like giving the book in the preface." "Just so, Sir, telling in the preface what should be in the middle of the book." Boswell and Louisa are as well matched, for the time being, as Mirabell and Millamant—the one constantly imitating the swashbuckling exploits of "the hero of a romance or novel," the other relying on her training as professional actress. They enact a literary romance, giving tit for tat—all carefully rendered by a narrator who pauses to tell us how he does it: "I think such conversations are best written in the dialogue way." With the self-conscious bravado of telling us how it is "best written," Boswell presents two actors playing out a romance, staged in the manner of the Restoration comedies he adored.

Boswell presents this comedy of love beautifully, depicting his solemn ardor, ingenuous anticipation, and disingenuous motives. We view him, for example, utterly dependent on particular models of behavior. As he approaches the glorious moment of consummation, arriving at the inn for their night of love, "I here thought proper to conceal my own name of Mr. Digges." Digges became famous enacting Boswell's favorite role of Macheath; so Boswell presents Boswell imitating Digges playing Macheath. He knows very well what he is doing, but not why. He senses only that he is half in love with love, and half in love with easeful art.

The full effect of the ultimate conquest of Louisa depends heavily upon Boswell's retrospective present, which captures his original "trembling suspense." It is astonishing to learn that when Boswell wrote this scene, he had probably already realized he had contracted veneral disease. At this moment Boswell selects and controls the material to tramatize the insufficiency of the hero's awareness, for the sake of the story. Instead of revealing the disastrous denouement, Boswell presents the lover contemplating his "fair prize . . . pleasingly confounded to think that so fine a woman was at this moment in my possession." On the verge of fulfillment, it is the *idea* of the achievement which he finds, as he elegantly states, so "elevating." His hyperbolic rapture expresses a transient but exultant sense of selfhood. Ironically, his untrammeled and unquestioned egoism measures how much he needs to learn.

> Good heavens, what a loose did we give to amorous dalliance! The friendly curtain of darkness concealed our blushes. In a moment I felt myself animated with the strongest powers of love, and, from my dearest creature's kindness, had a most luscious feast. Proud of my godlike vigour, I soon resumed the noble game. I was in full glow of health. Sobriety had preserved me from effeminacy and weakness, and my bounding blood beat quick and high alarms. A more voluptuous night I never enjoyed. Five times was I fairly lost in supreme rapture. Louisa was madly fond of me; she declared I was a prodigy, and asked me if this was not extraordinary for human nature. I said twice as much might be, but this was not, although in my own mind I was somewhat proud of my performance.

No sooner is this Olympian feat consummated than it becomes stuff for the artist, who "can with pleasure trace the progress of this intrigue to its completion." The performer is never satisfied; sinking to rest in Louisa's "snowy arms," he could not "help roving in fancy to the embraces of some other ladies which my lively imagination strongly pictured." We are likely to conclude that the hero's romantic illusions and self-delusions, rampant sexual braggadocio, and instant fickleness make him a fitting victim of "Signor Gonorrhea." The expectations Boswell aroused in introducing Louisa and characterizing himself are satisfied by this comic reversal, but Boswell is far from considering the turn of events funny or appropriate.

It is at precisely this point that we discern the limits of narrative comprehension, for the unhappy consequences of Boswell's delight in his "godlike vigour" never precipitate any exploration of events or motives. When he discovers his blight shortly thereafter, he suspects that Louisa has deliberately gulled him, and callously upbraids and rejects her, even though she may have infected him unknowingly and unwillingly. The reader's view of Boswell may differ considerably from Boswell's view of himself as always more sinned against than sinning. But Boswell is incapable of determining, or even investigating, the moral implications of his behavior. He is too close to the experience and remains trapped in a histrionic and unreflective posture. Judgment and Passion, Boswell notes in another context, "are very different."

Moreover, the rounded, relatively comprehended, and fully rendered quality of the romance, up through the voluptuous night, does not characterize the whole *London Journal*. This episode stands out, and critics tend to rely on it, as if it typified the entire book; but not every sequence has been so well incorporated into the story. If the resolution of the affair with Louisa fails to satisfy our need to understand and evaluate, Boswell leaves a seemingly inordinate number of other subjects even less fully illuminated. We are unsure, because Boswell has no idea, what to make of his hysterical fright following a public execution, when he must sleep in the same bed with a friend three nights running to ward off the demons. And what is the source of his obsessive confessions of myriad transgressions to nearly any authoritative figure who would listen? And what about his half-buried, deeply conflictive relations with Laird Auchinleck? Fears, guilt, and parental approval are some of the most interesting "themes" of the *London Journal*, but they remain incipient or latent—certainly revealing but presented in troubled confusion. The ways in which he will broach and then evade such provocative details evidence both his desire for honesty and the boundaries of his understanding. Boswell is much like Moll Flanders, who also presents but cannot fully comprehend her plight. Both characters struggle with a variety of fears and conflicts, without always illuminating the source or nature of the issues.

As the Louisa saga illustrates, Boswell is sometimes overweening and occasionally downright confounded. Often there is very little artful discrepancy between Boswell as observer and participant, because both have the same urgent priority. His most important quest is for a trustworthy identity in the midst of all his confusing experience. One example of the many, many ways he phrases it follows:

> Now, when my father at last put me into an independent situation, I felt my mind regain its native dignity. I felt strong dispositions to be a Mr. Addison. Indeed, I had accustomed myself so much to laugh at everything that it required time to render my imagination solid and give me just notions of real life and of religion. But I hoped by degrees to attain to some degree of propriety.

For Boswell is on a pilgrimage seeking mature purpose—his terms are propriety, dignity, consistency—and the *London Journal* comprises notes toward this supreme fiction of his own reliable authority.

Consider his evening at the Gould home in the light of his search for dependable selfhood; it is typical in that Boswell as narrator recounts his experience not to assess it but to prove something to himself:

> The Colonel had been debauching the night before and was in bed, but Mrs. Gould insisted that I should eat a family dinner with her and the children, which I did very happily. Miss Fanny [age seven] and I are now very good friends. "I am sure," said she, "Sir, if I like any man, I like you." She sat on the same chair with me after dinner, and sung and read very prettily. About six, Mr. Gould came down to us. I gave him a genteel lecture on the advantage of temperance, and made him acknowledge that the pain of rioting much exceeded the pleasure. He was heavy, but I was lightsome and entertaining, and relieved him. I drank tea and sat the evening gay and happy, just in the way I could wish.

In Boswell's narrative, Colonel Gould exists to hear the "genteel lecture" the hero is delighted to deliver; Gould is a foil to dramatize the virtue of Boswell. The account of bantering with the little girl Fanny demonstrates Boswell's most treasured trait, his capacity to provide agreeable company to nearly anyone, from Johnson and Rousseau to heavy-headed rioters and little girls. But Boswell is doing more than entertaining and enlightening the Gould family in this vignette: he is acting as substitute father at a "family dinner," while the Colonel sleeps off his debauchery. Boswell plays the role of the warm, candid, sympathetic patriarch, implying (without ever expressing) criticism of his own father. He gives us the scene not just because it occurred, but to present himself playing a demanding part with ease and grace.

Does he know what he is doing in such scenes? Not always. Every mask he tries on—lover, rogue, officer of the Guards, paterfamilias—fits in some meaningful way and tests a potential identity. Once he tries to purchase a fancy sword without money, on the credit of his "external appearance and address," and considers his success "much to my honour." Later he impersonates the very opposite part, "a complete blackguard," with costume, props, and idiom suiting an unsavory adventure with a tart. Significantly, Boswell notes, "My vanity was somewhat gratified tonight that, notwithstanding of my dress, I was always taken for a gentleman in disguise." The search for one unified entity called "self" is futile, however, for Boswell never could define himself, and so turned doggedly and sometimes brilliantly to his journals to forge a self. To any reader of the *London Journal,* and perhaps dimly to himself, Boswell is fascinating precisely because he seems to have no character at all. "I was rational and composed, yet lively and entertaining. I had a good opinion of myself. . . . Could I but fix myself in such a character and preserve it uniformly, I should be exceedingly happy. I hope to do so and to attain a constancy and dignity without which I can never be satisfied." Protean, or chameleonlike, he assumes assorted roles and emulates various models. "The mind," said Hume in the *Treatise of Human Nature,* is "a kind of theatre, where several perceptions successively make their appearance; pass, re-pass, glide away, and mingle in an infinite variety of postures and situations. There is properly no *simplicity* in it at one time, nor *identity* in different." Boswell inspects the "feelings of his heart" and his "external actions" in quest of that dependable and consistent identity he always sought and never located.

Boswell embodies, we might say, a very "Humean" notion of personal identity, even if he does not know it. In the process of exploring the "infinite variety of postures and situations" he describes in the *London Journal,* he is trying to discover, or to *create,* a true self which he does not yet know. He believes, or hopes, he has succeeded by the end of the journal. The last few pages include several conversations with Johnson, mostly about Boswell's growth and future. "I asked him, if he was my father, and if I did well at the law, if he would be pleased with me." Johnson is encouraging, particularly with respect to Boswell's spiritual development. "I returned him many thanks for having established my principles." So a newly principled Boswell resolves to study, according to his father's wishes, and "may in time, perhaps, apply to the law in Scotland." He and Johnson make an excursion to Harwich clearly designed to mark a culmination, and in the last journal entry, meditating on his change, he exclaims, "How different is my scheme now! I am now upon a less pleasurable but a more rational and lasting plan. Let me pursue it with steadiness and I may be a man of dignity." We are likely to see some progress but no transformation. Even without subsequent journals, we must anticipate a life of lapses and frustration. Like *Moll Flanders,* the *London Journal* ends with a kind of "conversion" which does not seem authentic or persuasive.

Boswell desperately wants us to like and admire him, and to accept his final resolution to follow "a more rational and lasting plan," but he is much too shallow a critic. Even at the end there are radical disparities between his ideals and his actions: "Since my being honoured with the friendship of Mr. Johnson, I have more seriously considered the duties of morality and

term) and on notional modulations as "ornament." We need not then quarrel
with his theory while describing it, but must recognize what it means in
our own terms.

His most direct statement in defence of his system of elaboration refers
to a passage of narration in the *Western Islands*. If *things must* be his reason
for writing, his main theme, they can yet be adorned with clustered notions.
Lord Monboddo wrote to Boswell that Johnson's language was too rich.

> JOHNSON. "Why, Sir, this criticism would be just, if in my
> style, superfluous words, or words too big for the thoughts, could
> be pointed out; but this I do not believe can be done. For instance;
> in the passage which Lord Monboddo admires, 'We were now
> treading that illustrious region,' the word *illustrious,* contributes
> nothing to the mere narration; for the fact might be told without
> it: but it is not, therefore, superfluous; for it wakes the mind to
> peculiar attention, where something of more than usual impor-
> tance is to be represented. 'Illustrious!'—for what? and then the
> sentence proceeds to expand the circumstances connected with
> Iona."

Johnson is giving the reason that justifies all epithetical or nonrestrictive
modification. When we use any word to tell not what thing we mean but
only under what aspect we mean it, we have taken the first step away from
plain style. The second step is to multiply the aspects under which we refer
to a single object. The third, and extreme Johnsonian, step is to multiply
aspects (or words apparently expressing different aspects) so that within the
range of relevance they overlap—which is "multiplication for emphasis."

The question whether his style was a way of saying the same thing
over and over—that is, giving the same meaning over and over—seems to
have occurred to Johnson but not to have worried him. Had he been forced
to the wall, he would probably have admitted, needlessly, that elaboration
involved repetition. The unshakable sense which all writers must have that
a multiplication of notions about one thing is not a repetition of one meaning
would have compelled him to defend his practice, but his bias for talking
of nature and facts, and not of meaning, would have made him plead guilty
of repetition and defend it as ornament. Or, he might have resolved the
conflict in another way, and indeed has left some hints that he partly did
so. "Words," he says in the *Preface to the Dictionary,* "are seldom exactly
synonymous; a new term was not introduced, but because the former was
thought inadequate: names, therefore, have often many ideas, but few ideas
have many names." If few ideas have many names, that is, if each idea has

religion and the dignity of human nature. I have considered that promiscuous concubinage is certainly wrong. . . . Notwithstanding of these reflections, I have stooped to mean profligacy even yesterday. However, I am now resolved to guard against it." And there have always been chasms between his public ebullience and private regrets:

> When my father forced me down to Scotland, I was at first very low-spirited, although to appearance very high. . . . I found myself a very inferior being: and I found many people presuming to treat me as such, which notwithstanding of my appearance of undiscerning gaiety, gave me much pain. I was, in short, a character very different from what GOD intended me and I myself chose.

This is nearly as disconcerting to us as it is to Boswell. So many various selves leave us unsure which is the real James Boswell. Since he so often reveals himself in behavior as a poseur, acting out roles, we naturally wonder how authentic or contrived his narrative may be. His mercurial, theatrical, and evanescent expression of personal identity is close to the spirit of *Tristram Shandy*. Because he was impressed by Sterne's writing, he would be pleased with this comparison; but some of the implications are distinctly unflattering.

Much of Boswell's unceasing self-exposure willfully avoids the introspection that might lead to understanding. To palm off songs of self as confessional hymns is an old ploy, of course, and even Augustine (a more unsparing self-analyst) has to recognize the fine "difference that there is between presumption and confession." Certainly there are sections in the *London Journal*, such as bits of the Louisa episode, where Boswell verges on irony: a somewhat wiser observer commenting on the foibles of a slightly more naïve participant. Usually the distinction is negligible; Boswell often fails to indicate how foolishly he acts, and seems sure to persist in his folly. The observer is frequently unwilling or unable to direct critical responses toward the participant because he has not always understood himself well enough.

How, for instance, do we read the following party dialogue with Lady Northumberland, in which the hero aggressively presses for helpful introductions? She fends him off: "Why don't you go to Court, Mr. Boswell? I'm sure that's a cheap diversion; it costs you nothing, and you see all the best company, and chat away. It is the best coffee-house in town." Does Boswell consciously play the *ingénu* to parry her thrust when he asks: "But ought I not, Madam, to be introduced first?" To which the Lady rejoins,

"You should, Sir. To be sure, some people do go and stand there without being presented. But that would not be right for *a man of your rank*." Her Retort Courteous and Reproof Valiant convey exactly how Boswell strikes this acquaintance, but are we supposed to concur with her? If it is a critical and comical assessment of the hero's imprudence by a more discreet narrator, it is insufficiently articulated. Boswell is often too busy applauding his performances and forgetting his transgressions to see what he might otherwise see, his real state.

This is, I realize, a fairly stringent judgment of Boswell's "real state"; in fact I am loosely paraphrasing Johnson's summary characterization of Richard Savage. We must remember that Boswell wants us to adopt his view of himself, implicitly made from a higher level of awareness, above all the blooming, buzzing confusion. The proper response to such requests for assent is vigorous skepticism. "The great thing to be recorded," Johnson impressed upon Boswell, "is the state of your own mind" and you should write down every thing that you remember." Boswell was afraid that his journal might then contain "all sorts of little incidents." Johnson's reply is sanction: " 'Sir,' said he, 'there is nothing too little for so little a creature as man. It is by studying little things that we attain the great knowledge of having as little misery and as much happiness as possible.' " Certainly Boswell could see no larger workings of providence in his experience, as did Augustine or Bunyan, though he would have liked to. The hero of the *London Journal* is nearly overwhelmed by the need to find a self amid all those "little incidents," to prove he exists, and to show why he deserves to. Boswell's continuous exploration of roles and models, in search of "great knowledge," and the witty consciousness which remarks at times upon such serious play give us a rich but limited perspective. To use his age's Lockean categories, Boswell has an abundance of wit but a deficiency of judgment.

As the later journals document with agonizing candor, Boswell spent the rest of his life trying to resolve the conflicts with which he grappled in London in the winter of 1762–63, never achieving that unity of being to which he aspired. And yet his prodigious talents and overwhelming needs eventually conspired to produce (in the words of an otherwise implacably hostile Macaulay) a book "likely to be read as long as the English exists, either as a living or as a dead language." The relationship between Boswell's personality and the *Life of Johnson* has been explored many times since the biography appeared in 1791, and continues to entice modern readers. Although this is not the place to summarize that celebrated controversy, my argument connecting the degree of narrative coherence in the *London Journal* and the author's personal strife inevitably raises similar questions about Boswell's greatest work, the *Life of Johnson*.

Basically, Boswell succeeded so splendidly as a biographer because he was able to subordinate himself to his subject:

> this extensive biographical work, however inferior in its nature, may in one respect be assimilated to the ODYSSEY. Amidst a thousand entertaining and instructive episodes the HERO is never long out of sight; for they are all in some degree connected with him; and HE, in the whole course of the History, is exhibited by the Authour for the best advantage of his readers.

This sustained vision is in itself a remarkable feat, since Boswell must surely be one of the most self-absorbed individuals in literary history; yet "subordination" does not exactly mean that Boswell purged himself from the pages of the *Life*. Boswell develops the "double consciousness of himself," that simultaneous sense of being both participant and observer, in new and apt ways. In the *Life*, Boswell's dual role is considerably more consistent and controlled than it is in the *London Journal*.

Boswell the character has a variety of guises in the story of Samuel Johnson—gadfly, jester, inquisitor, stage manager, host, *ingénu*, disciple—but all his roles provide a foil for the grandeur of the hero. As Gloucester reenacts the major theme of *King Lear* in a minor key, Boswell's melancholy and quest for certainty help us comprehend the full glory of Johnson's life. Again and again, Boswell contrasts his "Shandean" or "Humean" self with Johnson's monumental stability. Thus the evanescence and multiplicity of the hero's identity in the *London Journal* persist in the *Life*, but with a new purpose; no longer the chief concern of the narrative, Boswell's "wretched changefulness" clarifies and magnifies the "steady vigorous mind" of the central subject.

For example, one topic that troubled Boswell throughout his life was religious faith and fear of annihilation. In the *London Journal*, he constantly tested his mettle by attending public hangings, but he fails to analyze his condition; he presents himself as terrified and confounded. One of the great scenes of a later journal depicts Boswell visiting David Hume on his deathbed, to see for himself if the great atheist would finally recant (*Boswell in Extremes*). It is an incredible interview—the young man ingeniously and ingenuously probing, the dying philosophe as staunch and genially ironic as ever. The scene haunted Boswell for years because he shared some of Hume's skepticism but needed the certainty of orthodox piety. Death and the prospect of resurrection are a leitmotif of the journals, but Boswell never explains why. In the *Life*, freed from the burden of self-analysis, he uses the theme to illuminate Johnson's hard-won convictions. Boswell may not have the answers, but he plainly knows what questions to ask:

When we were alone, I introduced the subject of death, and endeavoured to maintain that the fear of it might be got over. I told him that David Hume said to me, he was no more uneasy to think·he should *not be* after this life, than that he *had not been* before he began to exist. JOHNSON. "Sir, if he really thinks so, his perceptions are disturbed; he is mad: if he does not think so, he lies. He may tell you, he holds his finger in the flame of a candle, without feeling pain; would you believe him? When he dies, he at least gives up all he has." BOSWELL. "Foote, Sir, told me, that when he was very ill he was not afraid to die." JOHNSON. "It is not true, Sir. Hold a pistol to Foote's breast, or to Hume's breast, and threaten to kill them, and you'll see how they behave." BOSWELL. "But may we not fortify our minds for the approach of death?"

The other aspect of Boswell's "double consciousness" is embodied by the narrator. In the *London Journal* there is an inconsistent narrative viewpoint, capable of incidental ironic perspectives but limited by confused egocentricity. While the character Boswell continues to flounder in the *Life*, the narrator attains a large measure of the authority young Boswell sought so ardently in the *London Journal*. The brilliance of the biographer is precisely what the autobiographer could not attain: a thorough exploration of the hero's behavior, revealing and assessing his spiritual essence. There is probably no better example in the *Life* than the famous passage which follows Boswell's self-conscious pursuit of "the subject of death." Notice how far Boswell has progressed—from the engaging, unreliable narrator of the *London Journal* to the mature judge of value and character (both his own and Johnson's) in the *Life:*

Here I am sensible I was in the wrong, to bring before his view what he ever looked upon with horrour; for although when in a celestial frame, in his "Vanity of human Wishes," he has supposed death to be "kind Nature's signal for retreat," from this state of being to "a happier seat," his thoughts upon this aweful change were in general full of dismal apprehensions. His mind resembled the vast amphitheatre, the Colisaeum at Rome. In the center stood his judgment, which, like a mighty gladiator, combated those apprehensions that, like the wild beasts of the *Arena,* were all around in cells, ready to be let out upon him. After a conflict, he drove them back into their dens; but not killing them, they were still assailing him. To my question, whether we might not fortify our minds for the approach of death, he answered, in a passion, "No, Sir, let it alone. It matters not how a man dies, but how he lives. The act of dying is not of importance, it lasts so short a time." He added, (with an earnest look,) "A man knows it must be so, and submits. It will do him no good to whine."

Few people maintain the reductive view that Boswell was simply fortunate enough to know Johnson and diligent enough to parrot his conversations. Still, it is important to affirm that he could produce the *Life* because (and only because) he had a conception of his subject precise enough to organize reams of material and dynamic enough to sustain an epical narrative. "Boswell's great subject," as William C. Dowling argues, is "the hero in an unheroic world." As Dowling demonstrates beautifully, Boswell imagined Johnson as an epic hero living in a debased environment—as if Aeneas were suddenly transported into *Mall Flanders* or *The Dunciad*. As a biographer Boswell continues to convey narrative authenticity, ostensibly holding up the mirror to reflect life artlessly: "I cannot allow any fragment whatever that floats in my memory concerning the great subject of his work to be lost." But we know that this is not so. Inclusive as the *Life* is, it presents a stable and clearly focused image of the hero—a figure considerably larger than life. Johnson exists in Boswell's narrative as the incarnation of the sublime—the scourge of "modern cant," insisting always on the moral implication of fine distinctions, struggling resolutely against "morbid melancholy" (Boswell's version of the hero's *hamartia*), finally dying with philosophic fortitude, and eternally commanding our "admiration and reverence." Boswell includes many examples of the various temptations with which Johnson struggled, such as sloth, pride, and anger; he omits many incidents which might appear unbecoming a hero's steadfast resolve, muffling his amorous inclinations and other less oracular, more abandoned moments.

Boswell is also able to use the kind of material that had seemed unintegrated in the *London Journal* to dramatize the theme of the *Life*. In other words, in the thirty years between the *Journal* and the *Life,* Boswell discovered a metaphoric meaning in the daily contingencies that beguiled and thwarted him: he transformed "what happened" into a symbolic vision of the world disintegrating around Johnson. The whole tumultuous flow of the century's events—personal losses and triumphs, disputes about literature, politics, and religion—represents the fragmented, fallen world in which Johnson suffered, endured, and inspired lesser mortals such as Boswell and his readers. While the hero of the *London Journal* revels in and is very nearly swamped by the flux of his experience, the hero of the *Life of Johnson* combats the beasts in his private arena and transcends the conditions of his existence: "What philosophick heroism was it in him to appear with such manly fortitude to the world, while he was inwardly so distressed! We may surely believe that the mysterious principle of being 'made perfect through suffering' was to be strongly exemplifed in him."

One final factor accounts for the increased coherence of the *Life of Johnson:* Boswell knew better what he was doing because he was refining an established literary genre. Biography was immensely popular and highly valued—the "part of literature . . . I love most," admitted Johnson—and many of their conversations concern its nature and purpose. Johnson devoted *Rambler* No. 60 to the subject, and of course produced life-stories throughout his career. Although the evolution of biography is a large and complex topic, the salient point here is that Boswell clearly had a tradition in which to work. He specifically cites a contemporary model, Mason's *Memoirs of Gray,* and a classical authority, Plutarch ("the prince of ancient biographers"). Boswell's biography demonstrates the classical and Johnsonian value of illustrating moral virtue, but it differs from anything Plutarch, Mason, or Johnson ever wrote in revealing its subject through "the most minute particulars." We might call the result a kind of empirical hagiography, the story of a moral *exemplum* constantly challenged and affirmed through mundane experience. Juxtaposition of the ideal and the real is of course a structural principle of many literary works, and it helped teach Boswell how to organize and present the story of Johnson's life. Moreover, the biographer could rely on the reader's curiosity and concern for even the smallest "particulars" about so celebrated a subject.

As a journalist Boswell had much less help. Johnson did encourage his efforts, and in fact composed his own autobiographical narrative, only to dispatch it finally to the flames. Yet Johnson's repudiation underscores the difficulty eighteenth-century writers had in completing their own life-stories. Dryden enunciates the typical neoclassical retience: "Anything, though never so little, which a man speaks of himself, in my opinion, is still too much. . . ." Boswell was not about to be stifled by musty notions of decorum, but he lacked models for procedure, and we can see this reflected in the uncertain narrative structure of the *London Journal.*

As a time when every pblic figure is compelled to engrave his recollections for the ages, it is worth remembering that first-person factual narrative had to struggle for recognition and respect. Early life-stories tended to be conversion narratives, and spiritual premises simultaneously justified and organized the mode. Boswell did sense, or yearn for, some vague connection between himself and the spiritual autobiographers of yore, but the parallels primarily measure the painful and ludicrous disparity between their sacred visions and his secular struggles. Without divine sanction, auto-biographers and journalists of the Restoration and eighteenth century usually kept their works to themselves or waffled between means of self-presentation. One autobiographer who did publish his story, Colley Cibber, thus certified his candidacy (at least to Pope) for a niche in *The Dunciad;* more dignified writers, such as Franklin and Gibbon, proceeded by fits and starts, leaving disparate segments and versions to twentieth-century editors. Thus the kinds of books which might have helped Boswell—Pepys's *Diary,* Franklin's *Autobiography,* Gibbon's *Memoirs,* and Rousseau's *Confessions*—had not yet appeared. Since the *London Journal* seems most successful when Boswell has a role to act and realizes a few of its implications, as in the Louisa episode, it is tempting to speculate that, with more time, increased wisdom, and more models of first-person factual narrative, he might well have made even more inspired use of his personal experience. Given the facts of the matter, the embryonic state of autobiographical narration, and his vantage point, his achievement is astonishing: he created a character who will always compel our fascinated interest and arouse our critical responses. No less remarkable are the growth of his imaginative vision and the development of his narrative mastery. By the time he composed the *Life of Johnson,* he was able to dramatize himself in the multifaceted but unified role of biographer, and to depict a fully human yet grandly heroic Johnson. From the wistful youth consoling himself with impersonations of Macheath, Tristram, and Aeneas, he matured into our greatest biographer.

WILLIAM C. DOWLING

A *Plutarchan* Hero:
The Tour to Corsica

"I said to General Paoli," wrote Boswell in 1783, "it was wonderful how much Corsica had done for me, how far I had got in the world by having been there. I had got upon a rock in Corsica and jumped into the middle of life." Boswell probably wrote the remark down because he was taken with his bon mot, but it is scarcely an exaggeration. In February 1768, at the age of twenty-seven, Boswell permanently emerged from literary obscurity with the publication of his *Account of Corsica: The Journal of a Tour to That Island, and Memoirs of Pascal Paoli.* Only readers who have taken an interest in Boswell's literary career will perhaps recall how successful the book really was: immediately after its first publication *Corsica* went through two more English and several (pirated) Irish editions, was translated into French, Dutch, German, and Italian, and won Boswell an international literary reputation greater than that of either Goldsmith or Johnson.

Boswell published his *Tour to the Hebrides* and *Life of Johnson,* the two works that guaranteed his permanent place in literature, in the ten years prior to his death. In the earlier years it was *Corsica* that established his literary identity: "Corsica Boswell" was, like "Dictionary Johnson," the figure with which a large contemporary public was most familiar. In a sense the response to *Corsica* marked the high point of Boswell's career as a living writer, for in that book Boswell appealed to the mind of Europe in a manner that the *Tour to the Hebrides* or the *Life of Johnson* could never have done. But if the historical moment in which *Corsica* was written accounted for much of its success, it is wrong to infer that the book made Boswell's literary

From *The Boswellian Hero.* © 1979 by the University of Georgia Press.

reputation because a large European reading public, entranced by Rous-
seauistic notions of primitivism and liberty, was waiting to lionize the first
young man who should write a book about a peasant rebellion. In responding
to *Corsica* Boswell's readers were responding primarily to Paoli, a figure
closer to the heroic world of Plutarch than to that of the *Contrat Social.*

For the modern reader who wishes to approach the *Tour to Corsica* as a
literary work, a brief description of the background of events against which
the book was written will suffice. The island of Corsica, under the domination
of the Republic of Genoa since the fourteenth century, was in revolt. Over
a period of about thirty years the islanders had driven their Genoese rulers
from the interior of Corsica and forced them to take garrisoned positions in
towns along the seacoast. In 1764 the Genoese called upon France for aid,
and French troops were sent to protect the fortified towns. Considering the
formal alliance between France and Genoa in the matter of Corsica, relations
between the Corsican rebels and the French troops stationed on the island
were surprisingly polite. It was Genoa and the Genoese whom the Corsicans
hated and from whom they were determined to win their independence after
four centuries of harsh rule.

This much, or a little more, Rousseau knew when he first praised the
Corsicans for their valiant defense of liberty, and Boswell knew when, fresh
from his remarkable siege of Rousseau at Môtiers, he set out for Corsica.
There were, to be sure, certain hardheaded citizens of the diplomatic community who shared no romantic illusions about the island: "to Chesterfield,
who reflected the view of the diplomats of Europe, the people were a 'parcel
of cruel and perifidious rascals,' " and Lord Holland, even in the face of
Boswell's overwhelming success with *Corsica,* pronounced them "the vile
inhabitants of one of the vilest islands in the world, who are not less free
than all the rest of their neighbours." But diplomats, burdened as they are
with factual reports, are denied the helpful insufficiency of information that
allows the rest of us to romanticize at will. Today the actual character of
the Corsicans and the merits of their cause are perhaps impossible to ascertain.
In Boswell's time the significance of the events on Corsica was that they
were actual, and this alone had great appeal in a political context so far
dominated by theory.

Corsica as a ready-made symbol drew the attention of political theorists
whose concept of liberty, and whose notions of the human state most con-
ducing to liberty, needed illustration; "a generation profoundly stirred by
theories of the progressive corruption of governments and the glories of the
state of nature," as F.A. Pottle puts it, "found that it no longer had to look
to the remote past or the world of ideas for its example of the good state,

or at least of a state which held promise of becoming good." In Frederick of Prussia's *Anti-Machiavel,* therefore, contemporary readers came across a reference to Corsica "in which this 'little handful of brave men' were cited to prove how much courage and natural virtue the love of liberty bestowed upon men" and in a famous passage of the *Contrat Social* (1762) reflected on Rousseau's remark that "in the midst of almost hopeless governmental corruption, there was one country still capable of legislation, and that he had a presentiment that the little island of Corsica would one day astonish Europe."

Rousseau's remark led in turn to the complicated business of Corsica's constitution. The affair is rather too involved to go into here, but the essential facts are simple enough: as a result of the passage in the *Contrat Social,* Rousseau was invited, or thought he was invited, by the rebel leaders of Corsica to compose a constitution on which the government of the island was to be founded after it had won its independence. He actually began the project. As the very idea of a constitution written *en philosophe* indicates, what Rousseau and his fellow theorists saw in Corsica was a utopian potentiality. Though it was perhaps a general scarcity of information which led Rousseau to comment on Corsica's promise as an independent state, it was clear to some Corsicans that this promise could best be fulfilled if the state engaged a Rousseau to write it into being. The emphasis is not on Corsica itself but on process, on becoming; the island is only the local habitation of a theory.

When he made his tour to Corsica, Boswell was in his period of greatest allegiance to Rousseau's social and political theories. But what is too little noted is that neither Rousseau nor Boswell knew very much about Corsica and that what both of them saw in Corsica was a grand potentiality for idealization. We have Boswell's response in *Corsica;* about Rousseau's we can be less sure, for the constitution of Corsica was never finished (and, since Corsica lost its war of independence, it could never have been put into effect). What we do have of Rousseau's constitution, however, forms an important commentary on Boswell's portrait of the islanders. Corsica as a free state, according to Rousseau's prescription, was to form a society simple, virtuous, peaceful, and independent: "the object was to turn the Corsicans into a nation of farmers, and very literally to beat swords into plough-shares. The island was to be self-supporting and independent of commerce with its neighbours. 'Le seul moyen,' wrote Rousseau, 'de maintenir un État dans l'indépendance des autres est l'agriculture [the only means of maintaining a State in independence is agriculture].' For this reason his entire plan is a 'système rustique.' "

The picture is utopian, and behind it, in nearly undisguised form, is the myth of the Golden Age dressed up as modern political theory. I have little doubt that it was this utopian potentiality, and Corsica's more practical potentiality for complete self-sufficiency ("un État dans l'indépendance des autres"), that initially attracted Boswell to Corsica, though he was to develop the implications of both in a manner that Rousseau would have found uncongenial. In any event Boswell arrived in Corsica in a frame of mind that entirely accounts for the character of the book he later wrote: "the *Account* and the *Journal and Memoirs*," William Siebenschuh explains, "form a single and continuous piece of propaganda and were intended to function together to influence public opinion in Britain." As important, Boswell shared with Rousseau at this point a tendency to romanticize the Corsicans themselves, not their leader.

When Boswell arrived in Corsica, however, he was not long in hearing from the islanders themselves about the character of Pascal Paoli. From the time Boswell meets Paoli, or, more properly, from the time he first divines Paoli's real role on Corsica, his tendency to idealize takes a new direction entirely. The result, to those of us who are able to gaze back at *Corsica* through the *Tour to the Hebrides* and the *Life of Johnson,* will seem natural, even inevitable: after Boswell's meeting with Paoli, everything is subordinated to the figure of the hero. The tendency that Boswell shared with Rousseau, to celebrate the Corsicans for their bravery in defense of liberty, is utterly transformed, and Boswell ends by idealizing the Corsicans themselves not to illustrate any social or political theory but to provide his hero with a proper moral setting.

Boswell's gravitation toward the figure of Paoli as hero accounts in part for what the modern reader will perceive as a small paradox: given the historical moment and the influence of Rousseau's theories on Boswell, *Corsica* might be described as a reactionary book. The ancient ideal of the Philosopher King and implicit suggestions of a conscious feudalism animate Boswell's portrait of Paoli and the Corsicans much more than the current of democratic or egalitarian ideas that we see today as having led to the American and French revolutions. In this, as much as in his simpler tendency to find and idealize a hero, Boswell was showing an attitude that was to remain consistent throughout his literary career. Intellectual historians tell us that there is a large and inevitable conservative component in any set of radical ideas, and the contemporary success of Boswell's *Corsica* illustrates the point perfectly. In the *Tour to the Hebrides* and the *Life of Johnson* one inevitably notes the relation of Boswell's concept of the hero to a conservative ideal, but it can only surprise us to find that same ideal at work in the *Tour to Corsica,* a book that purports to be about liberty and political rebellion.

At the same time, one cannot really disagree with the usual contention that the intellectual climate of the mid-eighteenth century was such that a book about any rebellion like the one in Corsica was likely to be warmly received. But, properly speaking, it was Boswell's *Account of Corsica,* the quasi-scholarly study of Corsican history and politics which preceded his personal journal, that satisfied this topical interest. Even with the climate of opinion as it was, I would guess that the *Tour to Corsica,* revolving around the portrait of Paoli, was accepted more for its literary than for its topical appeal. This at any rate is what Johnson had in mind when he uttered what is perhaps the most famous criticism of *Corsica:* "your History was copied from books; your Journal rose out of your own experience and observation. You express images which operated strongly upon yourself, and you have impressed them with great force upon your readers. I know not whether I could name any narrative by which curiosity is better excited or better gratified."

Johnson was correct. It is Boswell's *Tour* that survives, and properly so, for it belongs to literature. The image that operated most strongly on Boswell's imagination, as Johnson indirectly acknowledges, was the image of the hero. The book whose title we today shorten to *Corsica* is of course the second part of Boswell's account of the island, the first-person narrative that Johnson calls his journal. This short work, so successful in its own time, is at once a fine job of historical reporting and a small literary classic, and it does much to define the nature of Boswell's later achievement. For when Boswell set out for Corsica with an unconscious intention to idealize the Corsican people and their fight for liberty, he participated in the attitude of such philosophes as Rousseau and, more generally, in that main current of "progressive" ideas we now associate with the Enlightenment. But as soon as that tendency to idealize is shaped by the dominant figure of the hero, we have the first expression of an impulse that was to remain consistent with Boswell through his entire literary career.

II

In literature, especially high-mimetic literature, we are accustomed to the notion of an idealized social or political order which forms a background to the actions of the hero. Reference to this order may be implicit, as with the *comitatus* relationship in *Beowulf,* or explicit, as with the fellowship of the Round Table in *Sir Gawain* or the *Morte Darthur,* but it is there, the indispensable context for our understanding of the hero's character. In the *Tour to Corsica* we have an analogue of this familiar motif in Boswell's portrait of the islanders. The reader of the *Tour* is intended to view Paoli as a character in history and not in epic or tragedy, but just as his resemblance to the high-mimetic hero is calculated, so is the support it gains from Boswell's description of Corsican society.

In idealizing Corsican society, Boswell is locating Paoli as hero within an order that makes his heroism comprehensible and consistent. The device is conventional, and its importance perhaps becomes clear when we consider that the hero *outside* such an order is a traditional type of madman—the psychotic Napoleon sitting in the psychiatrist's waiting room, for example. Without the social context Boswell supplies, Paoli would appear in the *Tour to Corsica* as a figure not heroic but ludicrous, and the solemnity with which Boswell treats certain aspects of his character—his claims to second sight, his moments of spontaneous oratory—would become, if anything, hugely comic. What prevents this from happening is the presence, around Paoli, of people who believe in him as a hero and whose moral qualities underscore his own high moral character.

The character of the Corsican people as Boswell draws it, however, places them in a simpler world than we associate with either epic or tragedy and arises not least from their situation as inhabitants of an island. Islands are not necessarily literary symbols, though (like roses) they are perhaps as often as they are not; what makes an island symbolic is the stress the narrator lays on its remoteness from the known world, from the familiar, the everyday, and quite often the corrupt. Boswell's portrait of the Corsican people lays great moral emphasis on the remoteness of Corsica from Europe, or more precisely from European consciousness. (Similarly, in the *Account of Corsica*, which precedes the *Tour*, Boswell goes to some lengths to identify Corsica's long line of political oppressors with the corrupt world from which Corsica is separated by the sea, the world of secret treaties, expedient alliances, broken promises, power policies, and Machiavellian statecraft generally.) This is why the Genoese, as the villains of the *Tour*, are portrayed as the local representatives, merely, of an advanced but decayed civilization, as intruders in a simple rural world.

The separation of Corsica from the rest of Europe is thus a moral as well as a geographical fact. In discovering this symbolic significance in the island situation of the Corsicans, and in the difference between the national characters of the Genoese and the Corsicans, Boswell is in one sense aligning Corsica with the utopian islands of western literature, with Plato's Atlantis, More's Utopia, Bacon's New Atlantis. Corsica simply as an island would not necessarily possess this utopian signifiance, but Boswell in the *Tour* is describing Corsica during its battle for independence and (more important) Corsica under Paoli. For Boswell these are crucial factors, enabling him to present Corsican society as a potentially ideal order struggling to assert itself against corrupt and crushing opposition. The effect of this is to place Boswell, as the only European who has come to Corsica and grasped the moral significance of what is happening there, in the position of Raphael Hythloday. This is the meaning of Paoli's plea that Boswell tell his story to the British court: "tell them what you have seen here. They will be curious to ask you. A man come from Corsica will be like a man come from the Antipodes."

As Boswell makes clear from the beginning, he has been drawn not to a place but to a drama of events, an ideal actually working itself out in the state of nature: "Corsica occurred to me as a place which nobody else had seen, and where I should find what was to be seen nowhere else, a people actually fighting for liberty and forming themselves from a poor, inconsiderable, oppressed nation into a flourishing and independent state." At the beginning of the *Tour* Boswell offers himself as a typical representative of European culture, unsure about what he is going to find on Corsica but prepared to meet with a civilization that, insofar as it is different from his own, will be primitive and barbaric. His first picture of Corsican life is based on a conversation with a British naval officer who has visited several ports on the island and who solemnly assures Boswell that he is risking his life "in going among these barbarians," for his own surgeon's mate had once gone ashore on Corsica "to take the diversion of shooting and every moment was alarmed by some of the natives who started from the bushes with loaded guns and, if he had not been protected by Corsican guides, would have certainly blown out his brains." The British officer's account belongs to the genre of imaginary adventures in which white men sail beside savage coasts, pursued by painted barbarians who run along the shoreline howling and brandishing spears.

The officer's encapsulated portrait of the Corsicans as savage barbarians is the exact reverse of the romantic primitivism that Boswell eventually appeals to in idealizing Corsican society. But for now it is offered as typical of the average European's attitude toward Corsica, one which will be displaced to great effect by a view of the Corsicans not as savages but as people virtuously close to simple nature. This second view begins to emerge with Boswell's first sight of some actual Corsican natives, who emerge suddenly from the idyllic landscape: "the prospect of the mountains covered with vines and olives was extremely agreeable, and the odour of the myrtle and other aromatic shrubs and flowers that grew all around me was very refreshing. As I walked along, I often saw Corsican peasants come suddenly out from the covert; and as they were all armed, I saw how the frightened imagination of the surgeon's mate had raised up so many assassins." As dusk gathers, and Boswell continues on his way, he thinks of some lines from Ariosto: "e pur per selva oscure e calli obliqui / Insieme van senza sospetto aversi [they go together without fear, though through dark woods and winding paths]." The error of the British officer, in other words, and of his surgeon's mate, has been one not of fact but of imaginative response: *hony soyt qui mal y pense*.

As Boswell begins to lose his European prejudice about Corsica, he responds with increasing admiration to the social character formed by the rude simplicity of life on the island. On his passage to Corsica by boat, he earlier glimpsed this character in his conversation with some Corsican natives—"they told me that in their country I should be treated with the greatest hospitality, but if I attempted to debauch any of their women I might expect instant death"—but with Boswell's arrival on the island the picture of a people formed by nature is filled in, and the young traveler from Britain beholds a nation of simple, hardy, virtuous citizens with a stern sense of honor and a profound potentiality for feeling shame. Boswell's description of the hangman of Corsica epitomizes the theme of honor and shame: "being held in the utmost detestation, he durst not live like another inhabitant of the island. He was obliged to take refuge in the Castle, and there he was kept in a little corner turret . . . for nobody would have any intercourse with him, but all turned their backs upon him."

This hangman is a Sicilian recruited by Paoli for the task, for no Corsican could be brought to agree to execute his countrymen, "not the greatest criminals, who might have had their lives upon that condition." From Boswell's description of the hangman's situation, there is perhaps little in this to surprise us: the life of the state executioner in Corsica seems only barely preferable to a quick death as a convicted criminal. But that, of course, is not the point, nor is it strictly the uprightness of Corsican criminals. In a state where the principles of personal honor and shame transcend those embodied in laws or religion, there is a potentiality for loyalty and honorable action that does not exist in more advanced, and therefore more cynical, nations. It is this aspect of the Corsican character that the hangman incident dramatizes: if the behavior of a society's worst element is thus controlled by an overwhelming sense of possible shame, what capacity for the same feelings will be shown by its best, even its ordinary, citizens?

Among Corsica's ordinary citizens, in fact, the principle of personal honor embraces a patriotism based on the related notion of national honor. Honor and patriotism among the Corsicans are part of an extralegal morality that leads to attitudes not found in more "civilized" states and from which Corsica's utopian promise in the deepest sense derives. The interplay of personal honor and loyalty to Corsica as a state appears in Paoli's account of his conversation with the nephew of a condemned Corsican criminal. The nephew's proposal is that his uncle be banished from Corsica, and he offers the guarantee of his family that the uncle will never return to the island. Paoli counters with a direct appeal to the young man's sense of national honor: " 'such is my confidence in you, that if you will say that giving your uncle a pardon would be just, useful, or honourable for Corsica, I promise you it will be granted.' He turned about and burst into tears, and left me, saying, 'I would not have the honour of our country sold for a thousand zechins.' And his uncle suffered."

The *Tour to Corsica* powerfully invokes, in such scenes, an attitude toward undeveloped human societies which the eighteenth century was finding increasingly persuasive and which will support Boswell's eventual appeal to the older myth of the Golden Age. Boswell himself, making sure that no one will miss the philosophical point, includes in the *Tour* an excerpt that nicely exemplifies the new primitivism, taken from a work surprisingly entitled *A Comparative View of the State and Faculties of Man with Those of the Animal World,* by a Doctor Gregory: " 'there is a certain period in the progress of society in which mankind appear to the greatest advantage. In this period, they have the bodily powers and all the animal functions remaining in full vigour. They are bold, active, steady, ardent in the love of liberty and their native country. Their manners are simple, their social affections warm, and though they are greatly influenced by the ties of blood, yet they are generous and hospitable to strangers. Religion is universally regarded among them, though disguised by a variety of superstitions."

From this, romantic primitivism dressed up as science, Boswell develops his complicated appeal to the myth of the Golden Age. Not *the* myth, one should say, for despite the eighteenth century's conversance with classical tradition, no single Golden Age myth had universal currency, and even if there had been one, Boswell's portrait of Corsican society contains elements that surely would not have been compatible with it. Yet Boswell moves inescapably toward that accumulation of mythic material we usually characterize as proto-pastoral, and his point of departure is the golden pastoral world we encounter in the *Georgics* or in certain poems by Horace. This is not, properly speaking, the golden age of mythic prehistory but a state in which existence is simple, peaceful, and self-sufficent, mostly because of its close harmony with nature, and which is an island in a busy, corrupt and mercenary world. It is the world we expect to come upon in classical literature when we discover a hardy, healthy people thriving on a bare sufficiency of acorns and water. This, as we have seen, is the world Boswell finds himself in when he temporarily leaves off riding horseback and joins his Corsican guides on foot: "when we grew hungry, we threw stones among the thick branches of the chestnut trees which overshadowed us, and in that manner we brought down a shower of chestnuts with which we filled our pockets, and went on eating them with great relish; and when this made us thirsty, we lay down by the side of the first brook, put our mouths to the stream and drank sufficently. It was just being for a while on of the 'prisca gens mortalium [primitive race of mortals]' who ran about in the woods eating acorns and drinking water."

The phrase that Boswell includes in his own stream of impressions is from Horace's second Epode, and readers of Horace will recall that this is the poem in which an idyllic invocation of the golden pastoral world is abruptly undercut by an ending which sets all that has gone before in a severely ironic context: "haec ubi locutus faenerator Alfius . . . [when the usurer Alfius had said this . . .]." The reminder of the outside world which Horace introduces in the figure of Alfius the usurer is not out of place in the *Tour to Corsica,* for we are not to take Boswell's identification of the Corsicans with the "prisca gens mortalium" simply and by itself, but always to recognize that he is describing a threatened state of virtuous simplicity, that his Corsica, like Horace's imaginary rural farm, exists only precariously in a world governed by corrupt men and mercenary motives. The Rome of Horace's Alfius is, in the *Tour,* a Europe which wishes to encroach on the ideal society existing in the interior of Corsica.

From this pastoral myth, classical in origin and association, Boswell moves to a closely related ideal, that of Christian religious retirement. The path Boswell takes through the island moves from convent to convent (there are few inns on Corsica) and repeatedly provides an opportunity to evoke the picture of honest, pious, hospitable monks, morally sustained in their holy life by the larger simplicity of the Corsican society that exists beyond the convent walls. Thus the worthy Rector of Cuttoli, to choose a typical figure, is "directly such a venerable hermit as we read of in the old romances," and thus life in the convent at Corte represents a peaceful and otherworldly idyll:

These fathers have a good vineyard and an excellent garden. They have between thirty and forty beehives in long wooden cases or trunks of trees, with a covering of the bark of the cork tree. When they want honey they burn a little juniperwood, the smoke of which makes the bees retire. They then take an iron instrument with a sharp-edged crook at one end of it and bring out the greatest part of the honeycomb, leaving only a little for the bees, who work the case full again. By taking the honey in this way they never kill a bee. They seemed much at their ease, living in peace and plenty. I often joked with them on the text which is applied to their order: "Nihil habentes et omnia possidentes [Having nothing, and yet possessing all things (II Corinthians 6:10)]."

Boswell is charmed by precisely those elements that this scene of religious retirement shares with the classical world of golden pastoral, the peacefulness and simplicity of life in the convent at Corte, its self-sufficiency and harmony with nature. This is another appeal to primitivism, and the simple piety of the monks is the only specifically religious coloring that Boswell adds to the picture. Those sterner motives that we usually associate with the impulse to leave the world and enter a monastery—a desire for self-abnegation and sacrifice, a conscious acceptance of a rigorous life devoted to self-examination and prayer—are excluded. Boswell's convent at Corte is close to the world of the *Ancrene Riwle* and far from the hair shirts and self-flagellation that is the other side of our idea of monastery life.

Yet the holy life of the fathers at Corte exists as precariously as does the rest of Paoli's tiny nation, and a force which is not strictly compatible with this idyll of simplicity and peace has arisen to defend it. No Golden Age myth, so far as I am aware, allows for the presence of an armed and warlike populace, for peace among men is one of the ideal effects of simple virtue and harmony with nature. Yet we recognize the Golden Age as an informing element in the background of romance and realize that some sort of reconciliation of apparent opposites has taken place when we encounter jarring violence in the pastoral landscapes of Ariosto or *The Faerie Queene*. There is no overt violence in the *Tour to Corsica,* but the possibilities of a symbolic disjunction are there, and it is a tribute to Boswell's modulation from the purely pastoral to the militaristic that we feel both to be parts of a consistent whole.

Boswell's portrait of the Corsicans as warriors has no one model, though its outline follows the idea of military simplicity and hardihood that we have agreed to call Spartan. Through it Boswell is able to remind us constantly that Corsica is a beleaguered state whose battle for independence is a moral as well as a military struggle, showing the forces of a corrupt outside world arrayed against the simple citizens of a political order that is uncorrupt and close to nature. Corsica is defended by citizen patriots whose ardor is closely related to her simplicity as a polity, and at times Boswell seems to be moving through scenes that recall the military and civil virtues of earliest

Rome. Because Corsica is in a state of siege, foreigners are viewed with suspicion, and it is deemed advisable at one point that Boswell get a passport to carry with him into the interior: "after supper, therefore, the Prior walked with me to Corte to the house of the Great Chancellor, who ordered the passport to be made out immediately. . . . When the passport was finished and ready to have the seal put on it, I was much pleased with a beautiful, simple incident. The Chancellor desired a little boy who was playing in the room by us to run to his mother and bring the great seal of the kingdom. I thought myself sitting in the house of a Cincinnatus."

The Corsicans as warriors belong, really, to the half-mythic world of Cincinnatus. The islanders are, as soldiers, brave, self-disciplined, inured to hardship, and have a sense of personal honor that finds its social counterpart in a total and all-inclusive patriotism. This portrait takes on a pastoral coloring, and the strictly military virtues of the Corsicans remind us more than anything else of the last six books of the *Aeneid,* of the world of Turnus and his compatriots, of simple bravery and battle carried out against a pastoral setting. Yet there are also elements which are not strictly associated with any classical context, and more than one passage in the *Tour* is likelier to recall the image of the American frontiersman, in his ideal and mythic state, than of Virgil.

De Toqueville, perhaps, or those who have called the frontier the American version of pastoral, would immediately recognize the symbolic background in Boswell's description of the "stately, spirited race of people" he finds at Bastelica: "they just came in, making an easy bow, placed themselves round the room where I was sitting, rested themselves on their muskets, and immediately entered into conversation with me"; or of this scene of Corsicans at their leisure: "the chief satisfaction of these islanders, when not engaged in war or in hunting, seemed to be that of lying at their ease in the open air, recounting tales of the bravery of their countrymen, and singing songs in honour of the Corsicans and against the Genoese. Even in the night they will continue this pastime in the open air, unless rain forces them to retire into their houses." When *Corsica* was written, the American frontier had yet to be mythologized, but Boswell's portrait of the Corsican soldiers anticipates the mythic impulse that would eventually make legends not only of the hardy frontiersmen of American folklore but of the ragged band of citizen soldiers who began a revolution at Concord and Lexington. The figures of the American myth arose from the eighteenth-century fable of man's freedom and dignity in the state of nature, and Boswell's Corsicans belong to their family.

Corsica in its state of siege, however, is not the American frontier, for

the rough simplicity of these scenes coexists with an idea of polite civilization
that even now is implicitly present in the rude interior of the island, awaiting
only the blessing of political independence to emerge. Rousseau's vision of
the state into which Corsica might develop after independence depended
heavily on an idea of agrarian anonymity: "la nation ne sera point illustre,
mais elle sera heureuse. On ne parlera pas d'elle; elle aura peu de consideration
au dehors; mais elle aura l'abondance, la paix et la liberté dans son sein [the
country won't be illustrous, but it will be happy. No one will speak of it;
it will get little consideration from outside, but it will have plenty, peace
and liberty in its breast]." For Rousseau, one suspects, Corsica in its present
primitive state already represented something of a philosophical ideal, and
he would only have been annoyed at any suggestion of change after independence. But Boswell was less convinced than Rousseau that any advance
in civilization involves an inevitable and proportionate advance toward decadence. Politesse is for Boswell a social ideal with considerable appeal, and
he envisions for the Corsicans a social development that will grow naturally
from their present simplicity of life.

Corsica after independence will become a nation increasingly self-sufficient in its economy and increasingly conversant, on a cultural level, with
more civilized states but preserving an integrity that will keep it aloof from
the rapacity, duplicity, and propensity for diplomatic intrigue that characterizes Europe. Corsica as a free island nation need stand no danger of
being swallowed up by the corrupt world represented by her Genoese oppressors. Even now one comes across certain scenes which promise that
Corsica will someday achieve a civilization as polished as any in Europe but
without degeneration into European luxury and decadence: "at dinner we
had no less than twelve well-dressed dishes, served on Dresden china, with
a dessert, different sorts of wine, and a liqueur, all the produce of Corsica.
Signor Barbaggi was frequently repeating to me that the Corsicans inhabited
a rude, uncultivated country and that they lived like Spartans. I begged
leave to ask him in what country he could show me greater luxury than I
had seen in his house."

Politesse out of rugged simplicity: we glimpse the same theme in
Boswell's visit to another Corsican household, where the music of any polite
European drawing room uneasily coexists with a more boisterous native
tradition: "after they had shown me their taste in fine improved music, they
gave me some original Corsican airs, and . . . a Corsican dance. It was truly
savage. They thumped with their heels, sprung upon their toes, brandished
their arms, wheeled and leaped with the most violent gesticulations. It gave
me the idea of an admirable war-dance." The ideal of polite civilization in

Corsica, however, is most significantly represented in the coastal towns garrisoned by the French. One would expect, as Boswell at first expects, the Corsicans to despise the French as hirelings of the hated Genoese. But in the period Boswell is describing, a pause in Corsica's war with Genoa, relations between the Corsicans and the French are unexpectedly cordial.

This pause in Corsica's war of independence determines the mood of the *Tour,* for it lends Boswell's portrait of the Corsican people a static quality, an opportunity for leisurely discovery that lies beyond the reach of any narrative that must describe a people caught up in the violent upheaval of war. The Genoese, having deserted the island during this time of uneasy truce, never enter into the narrative directly; we do not see the oppressors but feel their presence as the Corsicans must, as a remote and menacing force whose one purpose is to swallow up the ancient society existing in the interior of the island. And the French, whose military presence serves as a constant reminder that Corsica's liberty is yet to be won, seem on the human and cultural level almost sympathetic to Corsica and her cause.

As a symbol of polite civilization the French garrison represents the politesse of European culture preserved from luxurious excess by the rigors of a military situation: a Frenchman on Corsica, though he bring with him all the easy cosmopolitanism of Paris, is on Corsica still. At the end of his tour Boswell decides to depart for the mainland from Bastia. He finds the town an island within an island, whose ruler is the Count de Marbeuf, "a worthy, open-hearted Frenchman" whose agreeable personality derives, Boswell suggests, both from his being French and a long-time army officer: "such a character is gay without levity and judicious without a severity. Such a character was the Count de Marbeuf, of an ancient family in Brittany." And here, in Marbeuf's tiny dominion, exists that world of elegance and grace without which Corsican society, for all its rugged virtues, is incomplete: "next morning I waited on M. de Marbeuf. . . . He gave me a most polite reception. The brilliancy of his levée pleased me; it was a scene so different from those which I had been for some time accustomed to see. It was like passing at once from a rude and early age to a polished modern age, from the mountains of Corsica to the banks of the Seine."

This sudden transition from the wild interior of Corsica to the polish and ease of life in the French garrison allows us finally to view the two modes of existence in sympathetic contrast. And to see the beginning of a process at work, for the retreat of the Genoese from the island, and their replacement by the French, has introduced a formative influence on Corsican society: "perhaps indeed the residence of the French in Corsica has, upon the whole, been an advantage to the patriots. There have been markets twice a week at the frontiers of each garrison town, where the Corsican peasants have sold all sorts of provisions and brought in a good many French crowns which have been melted down into Corsican money." Not only has the lull in combat given the islanders time to look about them, it has given them a model to contemplate and a period of temporary peace during which they can begin to live the kind of life that will be theirs as a free society: "a cessation of arms for a few years has been a breathing time to the nation to prepare itself for one great effort, which will probably end in the total expulsion of the Genoese. A little leisure has been given for attending to civil improvements, towards which the example of the French has in no small degree contributed."

Boswell on his arrival in Corsica was the most typical of eighteenth-century travelers, the young man of good birth whose tour of Europe was regarded as the end of his formal education. Boswell's stay in Corsica has been an interlude—an important one, one in which he has gained a new perception of history and heroism and political morality, but an interlude just the same. The story that began with the anxious imaginings of a British surgeon's mate thus closes on a similar note. Paoli has sent, as Boswell's guide to Bastia, a Corsican named Ambrosio, "a stange, iron-coloured, fearless creature. He had been much in war; careless of wounds, he was cooly intent on destroying the enemy. . . . I was sure I needed be under no apprehensions; but I don't know how, I desired Ambrosio to march before me that I might see him." In Boswell's apprehension begins the restoration of distance that allows us to see his visit to Corsica as a romantic journey into a forgotten age and to understand his portrayal of the Corsican people as an excursion into something very close to myth.

III

Boswell's idealizing portrayal of the Corsican people is finally, however, a subordinate motif, for the *Tour* is really a book about Pascal Paoli, a man unknown, before Boswell introduced him, to the generality of educated Europeans but afterward acclaimed by them as a hero stepped out of antique times. Boswell's portrait of the Corsicans, we have seen, is an analogue of the idealized social order behind the hero of epic or romance, providing the dramatic context that makes the specific qualities of his heroism comprehensible. Yet if the picture of Corsican society offered in the *Tour* represents an ideal order that derives its utopian promise from the vigor and primitive simplicity of Corsican life, it is Paoli who sustains both that order and its promise. For the Corsicans as the citizenry of an unrealized commonwealth are Paoli's creation. Paoli alone has been able to bring out his people's best qualities and to suppress their worst, and he has become the symbol of their feeling for Corsica as a whole, if only because the whole would not exist without him.

In one sense, therefore, the *Tour to Corsica* appears to be dealing with the familiar theme of the great man in history, with the notion of the superior individual who, in a given historical moment, assumes power over people and the direction of events. We seem to be closest to this idea when we observe that Corsican society as we see it in the *Tour* exists only because Paoli, through sheer force of personality and moral character, has managed to bring order out of anarchy: only since he has become their ruler has the Corsican sense of personal honor been transformed into patriotism, their tendency to violence into bravery in war, and their state of existence, based on a bare agricultural subsistence, into a pastoral state holding forth the promise of becoming more. Corsica as an ideal society exists largely in Paoli's vision, and his islanders are willing to leave the matter of vision up to him, in effect to accept it at one remove, through their loyalty to their leader.

Yet Paoli does not represent what Sidney Hook has called the event-making man, the hero in history, for the nature of his heroism takes us in quite a different direction, away from the world of practical affairs and toward the world of the imagination. This involves the notion, mentioned earlier, of the past as imaginative refuge: throughout the *Tour* we see Paoli not merely as a mystic or visionary, but specifically as a heroic figure whose dream of the past is a response to his own unheroic age. The spiritual allegiance of the Corsicans to their leader is thus a participation in an illusion so compelling that for the time it has replaced reality. This is why we are aware of an idealized or even mythic quality in Boswell's portrayal of the Corsican people, for his narrative ultimately pictures a state of unreality, a state in which both the hero and his society, existing within a magic circle of illusion, live apart from the modern age.

Paoli is first felt in the *Tour* as an ideal presence. Though Boswell has arrived full of admiration for the Corsicans' struggle for liberty, he has had no intimation that behind their bravery and resolution stands the single dominant personality of a leader. But as Boswell, in his first travels through the island, discovers that every Corsican identifies the battle for independence with Paoli's aspirations for his people, he inescapably begins to perceive Paoli's role as an inspirational figure in Corsican history. The first impression is continuously reinforced, until, as Boswell tells us, he himself is almost ready to approach Paoli as someone more god-like than human: "when I at last came within sight of Sollacaro, where Paoli was, I could not help being under considerable anxiety. My ideas of him had been greatly heightened by the conversations I had with all sorts of people in the island, they having represented him to me as something above humanity."

The representations of the Corsicans, as we discover when Paoli enters the story, contain a largely imaginative truth. Paoli as a leader brings to life an idea of stoic heroism—a self-discipline taking the form of stern self-denial, a quality of true greatness which communicates itself in his manner—that takes us out of the decayed world of the mid-eighteenth century and into the times of antiquity. To encounter Paoli as a man is almost inescapably to be moved to considerations of past and present. In ancient times, Boswell tells us at one point, when noblemen were like princes in their power, they were open and affable: "some of our modern nobility are so anxious to preserve an appearance of dignity which they are sensible cannot bear an examination that they are afraid to let you come near them. Paoli is not so. Those about him come into his apartment at all hours, wake him, help him on with his clothes, are perfectly free from restraint; yet they know their distance and, awed by his real greatness, never lose their respect for him."

Such scenes appeal to something like the Renaissance fable of an aristocracy of virtue, that social myth which placed the beginnings of hereditary nobility in personal superiority; and, by extension, to the theme of decay which is the usual accompaniment to the myth of the Golden Age. By so much as Paoli differs from the decayed nobility of contemporary Europe does Corsica differ morally from the world outside, for Paoli's distance from the people he rules is one solely of personal authority. In the eighteenth century, with aristocracy at the beginning of its great modern decline but still retaining a good deal of ideological prestige, the idea had a special appeal. Boswell pictures his hero as a natural aristocrat in a natural setting, offering his audience an implicit comparison with their own modern aristocracy, whose place owes almost nothing to moral character and everything to riches, inherited political influence, and, above all, the accident of fate that made them noblemen rather than hostlers.

Paoli's manner returns Boswell again and again to the theme of stoic heroism, for in it, the quality of "real greatness" discovered in a man who walks the earth, lies Paoli's affinity with the heroes of ancient myth and history: "I observed that although he had often a placid smile upon his countenance, he hardly every laughed. Whether loud laughter in general society be a sign of weakness or rusticity I cannot say; but I have remarked that real great men, and men of finished behaviour, seldom fall into it." The idea is familiar enough to qualify as an eighteenth-century commonplace—Lord Chesterfield's *Letters* are always advising his son that well-bred men smile but do not laugh—but only as a matter of decorum, a social counterfeit of which Paoli's instinctive dignity is the original. Yet Paoli's greatness is far from being a matter wholly of instinct, for Boswell's conception of the hero demands a moral character shaped consciously, not a happy accident of human nature. The stoic strain in Paoli's personality has been carefully cultivated: "he observed that the Epicurean philosophy had produced but one exalted character, whereas Stoicism had been the seminary of great men. What he now said put me in mind of these noble line of Lucan:

> Hi mores, haec duri inmota Catonis
> Secta fuit, servare modum finemque tenere,
> Naturamque sequi patriaque inpendere vitam,
> Nec sibi toti genitum se credere mundo.

[Such was the character, such the inflexible rule of austere Cato— to observe moderation and hold fast to the limit, to follow nature, to give his life for his country, to believe that he was born to serve the whole world and not himself.]"
(*Pharsalia*, ii. 380–83 [Loeb, tr. J. D. Duffy]).

"He bids your breasts with ancient ardour rise," as Pope said in his prologue to Addison's *Cato,* "And calls forth Roman drops from British eyes": in translating Paoli's preference for Stoic philosophy immediately into Lucan's vision of heroic patriotism, Boswell is appealing less to history than to stoicism as a conscious ideal, reminding us that a man who has become great through an act of moral effort is superior to one whom the gods have simply appointed as fit to lead.

Boswell's emphasis on the role of mind and will in Paoli's greatness moves us in another direction, toward the ideal of the Philosopher King. Like the Guardians of Plato's *Republic,* Paoli has been educated from birth for the leadership of his people, and his personal notions of leadership are derived entirely from philosophy and history. With a memory "like that of Themistocles," Paoli has "the best part of the classics by heart," and he moves in an imaginative world where past and present are imperceptibly merged. "I have heard him give," says Boswell, "what the French call *un catalogue raisonné* of the most distinguished men in antiquity. His characters of them were concise, nervous, and just. I regret that the fire with which he spoke upon such occasions so dazzled me that I could not recollect his sayings so as to write them down when I retired from his presence. He just lives in the times of antiquity. He said to me, 'A young man who would form his mind to glory must not read modern memoirs, but Plutarch and Titus Livius.' " Boswell clearly is dazzled less by the conciseness, nervousness, and justness of the portraits in Paoli's catalogue raisonné (what might be called their rhetorical qualities) than by the amount of imaginative and moral energy that Paoli has put into them: "he just lives in the times of antiquity."

As with Boswell's appeal to myth in his portrait of the Corsicans, the idea of Paoli as an actual hero of antiquity uses time as a metaphor of moral integrity. The *Tour* is able to present us with the vision of a people living in a Golden Age, led by a Plutarchan hero, existing precariously in the midst of a degenerate modern world, precisely because Boswell has found a way to represent convincingly the idea of moral distance in temporal terms. And the metaphor does convince, as we see in the sentence with which the *Tour* ends, Pitt's famous pronouncement on its hero: " 'it may be said of Paoli, as the Cardinal de Retz said of the great Montrose, "he is one of those men who are no longer to be found but in the *Lives* of Plutarch." ' " Echoes of Pitt's reaction to Paoli are to be found throughout the record of contemporary response to the *Tour,* the response of a public whose only acquaintance with Paoli was through Boswell.

Boswell's usual means of associating Paoli with the world of the ancient heroes is the allusive. Allusion in the *Tour* is a straightforward affair, occurring most often when some aspect of Paoli's character brings to mind a parallel in myth, epic, or history. Outside Paoli's chamber, for instance, sleep five or six faithful Corsican dogs: "they are extremely sagacious, and know all his friends and attendants. Were any person to approach the General during the night, they would instantly tear him in pieces. Having dogs for his attendants is another circumstance about Paoli similar to the heroes of antiquity." Boswell then goes on to note parallels with Homer's descriptions of Telemachus and the family of Patroclus; to take such a passage out of context perhaps emphasizes in a way unfair to Boswell the artlessness of his mode of allusion. Yet the descriptive simplicity of the *Tour* is part of its strategy, and such allusions invariably work to deepen our sense of Paoli's moral affinity with an age that has passed away. To compare a Corsican leader to the warrior heroes of Homer because of something so incidental as his watchdogs could only be comic unless there were in fact a Homeric dimension to his character as we perceive it.

Even when the way of direct allusion is denied him, Boswell manages continously to surround his hero with the figures of classical myth and history. One of the stranger aspects of Paoli's character is his claim to second sight, in which the Corsicans universally believe. Boswell's appraisal, on the surface only a judicious weighing of the facts, finds means to introduce the appropriate parallels. It might be supposed, he says, that Paoli has promoted belief in his unusual talent "in order that he might have more authority in civilizing a rude and ferocious people, as Lycurgus pretended to have the sanction of the oracle at Delphos, as Numa gave it out that he had frequent interviews with the nymph Egeria, or as Marius persuaded the Romans that he received divine communications from a hind." Yet one cannot believe, decides Boswell, that Paoli would descend to such pious frauds, and the case is straightway dismissed. But the case itself has been secondary, for what memory retains is the parallel in other respects with Lycurgus, Numa, and Marius, ancient civilizers of rude and ferocious peoples.

All Boswell's allusions to the ancient world are rooted in a strong context of personal impression, for the heroic dimension of Paoli's character, a quality which reveals itself primarily in his manner, is something that can only register on individual perception. Before we can accept the imaginative orientation that makes Paoli seem more a hero of antiquity than a man of the modern age, we must assent to Boswell's spontaneous response to this aura of greatness. At the center of Boswell's Plutarchan portrait is a perception that occurs with the intensity of a vision: "I had often enough formed the idea of a man continually such as I could conceive in my best moments. But this idea appeared like the ideas we are taught in the schools to form of things which may exist, but do not: of seas of milk and ships of amber. But I saw my highest idea realized in Paoli. It was impossible for me, speculate as I pleased, to have a little opinion of human nature in him."

The very insubstantiality of the aura of greatness that surrounds Paoli suggests, however, the real meaning of the vision: it is not that Paoli has managed to recreate in real life the character of the imaginary hero but that Boswell, as he has come to know Paoli, has been insensibly drawn into the private and heroic world sustained by Paoli's imagination. Here again we are dealing with an idea of projected illusion so powerful as to have become a kind of alternative reality. This is the reality perceived by those who move in Paoli's presence, for what Paoli has found in his handbooks of greatness, in Plutarch and Livy, Boswell and the Corsicans discover in Paoli himself. The effect, as Boswell's talk of books and schools makes clear, is to undermine the idea of greatness as an abstraction and to rediscover it as an actual potentiality of human nature. Yet this in an unheroic age is a diminished potentiality, one which can express itself only in the manner and personality of the superior man.

There is in Boswell's Plutarchan portrait of Paoli a certain danger of excessive remoteness. Paoli's dream of the past, drawing substance from the imagined world of heroic antiquity, involves a stern image of heroism, one calculated to reveal him as someone singleminded, aloof, and hopelessly distant from his people and Boswell's audience. Boswell mitigates the sternness of the portrait in a manner that looks forward to his treatment of Johnson in the *Life,* presenting as counterpoint a side of Paoli's personality that appeals strongly to the benevolist ideal of the Good Man. As in the *Life,* the appeal is not directly to the theories of instrinsic moral sensibility advanced by writers like Shaftesbury, Hutcheson, and Butler, but to the simplified, popular, and somewhat sentimental version of those theories that was so strong an influence on eighteenth-century fiction and drama.

Paoli's benevolism is revealed in the way he deals with his role as governor of an unrealized commonwealth, symbolically analogous to the way a father deals with his children: he reproves wrongdoers, encourages rectitude, settles family disputes, and in general controls the tenor of Corsican life through a judicious bestowal of his approbation or disapproval. Each time Paoli appears in this paternal light, a submerged feudal metaphor informs the scene, for in the *Tour,* as often in eighteenth-century literature when we come across a benevolist character in a position of authority, an idea of romantic feudalism is in the background. But Paoli's benevolism is of course merged with the sterner demands of self-denial: "had he been a private gentleman, he probably would have married, and I am sure would have made as good a husband and father as he does a supreme magistrate and general. But his arduous and critical situation would not allow him to enjoy domestic felicity. He is wedded to his country, and the Corsicans are his children." This symbolic relationship becomes the medium in which is dissolved the distance between the hero of antiquity and ordinary men.

Paoli's benevolism is thus embodied in the nature of his aspirations for Corsica as a state. The main objectives are peace, simplicity, and plenty, and when Boswell offers a studied compliment likening the "brave and free" Corsicans to the ancient Romans, he is quick to disavow the analogy: "he received my compliment very graciously, but observed that the Corsicans had no chance of being like the romans, a great conquering nation who should extend its empire over half the globe. Their situation, and the modern political systems, rendered this impossible. 'But,' said he, 'Corsica may be a very happy country.' " If Paoli's response is a means of renouncing the rapacity of the modern European state, it involves too the renunciation of the ideal of leadership sanctioned by Boswell's Roman parallel. The feudal aspect of Paoli's relation to the Corsicans appears again in his devotion, as Corsica's leader, to the arts of peace: "he said the greatest happiness was not in glory but in goodness, and that Penn in his American colony, where he had established a people in quiet and contentment, was happier than Alexander the Great after destroying multitudes at the conquest of Thebes."

Yet Paoli does not see himself as the governor of a feudal state, for as hero of the *Tour* he lives, as it were, inside the metaphor of romantic feudalism that controls Boswell's perception of Crosican society. Here again we sense the imaginative appeal of Paoli's dream of the past: Paoli has brought order out of anarchy in Corsica through the solitary force of his personality, and this, rather than any conscious effort on his part, has brought the Corsicans to recognize in their leader the actual personification of the state. Thus we see Paoli as a magistrate who, when he does not take his place in court, is in some sense revealed *as* the court: "he remained in his own apartment, and if any of those whose suits were determined by the sindacato were not pleased with the sentence they had an audience of Paoli, who never failed to convince them that justice had been done them. This appeared to me a necessary indulgence in the infancy of government. The Corsicans, having been so long in a state of anarchy, could not all at once submit their minds to the regular authority of justice. They would sumbit implicitly to Paoli, because they love and venerate him." Only Paoli's strong personal presence behind the forms of government lends them validity in Corsican eyes, and we sense that if his presence were withdrawn Corsica would revert to anarchy and the forms would be swept away.

For Paoli, innocent of the sense in which his power derives from his own absorption in an imagined reality, this represents a purely practical problem. Since a bad man could in this situation become a tyrant, and since independent institutions are historically the best guard against despotism, the Corsicans must be brought to view government as something apart from the governing personality of a leader. Yet Paoli's measures in this direction, so apparently and hopefully practical, still reveal the essentially feudal and paternal nature of his relationship to his society: " 'our state,' said he, 'is young, and still requires the leading strings. I am desirous that the Corsicans should be taught to walk of themselves. Therefore when they come to me to ask whom they should choose for their Padre del Commune or other magistrate, I tell them, "You know better than I do the able and honest men among your neighbours. Consider the consequence of your choice, not only to yourselves but to the island in general." In this manner I accustom them to feel their own importance as members of the state.' "

For the Corsicans, however, living within that magic sphere of illusion associated with Paoli's private dream of the heroic past, their leader is the state. A full revelation of Paoli's heroic grandeur thus comes only when he drops his well-intentioned but somewhat theoretical attempts to dissociate himself from Corsica and speaks as the state. As when he deals with a Corsican turncoat: " 'sir,' said he. 'Corsica makes it a rule to pardon the most unworthy of her children when they surrender themselves, even when they are forced to do so as in your case. You have now escaped. But take care. I shall have a strict eye upon you, and if ever you make the least attempt to return to your traitorous practices, you know I can be avenged of you.' He spoke this with the fierceness of a lion, and from the awful darkness of his brow one could see that his thoughts of vengeance were terrible." Behind such a scene lies the entire authority of Boswell's portrait of Paoli and the people he leads, for everything is concentrated at moments like this in the figure of the hero. The Corsica of the *Tour* is Paoli's creation, and even Boswell's feudal metaphor is insufficient to account for a situation where the external order that surrounds the hero is so completely identified with his mind and imagination.

This symbolic identification of Paoli with Corsica leaves both the leader and his people sadly vulnerable, and it is in the notion of vulnerability that we discover the final meaning of Boswell's story. On one level this is the vulnerability of a heroic leader and an idyllic state surrounded by the corrupt and threatening world of European duplicity. The *Tour* ends with Boswell, now safely in England, receiving from Paoli an account of the latest intrigue against him and Corsica: "as I passed by Bocagno, I learned that a disbanded Genoese officer was seeking associates to assassinate me. He could not succeed and, finding that he was discovered, he betook himself to the woods, where he has been slain." This is the level on which eighteenth-century readers, taking the *Tour* as a story about political conflict, about oppression and the eternal struggle for natural liberty, made heroes of Paoli and the Corsicans.

At the same time, and on another level, the *Tour* is about the larger conflict of imagination and reality. For the mythic dimension of Boswell's portrayal of Paoli and his people involves a symbolic alignment of Corsica with the imaginary world of poetry and heroic legend, and of Europe with the dismayingly actual world of unheroic modernity. And eighteenth-century readers, looking to the *Tour* for confirmation of new doctrines of primitivism and natural liberty, undoubtedly responded to this as well, to the half-mythic vision of a Golden Age society governed by a hero out of Plutarch. Yet few, perhaps, would have perceived the sense in which Boswell's Corsica, beseiged by the world of the unheroic and the unextraordinary, belongs wholly to the imagination, representing a reality transformed by a memory of the heroic past. The vulnerability of Paoli and Corsica is on this level the vulnerability of myth, or the power of myth to give shape to human existence, in a world increasingly dominated by the actual.

The vision of Corsica as a mythic state returns us therefore to Paoli, whose dream of the heroic past is at the heart of the process of imaginative transformation. For though Paoli and his people exist together within an illusion so strong as to have replaced a less satisfactory reality, Paoli is yet an isolated figure: the heroic world of Plutarch and the peaceful world of the Golden Age, though both are versions of the imagined past, are different worlds, and they merge in the *Tour* only because they stand together in symbolic opposition to the modern age. It is thus submerged tension between hero and milieu that gives meaning to our sense of Corsica as Paoli's creation, and though Boswell and the Corsicans are drawn partially into Paoli's dream of the past, they cannot inhabit it as he does. That dream is finally a private dream, the response of a heroic spirit to an age in which heroism seems to have disappeared, and behind it we glimpse the ultimate theme of spiritual isolation.

JOHN BARRELL

"The language properly so-called": Johnson's Language and Politics

The analogy, often submerged, but often visible, between proper language and proper government, is to be found everywhere in Johnson's writings on language; and it will be worth discussing Johnson's attitude to correct English and to linguistic change in some detail, because it seems to have been he who first clearly identified the threat to the custom of language as now to be anticipated as coming from a new quarter. I want to begin the discussion of Johnson with two quotations in which the analogy is not made directly, but which indicate the similarity of Johnson's ways of thinking about government and about language. In the *Plan* of the Dictionary, as it were an advertisement for the work he was beginning to undertake, dedicated to the Earl of Chesterfield and published in 1747, he writes:

> To our language may be with great justness applied the ob-
> servation of *Quintilian,* that speech was not formed by an anal-
> ogy sent from heaven. It did not descend to us in a state of uni-
> formity and perfection, but was produced by necessity and
> enlarged by accident, and is therefore composed of dissimilar
> parts, thrown together by negligence, by affectation, by learning,
> or by ignorance.

In a much later work, *The False Alarm* of 1770, written to oppose the stand taken by the electors of the County of Middlesex after the exclusion of John Wilkes from the House of Commons, Johnson wrote:

From *English Literature in History 1730–80: An Equal, Wide Survey.* © 1983 by John Barrell. Hutchinson & Co., Ltd., 1983.

Governments formed by chance, and gradually improved by such
expedients, as the successive discovery of their defects happened
to suggest, are never to be tried by a regular theory. They are
fabricks of dissimilar materials, raised by different architects,
upon different plans. We must be content with them as they are;
should we attempt to mend their disproportions, we might easily
demolish, and difficultly rebuild them.

Laws are now made, and customs are established; these are our
rules, and by them we must be guided.

These passages are not of course a perfect match: the accidental nature
of language and of government is not the product of causes precisely similar,
and Johnson can admit of language, as he could less easily of government,
that it has been formed by ignorance as well as by wisdom—it may be, of
course, because all men have contributed to the formation of language, but
only some to that of the constitution. Besides, as governments are more
easily reformed than are languages, the possibility (or necessity) of reforming
them can hardly be insisted upon. But both passages agree in this, that our
language and our government cannot be discussed as if they are the products
of settled plans. Johnson may sometimes regret this in relation to language,
while he seems to approve it in relation to government; but in either case
he is clear that we cannot understand and certainly cannot improve language
or government by consulting what, on a rational view, *ought* to be the case.
The language, however haphazard, is the only one we have; it must be
understood in terms of what we do say, not what we should. Our constitution
also, however accidentally composed, is perhaps more tendentiously represented as the only one available: "we must be content," for "laws are now
made, and customs established; these are our rules, and by them we must
be guided."

Precisely how Johnson defines what custom is, I will discuss later. I
first want to point out that this insistence, on the necessity of being content
with the language and government we have, enables Johnson to avoid the
theoretical questions concerning the origin of language and government that
preoccupied so many political thinkers and linguists from Hobbes and Locke
and throughout the eighteenth century. In particular, in his writings on the
alleged political rights of the American colonists, Johnson departs from the
contractual language of Locke and Blackstone and looks forward to Burke
in displaying little interest in the notion of the origin of government in the
consent of the governed, and therefore in the notion that governments
continue to derive their authority from that continued consent. Similarly

his adherence to custom, in his discussions of language and politics alike, is not—as it had been to writers earlier in the century—a defence of custom as the expression of what a language community or a political community has *chosen* to do. Custom no doubt may in part owe its origin to choice, to consent; but once established, customs become, in effect, the laws of the state or the rules of the language, which command obedience from the mere fact of their existence, and which should not be regarded as being open to any but the most modest alteration.

Johnson's impatience with the notion of government as founded in consent is clear in his writings on the Middlesex electors who persisted in returning Wilkes as their Member of Parliament in defiance of the will of the Commons, and in his writing against the American colonists, whose defence of the notion was partly derived from a democratic reading of Locke's second *Treatise.* "The rabble," he says in *The False Alarm,* "will be always patriots, and always Supporters of the Bill of Rights"; and in *The Patriot* (1774), another anti-Wilkesite pamphlet, he wrote:

> he that has been refused a reasonable or unreasonable request, who thinks his merit under-rated, and sees his influence declin- ing, begins soon to talk of natural equality, the absurdity of *many made for one,* the original compact, the foundation of authority, and the majesty of the people.

Some of what this malcontent talks of, of course, is an evidently radical theory of government, but some of it is the general currency of political theory of whatever persuasion: the discussion of a government in the light of general concepts is for Johnson a sufficient mark of a disaffected dema- gogue, never mind the fact that his particular opinions on those concepts are not to be trusted.

But most clearly, perhaps, he attacks the theory of consent in *Taxation no Tyranny* (1775):

> That a free man is governed by himself, or by laws to which he has consented, is a position of mighty sound: but every man that utters it, with whatever confidence, and every man that hears it, with whatever acquiescence, if consent be supposed to imply the power of refusal, feels it to be false. We virtually and implicitly allow the institutions of any Government of which we enjoy the benefit, and solicit the protection. In wide extended dominions, though power has been diffused with the most even hand, yet a very small part of the people are either primarily or secondarily

consulted in Legislation. The business of the Publick must be done by delegation. The choice of delegates is made by a select number, and those who are not electors stand idle and helpless spectators of the commonweal, *wholly unconcerned in the government of themselves.*

Of Electors the hap is but little better. They are often far from unanimity in their choice, and where the numbers approach to equality, almost half must be governed not only without, but against their choice.

How any man can have consented to institutions established in distant ages, it will be difficult to explain. In the most favourite residence of liberty, the consent of individuals is merely passive, a tacit admission in every community of the terms which that community grants and requires. As all are born the subjects of some state or other, we may be said to have been all born consenting to some system of Government. Other consent than this, the condition of civil life does not allow. It is the unmeaning clamour of the pedants of policy, the delirious dream of republican fanaticism.

What is remarkable about this, of course, is the way that an account of the *status quo* is assumed to be, at the same time and without further justification, a defence of it. To the argument that every man *ought* to consent to his own government, Johnson simply replies that, in point of fact, every man does not—and the question of whether there ought to be a more active consent than a merely passive and tacit admission is dismissed without argument as unmeaning, the dream of republican fanaticism for a condition that civil life does not allow—so why bother to consider whether it should allow it or not? It is a fact that in populous countries, the voteless and a significant majority of the voters can have no say whatsoever in the government of themselves—and this, Johnson asserts, in countries (and by implication especially in Britain, "the most favourite residence of liberty) where power has been diffused with the most even hand." Any other means of organizing government is presented, and as a matter of fact, as impossible; and consent can have no meaning unless we take it at its lowest level—non-resistance. He does not consider, for example, whether an extension of the franchise would ensure a greater measure of consent among the governed, because as I have said he has very little interest in the notion of consent, whether it could be made effective or not. This is clearest perhaps in the remark, "How any man can have consented to institutions established in distant ages, it will be difficult to explain." When those institutions were established, the argument is, men may possibly have given their consent to them; but though we who inherit them cannot be said to consent to them, we are not therefore free to change them, and there is no point, for Johnson, in even pausing to consider whether that ought to be the case or not.

The same or a similar attitude is evident in the remark from the *Plan* to the Dictionary quoted a few pages back. Language, says Johnson, did not descend from heaven, a perfect system; but it is not, therefore, as Locke had argued, formed by a voluntary agreement among men to make this sound or combination of letters the mark of an idea. Language was produced by necessity and enlarged by accident; there is no view here of the agents— those who *choose* that the language should take this form or that; and though by its very agnosticism this becomes a more credible view of the origin of language than Locke's, it is also a refusal to consider the rights of the langauge community as an issue of any importance in the questions of how language is to be used, and on whose terms it is to be "settled." Johnson clearly regards this position as an important one to establish if he is to avoid suggesting that men are free to decide, or that one man is as free as another to decide what the rules of the language ought to be. However, if the Tory Johnson differs from many more "Whiggish" supporters of custom in law or language who see its origin in consent, he does so only to make more sure the process by which, in Blackstone's phrase, customs "receive their binding power, and the force of law"; and what he does is simply to avoid the complications (and, to his credit, the bad faith) involved in the libertarian rhetoric whereby free men are bound by customs they are supposed to have assented to freely, but which they may not dissent from or change. Johnson's notion of language, as of government, is quite openly and frankly one in which the majority should be idle and helpless spectators while the customs of the polite are converted into law.

In all that I have said so far, however, I have been comparing what Johnson takes to be the immutable actuality of the political situation, with what he hopes might become—but is not yet—the actual state of the language. The present actuality, as Johnson understands it, is of a language in a state of nature still requiring to be "reduced" to a state of civil society; and it is in terms of the connection between language and government that he makes the nature of his task as a lexicographer fully (but still problematically) explicit:

> When I survey the Plan which I have laid before you, I cannot,
> my Lord, but confess, that I am frighted at its extent, and, like

the soldiers of Caesar, look on Britain as new world, which it is
almost madness to invade. But I hope, that though I should not
complete the conquest, I shall at least discover the coast, civilise
part of the inhabitants, and make it easy for some other adventurer
to proceed farther, to reduce them wholly to subjection, and
settle them under laws.

There may be, as I believe there often is in Johnson's writings about language,
an irony in this—evident perhaps in the words "frighted," and "madness"—
in which Johnson may be half-mocking the loss of the sense of proportion
that he has incurred by devoting himself so entirely to lexicography—he
seems to do the same when, in the later *Preface,* he notes wryly that as far
as spelling is concerned "particular combinations of letters" do not have
"much influence on human happiness." The irony may here be reminding
us, and Johnson himself, that this is only a dictionary, and not a constitution.
But there is more to it than that: the irony challenges the scale, but not
wholly the nature of the comparison, a comparison reinforced by Johnson's
ambiguity about what or who it is that he seeks to "civilize," "reduce," and
"settle": the "inhabitants" are, in the first place, presumably the words of
the language, to be "settled" and "reduced to subjection" by having their
spelling, etymology and meanings fixed, and then by being organized al-
phabetically in the word list. But the anthropomorphism of the passsage
points also to the political nature of the task—in settling and subduing the
language, Johnson will also be settling and subduing the inhabitants of
England, the speakers of English. To neither point is it irrelevant that
Johnson sees himself as a *Roman* conqueror; though he is insistent that English
is not to be regulated by the laws of any other language, the aspiration is
that the language, the inhabitants, and their customs, might come under
a discipline like that of Latin grammar, the *pax romana,* and the Roman
law.

That the English language, if not the English people, is in need of
such discipline, is a point continually reiterated by Johnson, in metaphors
often openly political; and it is a point which becomes more important to
Johnson in the course of his work on the dictionary, and so is much more
insisted upon in the *Preface* than in the original *Plan.* In the earlier essay,
English is described as "our licentious language," and Johnson remarks of
the syntax, for example, of English, that it "is too inconstant to be reduced
to rules," as also are the inflections of many English verbs. In the *Preface,*
the tone of such remarks becomes much more emphatic, in proportion (as
we shall see) to Johnson's increasing doubts that there is any possibility of

civilizing the "inhabitants" of England. English began as a "wild and barbarous jargon," and has since been

> suffered to spread, under the direction of chance, into wild exuberance, resigned to the tyranny of time and fashion, and exposed to the corruptions of ignorance, and caprices of innovation,

with the result that it is now

> copious without order, and energetick without rules: wherever I turned my view, there was perplexity to be disentangled, and confusion to be regulated; choice was to be made out of boundless variety, without any established principle of selection.

That Johnson to some extent still regrets what he sees as the unanalogical character of English is everywhere clear from his tone: but what he can do about it, or whether he should do anything, is less clear to him, and at no time less clear than on the completion of the dictionary. The possibilities are of course for him as they were for Swift: to correct and improve, or simply to ascertain and fix. That Johnson is tempted by the first possibility is clear, but it is one he claims to have rejected. He can expel, as he says he has done in the preface to the popular shortened version of his dictionary, some "barbarous terms and phrases"—*malus usus abolendus est:* he can attempt to fix spelling by referring more to the etymology of words than to their current pronunciation; but there is much more that he cannot do. Thus, some unanalogical spellings "are not errours in orthography, but spots of barbarity impressed so deep in the *English* language, that criticism can never wash them away; these, therefore, must be permitted to remain untouched"; and in the grammar prefixed to the dictionary he seems to regret the passing of words such as "wherewith" and a number of others which were in fact more tenacious of life than Johnson realized—"thereby," "whereby," "hereafter," and so on—words which are "proper, useful and analogous," but which could not alas be revivified.

In fact, Johnson is usually far from convinced of the value—let alone the possibility—of improvements and corrections in the language, and it is worth paying close attention to the language he uses at such times. He sometimes sees such improvements as the suggestions of pedants, doomed to be ignored by those whose concern with language is practical, not limply theoretical. This is from the "Grammar":

> There have been many schemes offered for the emendation and settlement of our orthography, which, like that of other nations, being formed by chance, or according to the fancy of the earliest

writers in rude ages, was at first very various and uncertain, and
is yet sufficiently irregular. Of these reformers some have endeavoured to accommodate orthography better to the pronunciation,
without considering that this is to measure by a shadow, to take
that for a model or standard which is changing while they apply
it. Others, less absurdly indeed, but with equal unlikelihood of
success, have endeavoured to proportion the number of letters to
that of sounds, that every sound may have its own character, and
every character a single sound. Such would be the orthography
of a new language to be formed by a synod of grammarians upon
principles of science. But who can hope to prevail on nations to
change their practice, and make all their old books useless? or
what advantage would a new orthography procure equivalent to
the confusion and perplexity of such an alteration?

The second question here is what gives Johnson's most usual position on
what he calls such "innovations"—in the grammar he goes on to give examples of such schemes, "as a guide to reformers, or terrour to innovators."
In the *Plan* he had already announced that, in matters of orthography, he
proposed to follow the rule

> to make no innovation, without a reason sufficient to balance the
> inconvenience of change; and such reasons I do not expect often
> to find. All change is of itself an evil, which ought not to be
> hazarded but for evident advantage; and as inconstancy is in every
> case a mark of weakness, it will add nothing to the reputation
> of our tongue.

And the position is most firmly stated in the *Preface* itself, where he advises
would-be reformers of language "not to disturb, upon narrow views or for
minute propriety, the orthography of their fathers. It has been asserted, that
for the law to be *known,* is of more importance than to be *right.*"

The similarity between the position here taken by Johnson, and the
defence of the common law by Blackstone and of the unreformed House of
Commons as it was to be made by Johnson himself, and later by Burke, is
sufficiently clear: "it hath been," wrote Blackstone,

> an ancient observation of the laws of England, that whenever a
> standing rule of law, of which the reason perhaps could not be
> remembered or discerned, hath been wantonly broken in upon
> by statutes or new resolutions, the wisdom of the rule hath in
> the end appeared from the inconveniences that have followed the
> innovation.

Johnson's appeal to the "orthography of our fathers" is closely related to that deference to the wisdom of our political forefathers in framing the constitution and the law, and it is in this context that Johnson's hostility to "innovation" is to be understood: he uses the word, as it is sometimes used by Blackstone, often by Burke, and by Johnson himself in his political writings, in contexts where one can hardly doubt that such competent latinists have *res novae* in the back of their minds. It may certainly be so used in the laconic phrase just quoted from the "Grammar," "a terrour to innovators"—"terrour" here has the sense of the threat of severe punishment, even death, appropriate for revolutionaries but less so for academic linguists.

The correction and improvement of the language is no longer for Johnson, then, primarily to be resisted on the grounds that it was at the start of the century, as an attempt to impose uniformity on language by a divine right of grammarians; it is resisted now on the grounds that "all change is of itself an evil," which involves an exchange of "stability" for "confusion"; and that such remarks have political implications is clear in Johnson's remark that "for the law to be *known,* is more important than to be *right.*" The fear is of a reorganization of society or of language that may possibly produce better laws, but will more probably produce anarchy. The innovators of language still sometimes retain, for Johnson, the characteristics of pedantic antiquarians with an absurd fondness for the obsolete. More often however, they are revealed as more dangerous modernists with no respect for established forms, in his reaction to whom Johnson himself can take on something of the tone of the antiquarians he ridicules, for example in his willingness to defend the "corruptions" of language, as he understands them, when they are sanctioned by time, in terms which anticipate to a remarkable degree Burkes's willingness to defend the system of Old Corruption in the unreformed House of Commons—rotten and pocket boroughs, sinecures and pensions—against the reforming zeal of philosophical radicalism. In Johnson's late and very Burke-like political writings, the dangers of pedantry have been entirely forgotten, and "innovators" in politics are unambiguously identified as inhumane rationalists who cannot grasp the value of the security guaranteed by the persistence of custom, and who do not understand that the constitution, like all the works of merely human tongues and hands, and whatever Coke or Blackstone may say of its "perfection," *must* be in some measure imperfect.

To Johnson, therefore, the process of fixing and ascertaining the language was not, as it had been to Swift, a part of the same enterprise as that of improving and correcting it; rather its opposite. It is an attempt to ascertain what is customary usage, however vicious it may often seem, and to fix it beyond the reach of reformers and innovators, as well as beyond

that of those who, speaking and writing incorrectly, are likely to introduce
further corruptions into the language. It is in this context that we should
understand Johnson's impatience with theory—his lack of interest in the
question of the origin and purpose of language, and his pragmatic insistence
on usage—which relates to the sense we discovered in his political writings,
that simply to discuss political ideas, regardless of the object, was the mark
of a political malcontent. Thus, in the *Preface,* he seems to refer to Locke's
notion that words are the signs of *ideas,* but he is insufficiently interested
in the notion to avoid expressing the wish, two lines later, that these signs
might be made permanent, "like the *things* (my italics) which they denote"—
an expression which entirely misses the point of Locke's definition. "Grammar," he announces at the start of his own Grammar, "*is the art of using
words properly.*" What he means by "properly" we shall shortly discover, but
it is the emphasis on "use" that I want to point to here. Like other "practical"
grammarians of the mid century, Johnson has no interest in "rational grammar" or with the theoretical status of grammatical rules, but simply in the
necessity of speaking and writing in accordance with those rules, understood
as derived from the practice, not the theory, of language.

Johnson announces his intentions as a lexicographer at the start of the
Plan: his concern is with the "perpetuity" of the language, and his aim is
"to preserve the purity and ascertain the meaning of our English idiom."
As far as pronunciation goes, he is concerned to "fix" it, while accepting
that such variations as have already come into use cannot perhaps be eradicated: in the matter of the selection of words, careful divisions are to be
made, so that they may be kept, between "words of general use; words
employed chiefly in poetry; words obsolete; words which are admitted only
by particular writers, yet not in themselves improper; words used only in
burlesque writing; and words impure and barbarous." The latter are "carefully to be eradicated wherever they are found, and thus

> will our language be laid down, distinct in its minutest subdi-
> visions, and resolved into its elemental principles. And who upon
> this survey can forbear to wish, that these fundamental atoms of
> our speech might obtain the firmness and immutability of the
> primogenial and constituent particles of matter, that they might
> retain their substance while they alter their appearance, and be
> varied and compounded, yet not destroyed.

This, like the wish in the *Preface* that words might become as permanent
as things, is an aspect of that attempt to reify, precisely to "thingify," the
usage of English speakers, so that, as I said earlier, usage is hypostatized

and opposed to what people do actually say. Usage becomes, as it were, a general will, how people ought and how ideally they want to speak, whether they do speak or want to speak like that at all. This is related to an important idea of the constitution common to all who, in the eighteenth century, found themselves in the position of having to defend the revolution of 1688, but were anxious to minimize if not to deny the possibility of any future revolution: that the constitution is, so to speak, the established and permanent articulation of our liberty, which guarantees that liberty against our licence, rather than the immediate expression of our freedom, as a changing language or a changing constitution might announce a change in the will of the people. It is an idea of linguistic and political liberty in which most of the rhetoric is entirely concerned with regulation and restraint, such as Cowper uses in his lines on the Gordon Riots:

> Let active laws apply the needful curb
> To guard the peace that riot would disturb,
> And liberty preserv'd from wild excess,
> Shall raise no feuds for armies to suppress . . .
> She loses in such storms her very name,
> And fierce licentiousness should bear the blame.

The attempt is to define a language which will as far as possible (in the words of the Declaration of Right of 1689) bind "themselves, their heirs and posterities for ever"—the expression made much of by Johnson and Burke in their political writings, and attacked as meaningless by Paine in *The Rights of Man*.

Before we examine Johnson's estimate of his likely success in this undertaking, we should look further at his notion of usage, and ask, in particular, whose usage it was that he sought to fix, to make permanent. The immediate and most obvious answer can be found by leafing through the dictionary itself: like the OED, it is to be regarded as a dictionary of the written, not the spoken language, and of the written language as it is to be found in the pages of polite authors, though as far as possible purged of the barbarisms that from time to time even the politest have admitted. The earliest author generally cited is Sidney; and indeed Johnson remarks of writers before the Restoration that their works are *"the wells of English undefiled,"* the pure sources of genuine diction;

> From the authors which rose in the time of *Elizabeth,* a speech
> might be formed adequate to all the purposes of use and elegance.
> If the language of theology were extracted from *Hooker* and the

> translation of the Bible; the terms of natural knowledge from *Bacon;* the phrases of policy, war and navigation from *Raleigh;* the dialect of poetry and fiction from *Spenser* and *Sidney;* and the diction of common life from *Shakespeare,* few ideas would be lost to mankind, for want of *English* words, in which they might be expressed.

The claim for the authority of such writers, it must be noted, lies for Johnson less perhaps in their politeness than in their evident excellence as writers, and their linguistic purity is seen mostly as a matter of their being (unlike later writers) comparatively free of "*Gallick* structure and phraseology." From this it would seem that good usage is to be defined nationalistically, and is more likely to be found in a plain than in a sophisticated style—an attitude foreshadowed in such remarks in the *Plan,* as that "our language [is to] be considered so far as it is our own." In spite of his including some extraordinary latinisms in his word list—"dignotion," for example, or "exolete," or "incompossible," or "clancular"—this notion of Englishness seems to suggest that for Johnson good usage is a matter of speaking and writing plainly, without unnecessary sophistication or affectation.

This does not turn out to mean, however, that good usage is the characteristic of a wider social group than that of the "best speakers" in whom most eighteenth century grammarians locate it; as we will see by observing Johnson's remarks on such topics as dialect words, terms of art, and pronunciation.

> The English language has properly no dialects; the style of writers has no professed diversity in the use of words, or of their flexions, and terminations, nor differs but by different degrees of skill or care. The oral diction is uniform in no spacious country, but has less variation in England than in most other nations of equal extent. The language of the northern counties retains many words now out of use, but which are commonly of the genuine Teutonick race, and is uttered with a pronunciation which now seems harsh and rough, but was probably used by our ancestors. The northern speech is therefore not barbarous but obsolete.

This passage is a remarkable justification for choosing the words to be represented in the dictionary from the diction of the polite, while appearing only to be guided by a consideration of general usage and genuine Englishness. Thus the assertion that English has "no dialects" is probably aimed at the Scots, and is supported by the belief that regional varieties of English differ only "by different degrees of skill or care," which must certainly imply that polite writers are the models of good usage, because they are, not the most polite—that is, apparently, not the issue—but the most skilled writers. The value to Johnson of this position is that it represents English, not as a collection of different Englishes, one of them "official" but each of them with its own integrity and tradition, but as one language only, which some write better than others. The unity of the language community is represented not as something to be struggled for, but as something already there, and at the same time as the unity of all British writers is thereby asserted, the existence of a hierarchy of writers, and of social divisions within that community, is asserted also. The strategy is familiar to us by now: to represent the community as at once naturally unified, and naturally stratified.

Of equal interest is the assertion that the "oral" language of "the northern counties" (which may here include lowlands of Scotland) "retains" many words "now out of use." It is not barbarous, and indeed if we were to take here what Johnson proposes as the test of purity in the *Preface*—an adherence to the teutonic original of English, wariness of gallicisms—we might expect it to be commended as purer, certainly more permanent, than metropolitan English. This would be a conclusion clean counter to most contemporary opinions of dialect, which James Buchanan, for example, who sees the imposition of the metropolitan standard of English on Scotland as a means of bringing the two nations into harmony, characterizes not only as "vicious" but as "notoriously vague and unstable," "continually fluctuating." Johnson knows too much about language to fall into the same error, and can only avoid attributing to the "language of the northern counties" the virtues of permanence and stability by saying that northern words, apparently barbarous, are in fact "obsolete": there could be no clearer example, both of usage being defined as only the usage of the polite, and, in the process, of "usage" being hypostatized in order to be opposed to the words people do actually use. The standard of what is obsolete here can only be current metropolitan language, even though northern dialect words are precisely current, "retained," in the north. By this strategy Johnson can omit from his word list all sorts of words, of properly teutonic origin, on grounds which thus establish the primacy of polite usage whether it has the sanction of long-established custom or not; and the notions of the customary and the current can now be manipulated in such a way as to ensure that whatever is in London, is right for everywhere else.

Johnson is on easier ground, with Rice and Buchanan, on the matter of pronunciation, the durability of which he believes is of great moment to the durability of the language. Johnson offers as a rule that we should regard those as "the most elegant speakers" who are found "to deviate least from the written words": their pronunciation he describes as the "solemn" one, and he warns against using instead the "cursory" and "colloquial" pronunciation as a standard; for though the solemn is by no means "immutable and permanent," the colloquial is vague and uncertain, and liable to "capricious innovation." Grammarians who have based the standard of pronunciation on the cursory have often established "the jargon of the lowest of the people as the model of speech."

The polite clearly emerge as the guardians of the customary, and not of the merely current, in Johnson's discussion, in the *Preface,* of whether the specialized vocabularies of various trades, especially mechanical trades, should be included in his word list; and the less than polite now emerge as too fickle, mutable, inconstant, for their vocabularies to form any part of the permanent language. In his discussion of terms of art in general, Johnson applies different standards according to whether he is dealing with the language of the learned professions or of the mechanical trades. The former are generally included if they have acquired metaphorical meanings which have extended their use outside the professional circles in which they were originally used, or if they may be of use to readers or in the business of daily life. Johnson originally intended to include the vocabulary of the trades on the same basis, but found it impossible to do, as he frankly acknowledges—the defect, he insists, was unavoidable:

> I could not visit caverns to learn the miner's language, nor take
> a voyage to perfect my skill in the dialect of navigation, nor visit
> the warehouses of merchants, and shops of artificers, to gain the
> names of wares, tools and operations, of which no mention is
> found in books; what favourable accident, or easy enquiry brought
> within my reach, has not been neglected; but it had been a
> hopeless labour to glean up words, by courting living informa-
> tion, and contesting with the sullenness of one, and the roughness
> of another.

The note of apology, however, with which Johnson introduces his remarks on this topic, soon fades, and he makes it clear that he does not at all "lament" his "omissions";

> Of the laborious and mercantile part of the people, the diction
> is in a great measure casual and mutable; many of their terms
> are formed for some temporary or local convenience, and though
> current at certain times and places, are in others utterly unknown.

This fugitive cant, which is always in a state of increase or decay, cannot be regarded as any part of the durable materials of a language, and therefore must be suffered to perish with other things unworthy of preservation.

Here the "laborious and mercantile part of the people" appear as a mob, as the *mobile vulgus*—as the rabble whose "inconstancy" is lengthily described by Johnson in *The False Alarm* and *The Patriot*. The stability of the language of the *polite,* and the stability of their constitution are alike threatened by the mutability of the people, who properly considered, have no interest in either matter. They are no part of the true language community, which is now a closed circle of the polite whose language is now presented as durable and permanent; and they form no part of the political community—only "submission" is "the duty of the ignorant . . . they have no skill in the art of government, nor any interest in the dissensions of the great."

But however committed he was to the ideal of a permanent and durable language, Johnson was convinced that his labours were doomed to failure, largely because they involved an attempt to establish the written language as a standard for the spoken; and "sounds are too volatile and subtile for legal restraints." It is evident that between the written and spoken language there was for Johnson the same opposition as between the polite and durable, and the vulgar and inconstant languages—not least because the most elegant speakers pronounce words in a way closer to how they are spelled. Throughout Johnson's writings on language the greater permanence of the written is opposed to "the boundless chaos of living speech": the written language is law, the spoken is anarchy; and the dictionary is as it were the written, methodized account of customary usages, *leges non scriptae,* which attempts to preserve our liberties against the anarchic licence of our actual speech. But the attempt, as I have said, is felt to be vain; for there are at work

> causes of change, which, though slow in their operation, and invisible in their progress are perhaps as much superiour to human resistance, as the revolutions of the sky, or intumescence of the tide.

They include the growth and spread of commerce, and so an increasing contact with other languages; the division of society into laborious and leisured classes, whereby the latter have opportunity to expand the stock of knowledge and therefore of words; the increase in politeness, now again represented as a force for mutability, and always liable to introduce capricious figures of speech; and the spread of translations, which adopt too many terms and idioms from their originals. "If the changes we fear be thus irresistible," Johnson concludes,

> what remains but to acquiesce with silence, as in the other insurmountable distresses of humanity? It remains that we retard what we cannot repel, that we palliate what we cannot cure. Life may be lengthened by care, though death cannot be ultimately defeated: tongues, like governments, have a natural tendency to degeneration; we have long preserved our constitution, let us make some struggles for our language.

But when we remember Johnson's earlier remark, that "particular combinations of letters" do not have "much influence on human happiness" we may suspect an irony in Johnson's regret that we must "acquiesce" in the inevitable transformation of language, "as in the other insurmountable distresses of humanity"; and the ironic note is confirmed when we recall that at one point Johnson has described the lexicographer's task as to "embalm" language—the task of securing it from "corruption and decay" presupposes in these terms that it is already dead, as indeed by one of Johnson's metaphors it is. For the phrase "the boundless chaos of living speech" suggests precisely that the life of a language is in its speakers, and even, perhaps, in its less polite speakers, who depart most in their pronunciation from the written word, and from whom Johnson was unwilling to court "living information." "No dictionary of a living language ever can be perfect," he writes at the end of the *Preface,* "since while it is hastening to publication, some words are budding, and some falling away"; and that image of an organic process in language—"budding" here a metaphor taken from Horace, the best classical authority for the sovereignty of common usage—seems to suggest a pleasure taken in the mutability of language, and not a merely reluctant acquiescence.

It is an attitude reminiscent of one, at least, of Johnson's political essays—an early one, before the Middlesex election and the American War—*The Bravery of the English Common Soldiers*—where he sees that bravery as something achieved not merely in spite of the lack of regularity and discipline in the English army, but because of qualities intimately related to that lack—the independence, even insolence, of the "English vulgar," who are raised to acts of courage by being "impatient of reproach." It is a jingoistic and comforting vision of Englishness, whose trick is to pretend that in a democracy all are *free,* whether enfranchised or not; it confirms the free genius of the English against the servility of the French, and reassures a polite readership that the other ranks are as keen on giving the French a bloody nose as are the officers. It is in terms of the same reverence for English Liberty that Johnson expresses his fervent hope that no academy on the French model would be established in England:

> In absolute governments, there is sometimes a general reverence paid to all that has the sanction of power, and the countenance of greatness. How little this is the state of our country needs not to be told. We live in an age in which it is a kind of publick sport to refuse all respect that cannot be enforced. The edicts of an English Academy would probably be read by many, only that they might be sure to disobey them.
>
> If an academy should be established for the cultivation of our stile, which I, who can never wish to see dependence multiplied, hope the spirit of English liberty will hinder or destroy.

This jingoism, and Johnson's irony alike, may both be defensive, but they serve to complicate the more closed conservatism of most of his writing on politics and language; and they keep in play a libertarian ideology, which could be used, certainly, as a means of curtailing the liberty it pretended to endorse, but whose implications for both politics and language could be taken a good deal further than Johnson himself would have approved.

LAURA QUINNEY

Johnson in Mourning

For thou art heavenly, she an empty dream
—MILTON

It is well remembered that Johnson mistrusted "the dangerous prevalence of imagination," and it is likely that this mistrust would have influenced his literary criticism. Such apprehension seems active in two particularly uncompromising interrogations of poetic license—one from the *Life of Cowley* and the other from the *Life of Milton,* poets whose political activity and aesthetic practice Johnson had already found reason to think perverse.

Cowley, as it turns out, invented the passion and the woman of his poem "The Mistress." Frivolous as this invention is, it gives Johnson strange pause. He regards Cowley's fabrication as a kind of literary demonology, as the generation of a phantom, but one whose uncertain charm he is willing to evoke in echoes from his dearest authors, Shakespeare, Cervantes, and Pindar (never mind Cowley). To Johnson, the unreality of "The Mistress" has its own real depth: "The desire of pleasing has in different men produced actions of heroism, and effusions of wit; but it seems as reasonable to appear the champion as the poet of an 'airy nothing,' and to quarrel as to write for what Cowley might have learned from his master Pindar to call the 'dream of a shadow' " [*Lives of the Poets;* all further references to this text will be abbreviated as *LP*]. From this oddly loving invocation of shadows, Johnson moves to warn against their creation and indulgence. He portrays Cowley as a writer who dissipated himself in his fictions, like a daydreamer rioting in fantasy:

Published in this volume for the first time. © 1986 by Laura Quinney.

It is surely not difficult, in the solitude of a college, or in the
bustle of the world, to find useful studies and serious employment. No man needs to be so burthened with life as to squander
it in voluntary dreams of fictitious occurences. The man that sits
down to suppose himself charged with treason or peculation, and
heats his mind to an elaborate purgation of his character from
crimes which he was never within the possibility of committing,
differs only by the infrequency of his folly from him who praises
beauty which he never saw, complains of jealousy which he never
felt; supposes himself sometimes invited, and sometimes forsaken;
fatigues his fancy, and ransacks his memory, for images which
may exhibit the gaiety of hope, or the gloominess of despair, and
dresses his imaginary Chloris or Phyllis sometimes in flowers
fading as her beauty, and sometimes in gems lasting as her
virtues.

At Paris, as secretary to Lord Jermin, he was engaged in
transacting things of real importance with real men and real
women, and at that time did not much employ his thoughts
upon phantoms of gallantry.

A *Rambler* gravely and evocatively calls daydreaming "this secret prod-
igality of being" (No. 89). Though the picture of Cowley wreathed in such
self-stimulating fantasy is more comic than horrifying, Johnson also strikes
some gratuitously ominous notes. It is tipping the picture toward horror to
compare Cowley's amorous inventions to paranoid fantasies of criminal, and
even "treasonous" guilt. Johnson is surprisingly prepared to confuse indulgence in a literary convention with a case of psychosis, when he suggests
that, like any madman, Cowley lost track of his fiction's unreality, and
"heated his mind" with the imaginary events of his poetry. He was so far
entangled, Johnson implies, that he needed the world to set him free, for
at last, the passage concludes with eerie emphasis, "At Paris . . . he was
engaged in transacting things of real importance with real men and real
women."

What stops one here is not the association of danger and poetry, but
the extent to which Johnson has forced this association. Displeased to find
that "The Mistress" is not autobiography, Johnson devises a different biographical significance for it. But he pursues an uncharacteristic literalism in
assuming that Cowley had to have become psychologically involved with
his fictions. It is this inappropriately elaborated biographical reading that I
find most interesting.

Johnson undertakes such a reading again in an hostile paragraph on Milton, a paragraph whose obstinacy and evasiveness prove revealing. Johnson is reflecting on the autobiographical details of the invocations to *Paradise Lost,* when he finds opportunity for an episode of antirepublicanism:

> Milton, being now cleared from all effects of his disloyalty, had nothing required from him but the common duty of living in quiet, to be rewarded with the common right of protection: but this, which, when he skulked from the approach of his King, was perhaps more than he hoped, seems not to have satisfied him; for no sooner is he safe than he finds himself in danger, *fallen on evil days and evil tongues, and with darkness and with danger compass'd round.* This darkness, had his eyes been better employed, had undoubtedly deserved compassion: but to add the mention of danger was ungrateful and unjust. He was fallen indeed on *evil days;* the time was come in which regicides could no longer boast their wickedness. But of *evil tongues* for Milton to complain, required impudence at least equal to his other powers; Milton, whose warmest advocates must allow, that he never spared any asperity of reproach or brutality of insolence.
>
> (*LP*)

What sarcasm is here leveled against one of the more disarming and gentle passages in *Paradise Lost.* Johnson practices some subtle distortion of Milton's poetry in order to clear the way for this energetic denunciation, or else practices this denunciation in order to distract himself from Milton's poetry. This paragraph misrepresents the tone and emphasis of the Invocation to Book Seven (as if that lyrical interlude were just carping on the fantasy of "one just man"), as well as assuming, with strange bitterness, that Milton's investment in this view of himself was absolute, and that he here reproduced his full mind in all its unmediated "impudence." This last assumption—that Milton is almost uncomfortably accessible in his poem—shares the biographical literalism of the paragraph on Cowley (as, in both cases, Johnson seems prepared to show that poetry engages the dangerous prevalence of the narcissistic imagination).

I now wish to look at what Johnson has left out in this perversely irritated reading of Milton's invocation. He has left out its sadness. Bitingly he summons up every term of the famous list—the evil days and evil tongues, darkness and danger—until he comes to the last word, which in Milton turns the spirit around:

> Standing on earth, not rapt above the pole
> More safe I sing with mortal voice, unchanged
> To hoarse or mute, though fallen on evil days,
> On evil days though fallen, and evil tongues;
> In darkness, and with dangers compassed round
> And solitude . . .
>
> (23–28)

This list is so fluid that it is beginning to seem easy. Then the rhythmic singularity of "And solitude" startles it. The word itself is surprising, since it is the only one in the series without moral nuance. Milton has his verse interrupt its rehearsal of an aggrandizing fantasy, to remember the experience of pain without grandeur or purpose. In this state, recalled to his separation from the world—all passion, all passivity—Milton can evoke the other-worldly warmth of his Muse: "yet not alone, while thou/Visit'st my slumbers nightly" (28–29).

Johnson chose to ignore this pathos in his account of the second invocation. Not that, given the context, he had any use for it: but then, he made the context. He chose to be angry with Milton, as with Cowley, and he facilitated his anger by means of a somewhat awkward biographical fallacy. It is as if he preferred to be angry, or more profoundly, wished to preserve a model of poetry—of poets' relationships to their work, and his own relationship to them—in which a response such as anger would be appropriate.

Johnson's loyalty to this model was established early in his career. In his first writing on Milton, he temporarily abandoned the model, but, after an uncertain pause, gratefully recovered it. Roughly thirty years before he wrote the *Life of Milton*, Johnson lent his support to the efforts of William Lauder, who was, through a not very clever ruse, busy to charge Milton with plagiarism. Lauder had found a Latin translation of *Paradise Lost*, and interpolated passages from it into some of Milton's known Latin sources; he then passed these off for the originals ("An Essay on Milton's Use and Imitation of the Moderns in His *Paradise Lost*," 1750). He was detected in short order, but not before Johnson had written Lauder's Preface, a mistake he was now forced to undo by writing Lauder's retraction. Johnson offered this revisionist scholar only a distant and tentative concurrence, it is true (his disinterested Preface represents the pamphlet as a penetrating source study, not as an exposé); yet in his willingness to cooperate, Johnson seems to have dallied with a wish fulfillment.

But if he wished to eradicate Milton's authority, he was relieved to reinstate it. The Preface as well as the retraction carefully preserve Milton's

special status; only in the subtle differences of their figural language do these
two essays reveal what stake has been hazarded. Aside from one bow to "this
mighty genius," the Preface avoids recalling the agency of Milton. *"Paradise
Lost,"* "the work," and similar phrases take over as the subjects and objects
of Johnson's sentences, as when, for example, he pictures the poem's development in silent self-propulsion: [Voice of Lauder] "Having thus traced
the original of this work, I was naturally induced to continue my search to
the collateral relations, which it might be supposed to have contracted, in
its progress to maturity." Here is a difficult interpenetration of anthropo-
morphic and denaturalizing language; the poem may grow up and marry,
but its extension is purely contractual, and its "maturity" as artificial as a
bond's. Johnson uses these metaphors from law and, elsewhere, from architecture to elude the organic model of authorship and composition. A
poem engineers itself, or is engineered by some remote, anonymous builder.
So Johnson's figures imply, when he explains that source study aims to
provide

> a view of the fabric gradually rising, perhaps from small begin-
> nings, till its foundation rests in the centre, and its turrets sparkle
> in the skies; to trace back the structure, through all its varieties,
> to the simplicity of its first plan; to find what was first projected,
> whence the scheme was taken, how it was improved, by what
> assistance it was executed, and from what stores the materials
> were collected, whether its founder dug them from the quarries
> of nature, or demolished other buildings to embellish his own.

In this extended metaphor, literature makes its appearance as a depersonalized
artifact, shaped by impassive intervention and far remote from psychological
verisimilitude.

From this experiment with an autonomy for literature, Johnson returns
to the familiarity of the poets. His retraction restores Milton to authorship
and sublimity, and paternal dominion, as it restores Johnson to his place
in a hierarchy of human relations. This alteration can be seen in the altered
configuration of one particular metaphor—the figure of the sun coming out
from behind the clouds. In the Preface, Milton's poem shakes off its shady
author to emerge in independent glory. With this assertion of independence,
the essay, like a manifesto, begins: "It is now more than half a century since
the 'Paradise Lost,' having broke through the cloud with which the unpop-
ularity of the author, for a time, obscured it, has attracted the general
admiration of mankind." But in the retraction, the metaphor recovers its
original Shakespearean configuration, testifying to the invincible sovereignty

of Milton, king and father: now, with the detection of Lauder's forgeries, "the shade which began to gather on the splendour of Milton [has been] totally dispersed." The retraction throughout displays excessive guilt and egregious humility, treating the attack on Milton as an attack on "truth" and "mankind," and hastening to reconsolidate Milton's authority by reserving for him the language of monolithic power.

As if the outcome of this crisis motivated the unusual consistency, or conservatism, of his writing, Johnson remained forevermore faithful to this lionization of Milton, and to the personalization of literature. It is clear from his interest in biography that he wished above all to sustain the company of the poets. He was for this reason willing to overcathect occasions for anger, such as the memory of Milton's politics, or his personal failings, or his use of blank verse. Johnson is then able to make reparation with tender and remorseful acknowledgments, often staying his regrets until final, sonorous paragraphs. At the end of the Life of Milton, he transforms Milton's "impudent," self-imposed isolation into heroism, and turns his own recalcitrance to mourning:

> But, of all the borrowers from Homer, Milton is perhaps the least indebted. He was naturally a thinker for himself, confident of his own abilities, and disdainful of help or hindrance: he did not refuse admission to the thought or images of his predecessors, but he did not seek them. From his contemporaries he neither courted nor received support; there is in his writings nothing by which the pride of other authors might be gratified, or favour gained; no exchange of praise, nor solicitation of support. His great works were performed under discountenance, and in blindness, but difficulties vanished at his touch; he was born for whatever is arduous; and his work is not the greatest of heroick poems, only because it is not the first.

> (LP)

Yet this account of Johnson's fondness for biography does not quite explain why he obscures the pathos of the Invocation to Book Seven. In order to explore this problem, I'm going to look at another example of the suppression of pathos in the Life of Milton. Here also Johnson treats a powerful moment in Milton's poetry as if it were mediocre and trivial, little interesting except from a biographical point of view. In an especially brisk paragraph, Johnson summarizes some vicissitudes of Milton's domestic history:

> About this time his first wife died in childbed, having left him three daughters. As he probably did not much love her, he did

not long continue the appearance of lamenting her; but after a short time married Catherine, the daughter of one Captain Woodcock of hackney; a woman doubtless educated in opinions like his own. She died, within a year, of childbirth, or some distemper that followed it; and her husband honored her memory with a poor sonnet.

(LP)

It is long since "Methought I saw my late espoused saint" has been considered "a poor sonnet." If Johnson was indifferent to the poem, indifferent enough to dismiss it with an almost ostentatious economy, he may have chosen this chill response out of loyalty to a standard more compelling than taste.

Boswell reports what would seem to be a similarly motivated elision in the *Life of Parnell*. Parnell was promoted to a vicarage, "But," says Johnson, "his prosperity did not last long. His end, whatever was its cause, was now approaching" (LP). To produce this disinterested summary, Johnson struck his first, and more sonorous, version: "But his prosperity was clouded by that which took away all his powers of enjoying either profit or pleasure, the death of his wife, whom he is said to have lamented with such sorrow, as hastened his end" [*Life of Johnson;* all further references to this text will be abbreviated as *LJ*]. This sentence echoes the famous conclusions of the *Preface to the Dictionary* ("I have protracted my work till most of those whom I wished to please have sunk into the grave, and success and miscarriage are empty sounds"); it is as if Johnson had suppressed the sentence in order to silence the echo of his own words. Boswell is alert to this suppressed resonance, remarking keenly, "I should have thought that Johnson, who had felt the severe affliction from which Parnell never recovered, would have preserved this passage" (LJ). Johnson was apparently very unwilling to allow, or acknowledge, such an identification with a widower. (I have found only one example, from a letter written not long after Elizabeth Johnson's death; and even here, Johnson is compassionating a friend, not a poem or a biographical subject.)

Johnson's diaries reveal that he was familiar with the experiences of "Methought I saw my late espoused saint." Yet they also testify to an ambivalence about his mourning which may have helped him to suppress potential identifications. A sermon written for his wife's funeral is peculiarly emphatic about the inaccessibility of the dead; in grief, "The whole mind becomes a gloomy vacuity, without any image or form of pleasure, a chaos of confused wishes, directed to no particular end, or to that which, while we wish, we cannot hope to obtain; for the dead will not revive; those whom

God has called away from the present state of existence, can be seen no more
in it; we must go to them; but they cannot return to us" (*Sermons*). This
urgent self-admonishing gave way, and, in a prayer composed a month later,
Johnson pleads, "O Lord, Governor of Heaven and Earth, in whose hands
are embodied and departed spirits, if thou hast ordained the souls of the
dead to minister to the living, and appointed my departed wife to have care
of me, grant that I may enjoy the good effects of her attention and minis-
tration, whether exercised by appearance, impulses, dreams, or in any other
manner agreeable to thy government" [*Prayers and Meditations;* all further
references to this text will be abbreviated as *PM*]. But the violence of these
wishes made him anxious; at the same date, he prays to be preserved from
"fruitless grief, or tumultuous imaginations" (*PM*), and a year later, he
remains fearful about the teleology of his mourning: "Apr. 29. 1753. I
know not whether I do not too much indulge the vain longings of affection;
but I hope they intenerate my heart & that when I die like my Tetty this
affection will be acknowledged in a happy interview & that in the meantime
I am incited by it to piety. I will however not deviate too much from
common & received methods of devotion" (*PM*). Johnson treats his own
grief as dubious and alien, to be suppressed in favor of ceremonies "common
and received."

   This anxiety about emotional deviation seems to have encouraged Johnson in some linguistic eccentricities. He developed the habit of using abbreviations and foreign phrases to allude to mourning—this in his private
papers, which he wrote for his reading alone, and many of which he succeeded
in destroying just before his death. Here he keeps detailed accounts of his
personal mourning rites, at the same time that he is driven to euphemism.
He reports praying for Tetty in church, and wants to confess his emotion,
but not without changing languages: "I repeated mentally the commendation
of her with the utmost fervour larme à l'oeil before the reception of each
element at the altar. I repeated it again in the pew, in the garden before
dinner, in the garden before departure, at home at night. I hope I did not
sin. Fluunt lacrymae" (*PM*). When he wants to say that he has cried, Johnson
flees to foreign phrases, as if there were a language within language where
sorrow might be contained. Later in the journal of his prayers, he stops
writing the words for death, using instead the abbreviations "θ" and "θφ,"
short for "dead" and "dead friends" (*PM*).

   It should be remembered that not only Latin and Greek, but also
French, belonged among the dead languages to Johnson: they were his literary
languages, confined to reading, writing, and quotation. Their silence no
doubt made them attractive to secrecy and euphemism. Johnson hid not

only his mourning, but his inner life more generally, under the cloak of such euphemisms; in 1784, he repented his "μ χ. 'αισχ-νο κεν β," apparently meaning that he had been racked by "melancholy, shameful thoughts," and "vain resolutions" (*PM*). Johnson allowed his sadness and anxiety to take harbor in dead languages. Without rising to speech, invisible pain transformed itself into their silence. Interestingly enough, the silent experience of reading undergoes the same transformation. In another ambivalently informative note, Johnson adopts Latin when he confesses his vulnerability to literature: [Good Friday, 1765] "Slept ill. Rose. Mr. Lye. To Church at the lesson; heard ill. Graham. Sat at home. Read Nelson, then read Temple. In reading Nelson thought on Death cum lacrimis" (*PM*). If Johnson's sadness fled to other languages, it pivoted on them, and returned in their literatures. Hester Thrale wrote (bringing us back to the question of Milton's sonnet), "Of the pathetic in poetry he never liked to speak" (*Anecdotes*). In spite of this continence, he could not resist Church Latin, for, Thrale goes on,

> It was not however from the want of a susceptible heart that he hated to cite tender expressions, for he was more strongly and more violently affected by the force of words representing ideas capable of affecting him at all, than any other man in the world I believe; and when he would try to repeat the celebrated *Prosa Ecclesiastica pro Mortuis,* as it is called, beginning *Dies irae, Dies illa,* he could never pass the stanza ending thus, *Tantus labor non sit cassus* [Let not such toil be in vain], without bursting into a flood of tears. . . .
>
> (*Anecdotes*)

In this account, Thrale candidly shows that what mattered to Johnson was not the sentiment so much as the rhetoric—the texture of spoken signifiers. The "force of words" disarmed him to such an extent that he suppressed them in silence, "never [liking] to speak" of moving poetry, and "[hating] to cite tender expressions." But in the silence of writing, he was much more willing to cite, and it is here that Greek and Latin quotations really figure. In that one example of his identification with a widower, Johnson reverts to Euripides under the pressure of distress [to Thomas Warton, 21 December 1754]:

> You know poor Mr. Dodsly has lost his Wife, I believe he is much affected. I hope he will not suffer so much as I yet suffer for the loss of mine.

Οἴμι· τι δ'ὄιμι; θνῆτα γὰρ πεπόνθαμεν.

[Alas! Yet why alas? For we were born to mortal fate.]

I have ever since seemed to myself broken off from mankind
a kind of solitary wanderer in the wild of life, without any certain
direction, or fixed point of view. A gloomy gazer on a World to
which I have little relation.

Quoting this Euripides actually seems to make Johnson change the
terms of his lament; sympathetic identification then yields to a wildly literary
language of solitude. It is as if Johnson felt his isolation, his "gloomy
gazing," to be bound up with the experience of Greek literature. He may,
in turn, have suppressed this association in Milton's case because Milton
wrote in the too audible words of the living language, English.

It is impressive to find literary pathos among the other phenomena,
God and Death, which Johnson buried in the silence of great anxiety. If
Thrale's remark is to be credited, then Johnson was reluctant to talk about
"the pathetic" in public, though he sometimes acknowledged his literary
distress in writing. This self-imposed muteness, this silent writing from
books to books, dramatically separates literature from what Johnson called
"the living world." Yet, along with the rest of his own work, diaries aside,
Johnson's writing on pathos is deliberately public, conscious, and glad of
its audience. It treats pathos as a place of isolating trauma from which one
hastens back to the world. In his notes to *Othello,* Johnson finishes his
plodding and weary emendations of the murder scene, then startlingly avows:
"I am glad that I have ended my revisal of this dreadful scene. It is not to
be endured." Johnson writes as if the encrypted horror of the scene were
closing over behind him, and he were once again free to speak amid human
company. This flight to "the living world" seems still more dramatic in his
famous remarks on the death of Cordelia. Only under the canopy of the
public opinion will Johnson divulge his pain at reading *Lear:* "And, if my
sensations could add any thing to the general suffrage, I might relate, that
I was many years ago so shocked by Cordelia's death, that I know not whether
I ever endured to read again the last scenes of the play till I undertook to
revise them as an editor." This admission, it will be remembered, appears
in defense of Tate's *Lear,* which Johnson seriously favored. His preference
for Tate makes it clear that by "shock" he meant something less refreshing
than the "sublime" of his contemporaries, which is openly associated with
pleasure and the desire for repetition.

Johnson's concern about the secret inhumanity of literature appears,
here and elsewhere, in his exaggerated reconstitution of the difference between books and "the living world." This difference, in turn, he exemplified

in his critical portraits of antiquarians, scientists, and scholars, whom he liked to represent as dusty and spectral. An Oxford fellow whom he had known in their shared youth he dismissed for being now "Lost in a convent's solitary gloom" (*LJ*). He favored such figures of immersion and attenuation in his pejorative remarks on book-learning. In a *Rambler* (No. 180) called "The study of life not to be neglected for the sake of books" (a superfluous command, one would think), he distinguishes "the scholastic race" as "Men bred in shades and silence." This Gothic vocabulary yields to still more unsavory language in another *Rambler* (No. 177), in which a former scholar confesses that he abandoned his studies when he found his mind "contracted and stiffened by solitude." This grave degeneration led to departures from companionability, a fault that, says the ex-student, "I soon discovered to be one of those intellectual diseases which a wise man should make haste to cure. I therefore resolved for a time to shut my books, and learn again the art of conversation; to defecate and clear my mind by brisker motions and stronger impulses: and to unite myself once more to the living generation." In keeping with the metaphor of disease, this passage describes the experience of the mind in highly palpable terms drawn from the experience of the body ("contracted," "stiffened," "defecate and clear," "brisker motions," "stronger impulses"). With this too vivid language, a contagious desiccation seems to creep from the student's books into his mind. This hidden figure of metastasis, the metastasis of death in fact, gives a special resonance to the student's resolve that he will "unite [himself] once more to the living generation."

This touch of the macabre is typical of the apotropaic distaste with which the *Rambler* chides pedantry, yet its dread of an encroaching, papery lifelessness is a red herring. With this motif of the arid pedant, Johnson misrepresents his anxiety about the effects of literary experience. Such moments are meant not to portray any real "danger" of scholarship, so much as they are designed to evoke the pathos of "the living world." In the character of Gelidus, the frozen scholar, Johnson invents a solipsist to chastise for being "unqualified to perform those offices by which the concatenation of society is preserved, and mutual tenderness excited and maintained" (No. 24). This figure is so absorbed in treatises and calculations that he has arrived at a zombie's self-sufficiency: "He spends his time in the highest room of his house, into which none of his family are suffered to enter; and when he comes down to his dinner, or his rest, he walks about like a stranger that is there only for a day, without any token of regard or tenderness. He has totally divested himself of all human sensations. . . ." What faint drollery there is in this description disappears when Johnson reaches his end, the sudden heightening of pathos with the return of the "living generation":

"Thus lives this great philosopher, insensible to every spectacle of distress, and unmoved by the loudest call of social nature, for want of considering that men are designed for the succour and comfort of each other." Gelidus, the figure of such perfect, "unmoved" "insensibility," is clearly a straw man, whom Johnson conjures up and dismisses on his way to something else. What seems to draw him here is the imperative to evoke sadness and apprehension for the fragility of people in their interdependence.

Johnson tends to represent "the living world" this way—as if it were cast into darkness by some unseen spirit of antagonism. "The living world" then turns out to be as much a tenuous shadow as it is a warm and vigorous presence. Johnson appears to have been riveted by this trope of the pathos of the living. (It will be noted that even in the case of the following passages, I take it for granted that the trope precedes its rationale. The rationale would here be the imminence of death, a fit candidate for the role of "unseen antagonist," but I am suggesting that existential affects such as the fear of death are derived and secondary in Johnson.) In his letters, he writes such plaintively urgent reminders as "I think it time we should see one another, and spend a little of our short life together," or "We that have lived to lose many that might have cared for us, should care a little for one another," or "When I see her again, how I shall love her. If we could keep a while longer together, we should all, I hope, try to be thankful." Why does "the living world" gather up such acute pathos? This acuteness indicates a superaddition of affect, a diversion of pathos from another place.

With Gelidus as its representative, the antagonist of "the living world" is that which has no affect, but remains "insensible" and "unmoved." Yet Gelidus seems to be a false antagonist. Let me turn to another passage on the pathos of "the living world." Johnson's *Rambler* on Suspirius, the gloomy prophet of "evil," ends by resuscitating the solemn duties of society:

> To hear complaints with patience, even when complaints are vain, is one of the duties of friendship; and though it must be allowed that he suffers most like a hero that hides his grief in silence . . . yet it cannot be denied, that he who complains acts like a man, like a social being, who looks for help from his fellow creatures. Pity is to many of the unhappy a source of comfort in hopeless distress, as it contributes to recommend them to themselves, by proving that they have not lost the regard of others; and heaven seems to indicate the duty even of barren compassion, by inclining us to weep for evils which we cannot remedy."
>
> (No. 59)

Johnson here describes two inverse phenomena—the heroism of grief hidden in silence, and the humanity of compassion stirred though in vain. What would it do to the solemn pathos of this sentiment to remember their shadows in literary experience—imaginary grief consigned to silence, and compassion made barren without human objects?

It seems that Johnson felt constrained to protect "the living world" against the dubious legitimacy of literary experience. If we return to Johnson's remarks on the death of Cordelia, we will see this constraint in operation. Here Johnson softens the requirements of mimesis in deference to the audience's susceptibility: "A play in which the wicked prosper, and the virtuous miscarry, may doubtless be good, because it is a just representation of the common events of human life: but since all reasonable beings naturally love justice, I cannot be easily persuaded, that the observation of justice makes a play worse; or, that if other excellencies are equal, the audience will not always rise better pleased from the final triumph of persecuted virtue." If all other excellencies are equal, a literary work should yield to the wishes of its audience's love, pleasure, and peace. This paradigm allows for a surprising redistribution of strength and vulnerability.

Literature does not call for sensitive treatment; on the contrary, here it is the play's freedom to be relentless, and the audience's weakness to need accommodation. Such a paradigm hints at literature's temptation to the perverse, and thus illuminates what is "so shocking" in the death of Cordelia. Earlier in his discussion, Johnson had begun to wonder at the play's "strangeness": "Shakespeare has suffered the virtue of Cordelia to perish in a just cause, contrary to the natural ideas of justice, to the hope of the reader, and, what is yet more strange, to the faith of chronicles." With gratuitous and inventive cruelty, the play propagates a death whose only end is its "shock" to the audience. This perversity could be called malice, if it had a human author, but since Johnson is careful to treat the play as impersonal and impassive, its painful affect seems to be born *ex nihilo*.

Yet that pain could still count as part of the "living world," as a lawful response to the painful representation of Cordelia's death. In other of his critical works, Johnson discovers phantom suffering that is stimulated by literature, not as a representation of life, but only as an insensible artifact. In these cases, the phantom suffering is acute enough, though not the same as the affect of pathos. The improvident Richard Savage grew passionately solicitous about his galley proofs, agonizing over the punctuation, revising and restoring it so often that Johnson calls him "dubious and irresolute without end, as on a question of the last importance." Turning to more dramatic language, Johnson expatiates: "the intrusion or omission of a

comma was sufficient to discompose him, and he would lament an error of
a single letter as a heavy calamity. In one of his letters relating to an
impression of some verses, he remarks that he had, with regard to the
correction of the proof, 'a spell upon him'; and indeed the anxiety with
which he dwelt upon the minutest and most trifling niceties, deserved no
other name than that of fascination" (*LP*). Despite some rueful humor, this
passage worries the asymmetry between Savage's affects and their object: out
of the most trivial and superficial features of literature is born an impressive
turbulence of the interior—doubt, agitation, lament, anxiety, obsession.
Here, and in the case of other writers, Johnson exemplifies the phenomenon
of phantom suffering as an obscurely fatal enthrallment to the foibles of the
signifier. Cowley was attracted to silly puns and conceits "by some fascination
not easily surmounted," or even, "by a kind of destiny" (*LP*).

But Johnson reserves a more poignant language of tragic infatuation
for Shakespeare himself: "A quibble is to Shakespeare, what luminous vapours
are to the traveller; he follows it at all adventures, it is sure to lead him
out of his way, and sure to engulf him in the mire. It has some malignant
power over his mind, and its fascinations are irresistable. . . . A quibble
poor and barren as it is, gave him such delight, that he was content to
purchase it, by the sacrifice of reason, propriety and truth. A quibble was
to him the fatal Cleopatra for which he lost the world, and was content to
lose it." It is odd to characterize punning as a suicidal passion. In order to
make it look so, Johnson portrays the quibble as an autonomous thing, an
eerie phantom that Shakespeare pursues in the *ignis fatuus.* Through this
invention, Johnson conjures up a tragic interiority which has accumulated
in response to the insubstantial and elusive surfaces of representation.

Johnson described a similar syndrome in the reader of *Paradise Lost,* a
syndrome of distress, that is, which arises from having experience with
literature, though not precisely from being moved by it. In a famous remark,
he assures us that *Paradise Lost* wants "human interest," but this, which
amounts to the absence of "the pathetic," does not prevent the poem from
becoming a source of pain:

> But original deficience cannot be supplied. The want of human
> interest is always felt. *Paradise Lost* is one of the books which the
> reader admires and lays down, and forgets to take up again. None
> ever wished it longer than it is. Its perusal is a duty rather than
> a pleasure. We read Milton for instruction, retire harassed and
> overburdened, and look elsewhere for recreation; we desert our
> master and seek for companions.
>
> (*LP*)

This passage slides precipitously from a criticism of blank "deficience" into a drama of indolence, anxiety, and guilt, mental torments that are familiar from the *Rambler* or from Johnson's own *Prayers and Meditations*. The reader begins with boredom, progresses to gloomy obligation, and concludes "harassed and overburdened," fleeing from the poem's harsh solitude to the comforts of "the living world." This unhappiness does not echo any pathos in *Paradise Lost,* but emerges out of its blankness, like Shakespeare's fatal "fascination" with puns.

In his theoretical account of literary affect and literary identification, Johnson does fleetingly envision the stimulation of a spurious interiority. He pauses in his essay on Shakespeare to consider the question of "how the drama moves, if it is not credited." The direct communication of affect is the issue here, and Johnson at first explains it in conventional terms, as the effect of a proleptic identification experienced at a safe distance: "[The drama] is credited, whenever it moves, as a just picture of a real original; as representing to the auditor what he would himself feel, if he were to do or suffer what is there feigned to be suffered or to be done. The reflection that strikes the heart is not, that the evils before us are real evils, but that they are evils to which we ourselves may be exposed." But at this point, Johnson swerves away from the old saw, to intimate the decay of that safe distance in a more perfect and literal incorporation of fictional affects: "If there be any fallacy, it is not that we fancy the players, but that we fancy ourselves unhappy for a moment." Here the security of prolepsis and the externality of representation disappear; instead of congratulating ourselves on our freedom from the characters' woes, "we fancy ourselves unhappy for a moment." Fictional unhappiness has been made real. (It remains to be seen how the qualification, "for a moment," will hold up.) Johnson now retreats from this implication, adding: "but we rather lament the possibility than suppose the presence of misery." What is signified in the transition from "fancying" ourselves unhappy to "lamenting the possibility" of unhappiness? The affect may be slightly different (though "lament" bears the traces of "present misery"), yet the process of internalization and realization remains the same. Johnson restores prolepsis, but without the recollection of fictionality. The internalization of spurious and unreal distress proceeds so successfully that its results remind Johnson of the imminence and the dread of death: "we rather lament the possibility than suppose the presence of misery, as a mother weeps over her babe, when she remembers that death may take it from her."

Earlier in the *Preface to Shakespeare,* Johnson makes statements which suggest not only the fatality of literary experience, but also its priority to experience of "the living world." His familiar argument that Shakespeare

wrote from Nature, that he "caught his ideas from the living world," actually
works to imply that the autonomy of Nature emerges late, in general history
and in individual development. It is historically belated, since, after gen-
erations of fabulists, Shakespeare was the first English writer to "[show] life
in its native colors." Readers before his time had in fact preferred the fabulists
because, Johnson strangely affirms, their exposure to literature preceded
their acquaintance with Nature, an inevitability which made them as cred-
ulous as children: "Nations, like individuals, have their infancy. A people
newly awakened to literary curiosity, being yet unacquainted with the true
state of things, knows not how to judge of that which is proposed as its
resemblance." If I understand this sentence rightly, Johnson is treating
"literary curiousity" as if it comes before the search to know Nature, and
in fact, stimulates it, as a means to understanding and evaluating books.
Earlier in the *Preface,* when he first exalts Shakespeare's fidelity to Nature,
and promises its comforts to individual readers, Johnson seems to be following such a chronology, though his use of it there is more troubled as
well as more consequential. He is preoccupied with the didactic potential
of literature, and with its approach to coincidence with life; but his tests
for this coincidence always involve isolated people who have come to books
first, and who sometimes remain isolated among them. The figures in this
paragraph apparently live in closets, and read in promiscuous solitude: "This
therefore is the praise of Shakespeare, that his drama is the mirror of life;
that he who has mazed his imagination, in following the phantoms which
other writers raise up before him, may here be cured of his delirious extasies,
by reading human sentiments in human language; by scenes from which a
hermit may estimate the transactions of the world, and a confessor predict
the progress of the passions." If a person is to gain his or her knowledge of
life through literature, what would be the fate of the confessor and the
hermit who were exposed first to the "delirious extasies" of some books, and
who tried to see the world through them? Johnson even says, above, that
writers other than Shakespeare "disguise the most natural passions and most
frequent incidents; so that he who contemplates them in the book will not
know them in the world," as if one's disorientation were experienced not in
reading, but in turning to life. Someone to whom books had come first
would be disoriented to find that the world does not coincide with literature,
but would continue to seek out such a coincidence in order to be relieved
from the restless tedium of this disorientation. This seems to have been
the case with Johnson, who hunted down occasions for literary gloom,
as is suggested by the following letter, with its talk of coincidence and
sorrow:

At Durham, beside all expectation, I met an old friend . . . I
thought her much decayed, and having since heard that the
Banker had involved her in his extensive ruin I cannot forbear
to think, that I saw in her withered features more impressions
of sorrow than of time.

> Qua terra patet, fera regnat Erinnys.
> [Where earth extends, there reigns the savage Fury.]

He that wanders about the world sees new forms of human
misery, and if he chances to meet an old friend, meets a face
darkened with troubles.

The "old friend" whom Johnson comes upon in his wanderings is the
quotation from Virgil, which he detects staring out at him from the face of
a former acquaintance. Here books do not illustrate life, but rather the
reverse. In fact, Johnson sometimes allows that the lessons of literature can
exercise this peculiar ascendency. That is the assumption behind his remarks
on didacticism and exemplarity, which were familiar concerns of his age,
but which he seems to have understood more subtly than his contemporaries.
He did not, for example, follow the simple model of exemplarity in which
an audience at *The Beggar's Opera* rises wishing to turn highwaymen (*LJ*).
His discussions of exemplarity grant to literature a power of influence whose
danger lies in its secrecy and silence. Literature stimulates the impulse to
imitation, but this imitation occurs without the authority of intention or
the check of consciousness.

In the famous *Rambler* No. 4, said to have been occasioned by the
popularity of *Roderick Random* and *Tom Jones,* Johnson claims that literary
realism is insidious, because it is insufficiently tendentious and selective. Its
"promiscuous descriptions" become alarming in the light of imitation without authority, whose unseen workings a good author would remember and
circumscribe: "But if the power of example is so great, as to take possession
of the memory by a kind of violence, and produce effects almost without
the intervention of the will, care ought to be taken, that, when the choice
is unrestrained, the best examples only should be exhibited; and that which
is likely to operate so strongly, should not be mischievous or uncertain in
its effects." It is hard to imagine how literature might be so well policed
as to ensure perfect "certainty" in its effects, and indeed, *Rambler* No. 4 is
so anxious about this necessity that it comes to seem considerably more
doubtful than confident of literature's moral efficacy. But what I want to
concentrate on is the mechanism of its dubious legitimacy—that is, on the
power of literary example to "take possession of the memory by a kind of

violence," and to "produce effects almost without the intervention of the will." This is a phenomenon of involuntary quotation, but as in Johnson's account of "how the drama moves," it is quotation transformed into interiority, literature echoed in "the living world."

In Johnson's works, the image of human authority is already a source of sadness. People who have painfully acquired the authority of knowledge and experience do not gain in power or substance, but in isolation and attenuation. To have authority in Johnson is to move in a fainter sphere, as a diminished thing amid insubstantial company. Rasselas best exemplifies the severity of this reverse, when he gives warning to some youngbloods: "Let us consider that youth is of no longer duration, and that in maturer age, when the enchantments of fancy shall cease, and phantoms of delight dance no more about us, we shall have no comforts but the esteem of wise men, and the means of doing good." The great pleasures of the narcissistic imagination do not dwindle into tamer satisfactions, but vanish altogether, and in their place rise the small, harsh "comforts" of selfless duty and mild esteem. This is the pathos of authority—to be requited with deprivation, loneliness, and self-loss ("But these were the dreams of a poet doomed at last to wake a lexicographer").

Johnson is willing to stir this pathos even out of Shakespeare's scant biography. Like others, Johnson enjoys the myth of Shakespeare's Adamic freedom, affirming that, unburdened by critics and precursors, he wrote "with the world open before him." But, in the course of Johnson's essay, this freedom turns into isolation and neglect. Without authorities to direct or approve him, Shakespeare had to guide himself, in silence and invisibility. A person of his time who wished to study Nature "was under the necessity of gleaning his own remarks, by mingling as he could in [the world's] business and amusements." And such solitary, uncertain research Shakespeare pursued, or so Johnson seems to be thinking when he writes, wistfully, "Shakespeare must have looked upon mankind with perspicacity, in the highest degree curious and attentive." His powers made him more watchful, though perhaps less regarded. Yet as a consequence of his originality, Shakespeare did not value his work, but joined his audience in the evanescence of the present: "It does not appear that Shakespeare thought his works worthy of posterity, that he levied any ideal tribute upon future times, or had any further prospect, than of present popularity and present profit. When his plays had been acted, his hope was at an end." In Johnson's imagining, the result of Shakespeare's authority was to make him abandon himself. The containment of his hope is especially sobering, since Johnson usually ascribes to hope such ebullience and tenacity. Authority then seems sad to behold, because it exacts the subject's erosion by his or her own advances. The Astronomer of *Rasselas* mourns this fatality, regretting that "I have purchased knowledge at the expense of all the common comforts of life."

But, despite his fondness for this trope, Johnson saw that the pathos of authority can be sheer fantasy, particularly when it is indulged by the narcissistic imagination. One can easily enough invent and then grieve for one's "lonely wisdom and silent dignity," in the words of an admonishing *Rambler* (No. 135). And this is what the mad Astronomer does. It is no less rueful that he should so naturally appropriate, and so pointlessly live out the pathos of tragic authority, than that his madness should have grown out of his "literary solitude" to begin with. With his chimerical burdens and self-imposed isolation, the Astronomer throws his life away on a fantasy of brave, afflicted greatness (or, as he grimly says, "I am . . . tempted to think that my enquiries have ended in error, and that I have suffered much, and suffered it in vain"). To contrast with this narcissistic effulgence, Johnson introduces a depressive "old man," who seems to be the Astronomer's self-demystified double. He is a "sage"—ancient, knowing, and cold. In consequence of his sanity and wisdom, his interest in others, and in himself, has dwindled to a pip; in fact, his description of his life is so summarily bleak that it angers and debilitates his audience, who were prepared to be moved and instructed by him. Between the Astronomer and the old man, authority makes its last sacrifice, abandoning the pleasures of narcissism, so that now, the old man insists, even praise is to him "an empty sound." In the perfection of his clear-sightedness, the sage does not allow himself the comfort of approving his "lonely wisdom and silent dignity," but only lingers on as a body awaiting death. "The transition from the protection of others to our own conduct is a very awful point of human existence," Johnson wrote to a friend; and it will now be seen how he could view this transition with such sadness. The "empty sounds" which float around the sage recall the "empty sounds" at the end of the *Preface to the Dictionary* ("and success and miscarriage are empty sounds"). To have attained the authority of wisdom and experience is to have grown out of the world of people into the world of "empty sounds," that is to say, into a world which echoes with the involuntary quotations of imitation without authority.

One night at dinner, in the last year of his life, Johnson engaged in a favorite debate on the prevalence of unhappiness. When he was asked how he could be so cheerful in company, and yet so obstinate in his affirmations of misery, he explained: "Alas! It is all outside; I may be cracking my joke, and cursing the sun. *Sun, how I hate thy beams!*" Here resurfaces that experience which Johnson had suppressed in the *Life of Milton*—that "solitude" of pained interiority and tragic separation from the world. In what are already Shakespearean cadences, Satan ranges in his isolation, cursing the stars: "to thee I call,/But with no friendly voice, and add thy name,/O sun, to tell thee how I hate thy beams/That bring to my remembrance from what state/ I fell, how glorious once above thy sphere" (IV, 35–39). These emptying words Johnson produces (though gaily) as the content of his interiority, as if his separation from the world were predicated on the memory and quotation of Milton. I am reminded here of Abraham and Torok on a case of endocryptic identification: "It takes some time to understand that he speaks and lives someone else's words and affects." In "L'object perdu—moi" (*SubStance* 43), Abraham and Torok describe this phenomenon as a denial of mourning, a secret incorporation of a lost loved object which allows you to miss yourself in her or his place. This secret, necessarily inventive incorporation makes it "possible to disguise under one's own traits a phantasy person endowed with entirely fictitious greatness and torments." These false affects, this false mourning, seem to have been the forms in which Johnson's literary experience expressed itself. He was close to suspecting that literature had imposed on him a spurious interiority, close enough to recognize such a phenomenon in theory, while regarding literary pathos, and his particular vulnerability to it, with ambivalence and distrust.

This distrust and its cause help to explain why, in his last work, Johnson pursued the task of making hopeless reparations to dead poets, why, that is, he sought the Oedipalization of literary space. The most exemplary of his hopeless reparations was in fact made in honor of his father. During a visit to Lichfield in 1781, Johnson disappeared for some hours; it transpired that he had been standing, hat in hand, at the corner in Uttoxeter where his father had used to set up his bookstall. In the fall of the winter in which he died, Michael Johnson had asked his son to make the trip to Uttoxeter market for him, but Johnson refused. He was now running this errand, fifty years late (*LJ*). This private ceremony has usually been interpreted as a simple kind of penance. Yet it seems strange that Johnson allowed himself so literal-minded and eccentric a ritual. I am inclined to think of it as more wishful than penitential, as a resumption rather than an exorcism. Johnson was busy remembering himself as a son. As in *The Lives of the Poets,* he wished to return to the Oedipal organization of the world, in response to the dubiety of literary experience, out of nostalgia for human authority.

GORDON TURNBULL

"Generous Attachment": The Politics of Biography in the Tour to the Hebrides

I looked on this tour to the Hebrides as a co-partnery between Mr. Johnson and me.

—BOSWELL

O God! Poor Scotland!
—PRINCE CHARLES EDWARD

Boswell's deeply perplexed national self-understanding, a consequence of eighteenth-century Scotland's political and cultural relation to England, fashioned much that is crucial in his practice as a public journalist, private diarist, and literary biographer. Pleased with ideas of his ancient Scots blood and genuinely regretful of Scotland's loss of national independence, he was nonetheless almost helplessly drawn southward by the attractions of England, suffering, at times acutely, from the anxieties of cultural dislocation. Once a vigorous and independent polity, Scotland was now subordinate to its larger and richer southern neighbor, and since the Union of the Crowns (1603) and the Treaty of Union (1707) had continued uncertain—having dwindled, to the minds of many, into a mere region or province—in the new Westminster-ruled political system of "Britain." "I am by birth," Boswell began a letter to the *Public Advertiser* in 1779, "a North Briton, as a Scotchman must now be called" (6 April 1779).

Boswell's cultural perplexity, so strong a part of his larger anxieties of selfhood and identity, arose in him with particular force in his friendship and literary association with Johnson, and his *Journal of a Tour to the Hebrides with Samuel Johnson LL.D.* addresses most directly the relation between himself as a Scot ("a gentleman of ancient blood, the pride of which was his predominant passion") and the English Johnson—"at bottom much of a *John Bull,* much of a *true-born Englishman.*" His record of the tour confronts, and (in its published form) aims at resolution of, the division in his own and the Scottish national self-perception. The major moments of the tour turn on paradigms of political union: the Boswell-Johnson "co-partnery" stands as the personal analogue to the political and cultural link, as it was perceived by Boswell in idealized or paradigmatic form, between Scotland and England. The interdependences of biographer and subject represent, for the biographer, an equality-in-secondariness, a "generous attachment" (an importantly repeated expression discussed in detail below) that enriches and aggrandizes, as it ensures the continued survival (literary immortality) of both partners. The text, a collaborative coproduction of Johnsonian utterance and Boswellian journalism, subtly announces itself as an exemplary issue of the common British nation Boswell saw as the fruit of the Union.

The public Johnsonian memoir must be understood as an edited version of the private Boswellian journal, seen, that is, in the context of the continuing autobiographical record of which it is a part. Boswell's early English and continental journals are (among other things) a record of travel. They register Boswell's protracted interrogation and testing of his Scottishness against other national and regional identities, and thoughts and conversations on the competing claims of the Houses of Stuart and Hanover on his cultural affiliation adumbrate the *Tour*'s major politico-biographical themes.

Two conversations, only some eighteen months apart, reflect the deep confusion in the young Boswell's national allegiances. In London on 17 January 1763, Boswell "fell upon political topics" with his Scots friends, the Kellie family (their father, the fifth Earl of Kellie, had been a colonel in the Jacobite army in the Forty-Five), and "all agreed in our love of the Royal Family of Stuart and regret at their being driven from Britain. I maintained," reports Boswell, "that their encroachments were not of so bad consequence as their being expelled the throne." In short, Boswell's journal continues,

> the substance of our conversation was that the family of Stuart, although unfortunate, did nothing worthy of being driven from the throne. That their little encroachments were but trifles in comparison of what Oliver Cromwell did. . . . That by the Rev-

olution [of 1688] we got a shabby family to reign over us, and that the German War, a consequence of having a German sovereign, was the most destructive thing this nation ever saw.

This, concludes Boswell, "was a bold and rash way of talking; but it had justice, and it pleased me." But a year and a half later, in Berlin on 23 July 1764, Boswell was discussing Jacobitism again, now with his distinguished Scots traveling companion, George Keith, 10th Earl Marischal. Heroic rebel leader in the Jacobite uprising of 1715 and an intriguer for the Old Pretender in its aftermath, Lord Marischal had grown bitter and disillusioned and had (unlike the fifth Earl of Kellie) taken no part for the Young Pretender in 1745. Though there was "something pathetic and generous" in Jacobitism, "as it was espousing the cause of a distressed and ancient royal house," Lord Marischal owned that the Stuarts had deserved to lose the throne of Britain. "I own so too," declared Boswell (the conversation with the Kellie family now forgotten). "I am sorry for them. I wish to forget them; and I love from my soul 'Great George our King.' "

Three weeks later in his German travels, Boswell records an evening's entertainment in terms that gesture implicitly but noticeably toward emotional resolution of this contradictory muddle. He found himself dancing with the Heriditary Princess, Augusta, sister of Great George our King. The pair made, Boswell wrote,

> a very fine English minuet—or British, if you please, for it was a Scots gentleman and an English lady that performed it. What a group of fine ideas had I! I was dancing with a princess; with the grand-daughter of King George whose birthday I have so often helped to celebrate at Old Edinburgh; with the daughter of the Prince of Wales, who patronized Thomson and other votaries of science and the muse; with the sister of George the Third, my sovereign. . . . It was noble to be in such a frame. I said to the Princess, "Madam, I return your Royal Highness a thousand thanks for the honour you have done me. This will serve me to talk of to my tenants as long as I live."

Around the Brunswick ballroom, Boswell and the Hanoverian Princess dance a miniature model of the Union, not English but British. His "group of fine ideas" trace the history of post-Union Scottishness, and the interplay of international political history and Boswell's individual history. The ideas bring into union the German George II (Boswell's memories of public royal birthday celebrations) and "Old Edinburgh," ancient seat of the Scottish

Stuarts; George II's son, the Prince of Wales, and James Thomson, whose career—as a Scottish poet reaching great fame in England—Boswell would like to emulate; and George III's sister and Boswell's own family estate, in the vision of the humble tenants of Auchinleck hearing of this event in the reminiscences of their Laird. Behind the unions in Boswell's fine ideas stands the central political fact of Boswell's time, the Union of Scotland and England.

Touring the Hebrides with Johnson some nine years after this minuet in Brunswick, Boswell danced a Highland reel on top of Duncaan on the island of Raasay with Malcolm MacLeod of Brae, one of the heroes of the Forty-Five who had helped the Young Pretender elude government forces and escape to France. Now, in the autumn of 1773, active Jacobitism was no more, but it remained alive as a sentiment, and the Highlands had become an idealized *locus* of old Scots patriotism. Johnson, among the best known English men of letters of his day, and one known to be averse to the Scots, had been associated in Boswell's mind since before their first meeting ("Don't tell him where I come from") with a glamorous English literary celebrity he yearned to experience. The tour through the Highlands and Western Islands with Johnson was for Boswell a major step in his much longer psychopolitical tour: he travels through the imaginative heartland of his lingering emotional attachment to an ancient independent Scotland— "Caledonia." In his journal, accounts from participants in the Forty-Five and its aftermath (notably Malcolm MacLeod, as well as Flora Macdonald, disguised as whose maid the Young Pretender was able to make his escape) weave in and out of the Boswell-Johnson record to provide a continuing interplay of national history and individual identity: the events on which Boswell quotes his informants are among those which have fashioned him as a political being. The text of this history seems to him inscribed on the very landscape through which he passes:

> I saw Loch Moidart, into which the Prince entered on his first
> arrival, and within which is a lesser loch called Lochninau, where
> the Prince actually landed. The hills around, or rather mountains,
> are black and wild in an uncommon degree. I gazed on them
> with much feeling. There was a rude grandeur that seemed like
> a consciousness of the royal enterprise, and a solemn dreariness
> as if a melancholy remembrance of its events had remained.
>
> (*Tour*)

Putting Johnson into this setting, into the company of some of the heroes of the Forty-Five, among the clans and chieftains who represented what now

survived of the old Highland ways of life, even into the very bed Prince
Charles Edward had slept in, allowed Boswell boldly to fuse the best of both
cultures (in his imaginative constructions of them) with claims on his affiliation. The Forty-Five was a last flourish of active sympathy for the over-
thrown Stuarts, the final blow (after the Union of Crowns and the Treaty
of Union) to Scottish independence and pride. For Boswell's generation,
whose initiation into national history came in the 1750s and 1760s, political
subordination to England was, indeed had long been, an established fact.
The Duke of Cumberland's defeat of the largely Highland forces at Culloden
had left the second Jacobite uprising only a romanticized glorious failure,
and Jacobitism a focus for elegaic or sentimental attachments to the idea of
an independent Scotland.

Without relinquishing his deep sympathy for the "pathetic and generous" cause, Boswell abandons the claims of "Scotland" on his cultural
allegiance, and finds in his biographical mission—to record the thoughts
and utterances of the Rambler—long-sought participation in the cultural
plenitude made possible by the Union. When Malcolm MacLeod guided
Prince Charles Edward in his Highland wanderings after Culloden, he was
Boswell's age at the time of the tour to the Hebrides. Jacobite bravery
remains only a fantasy heroism for Boswell, whose heroism is now social
and biographical. Just as the Highland craft and guile of Malcolm MacLeod,
Flora Macdonald, and their comrades guided the princely Pretender through
the Highlands, Boswell's considerable social guile and craft guide Johnson,
the Monarch of English letters, into and through spectacular encounters with
the Scots, for Boswell's biographical purposes. In Scotland, Johnson is cul-
turally "other," but unlike Boswell in London, is conscious that he represents
the conquering culture, that it is his nation to which Scotland has subordinated its identity. He is massive, static, English, solid: "Indeed," Boswell
wrote to Garrick from Inverness, "as I have always been accustomed to view
him as a permanent London object, it would not be much more wonderful
to me to see St. Paul's church moving along where we are now." Boswell
on the other hand is all social accommodation and pliability. It is he who
socially mobilizes Johnson for the Highlanders: "they observed that it was
I who always 'set him a-going.' The fountain was locked up till I interfered"
(*Tour*). On October 2, Boswell found himself dancing again, this time
unwillingly:

> I had written letters all forenoon. It was a very bad day, and at
> night there was a great deal of lightning. I was really fatigued
> with violent dancing. I do not like dancing. But I force myself

to it, when it promotes social happiness, as in the country, where it is as much one of the means towards that end as dinner; so I danced a reel tonight to the music of the bagpipe, which I never did before. It made us beat the ground with prodigious force. I thought it better that I should engage the people of Skye by taking a cheerful glass and dancing with them rather than play the abstract scholar. I looked on this tour to the Hebrides as a co-partnery between Mr. Johnson and me. Each was to do all he could to promote its success; and I am certain that my gayer exertions were of much service to us. Mr. Johnson's immense fund of knowledge and wit was a wonderful source of admiration and delight to them. But they had it only at times; and they required to have interstices agreeably filled up, and even little elucidations of his grand text.

(*Tour*)

Boswell, like his imaginative sense of Scotland in the Union, is a subordinate but vital accessory. The co-partnery of biographer and subject becomes an equality-in-secondariness.

The Scotland Boswell would preserve is a complicated fusion of a romanticized Highland patriarchy and an idealized sense of his family seat of Auchinleck. He aims his rejections at Lowland, Presbyterian, Whig Scotland—the Scotland, in other words, of his father, Lord Auchinleck. Boswell's initiation into his national history coincided with his own progress to youthful rebellion against the rule of his father. The history of the Stuarts fascinated Boswell in part because, as Frank Brady has put it, "they were dramatic in their recklessness and gallant in their daring rebellions. Like himself they had been confined and thwarted by strict gloomy Presbyterians." The inevitable collision between Johnson and Alexander Boswell is a culminating episode after the Highland and Hebridean part of the tour. Lord Auchinleck "was as sanguine a Whig and Presbyterian as Dr. Johnson was a Tory and Church of England man" (*Tour*). His hold on his son was strong, and would remain long after to trouble Boswell's later aspirations to a life in England. But in the *Tour,* the comically violent clash at Auchinleck marks the symbolic displacement of Alexander Boswell as the object of Boswell's cultural allegiance, and the installation of Johnson as his cultural father. The subjects that brought them into collision were, not surprisingly, Cromwell and the Commonwealth, Stuart rule, and the merits of Scots Presbyterians. Lord Auchinleck, a distinguished Scots judge, learned, literate, a classicist and bibliophile, was himself an accomplished talker for victory, and proves, unlike the Highlanders or the meek and silent professors at St. Andrews, a worthy adversary for the Rambler. The contest seems a tie, but Boswell's final word on the matter shows how he scored it: "They are now in another, and a higher state of existence; and as they were both worthy Christian men, I trust they have met in happiness. But I must observe, in justice to my friend's political principles and my own, that they have met in a place where there is no room for Whiggism" (*Tour*).

It had long been Boswell's ambition to unite Johnson and the family seat at Auchinleck, and

> as I wandered with my revered friend in the groves of Auchinleck,
> I told him that if I survived him, it was my intention to erect
> a monument to him, among scenes which, in my mind, were all
> classical; for in my youth I had appropriated to them many of
> the descriptions of the Roman poets.
>
> > (*Tour*)

Johnson—monumental, Augustan, Roman London—has come to Auchinleck's groves, the fixed embodiment of English metropolitan culture to which Boswell aspired, and against which he could only measure the disconcerting fluctuations in his own temperament, fluctuations that helped create in him a vision of a fixed, permanent, stable Johnsonian England, and a violently unstable Scotland, an amalgam of regional identities, petty bickering factions, and internal squabbles of all kinds, "a country filled with jarring interests and keen parties" (*Tour*).

That Boswell can give his account of this serious cultural disputation and resolution a nonetheless comical cast catches the tone of the whole *Tour*. Times are now such that cultural collisions are verbal and end civilly; they do not, as they did for the generation who fought in the Forty-Five, take the form of war. Great and violent action has now ceased: the stage is held not by the Wanderer (Boswell's most frequent designation of Prince Charles Edward) but by the Rambler, a hero of the mind, of the civilized life, whose wanderings are not usually among "black and wild" mountains and are without "rude grandeur," but are among words. Present heroes excel in the arts that the end of war has made possible—reading, writing, Conversation, touring the Hebrides. The *Tour* shows Scotland's past to be a long history of fighting, of wars with England, and, more frequently, of internecine strife in the form of tribal or dynastic fury among the old clans. Boswell notes, for example, the story of how, in violent retributive justice, the MacLeods smoked the inhabitants of the island of Eigg to death in a large cave to which they had fled. On the island of Coll, Boswell rummaged through a cabinet full of papers, and he records stories and letters about the numerous murders and territorial disputes involving that island. Significantly, the next clan fight he reports figures in a letter from Donald Cameron and Alexander MacDonald to Alexander Invernahyle, in which the writers, who are Jacobites, upbraid the Campbells, who are Hanoverians. With this sequence Boswell implies a direct continuity between the old clan barbarities, the war in the Young Pretender's cause, and its survival as the competing claims of the Houses of Stuart and Hanover for his allegiance.

In its sustained generic allusion to epic, in its celebration of the arts of peace and leisure that follow war, the *Tour* is post-Iliadic. It traces the course not of war but of wandering after war, of Boswell's cultural homecoming. Tragedy and tragic epic are now merely among the topics of conversation. *Macbeth,* fictional testimony to Scotland's long history of slaughter, can now be quoted and discussed in fun as, on the way to a now calm Forres, the travelers "drove over the very heath where Macbeth met the witches" (*Tour*). In the exchange on the *Iliad* between Johnson and Lord Monboddo (James Burnett) it is to scenes of cultural plenitude and of peaceful legislative procedure that discussion turns. But Boswell's "epic" can follow the movements of its displaced and wandering royalty only so far: Charles Edward can only fail gloriously and escape with courage and ingenuity. More than Homeric, the major epic antecedents are Virgilian—Augustan, Roman, like monumental Johnson in the groves of Auchinleck. Boswell is concerned to give shape and definition to the national identity of a people, the Scots, who though repeatedly baffled and defeated prove resilient, and survive through a Trojan/Latin-like fusion with England. Charles Edward's cry, "O God! Poor Scotland!" (*Tour*), uttered when he starts from troubled slumbers in a hut on Raasay, is the last gasp of ancient, independent Scotland. Boswell would signal his country's rebirth in Britain.

In Edinburgh near the end of the tour, the great Scots historian William Robertson pays Johnson a Virgilian compliment which Johnson rejects as exaggerated: " 'I am really ashamed of the congratulations which we receive. We are addressed as if we had made a voyage to Nova Zembla, and suffered five persecutions in Japan.' " Robertson and Boswell are attuned to a Virgilian significance in the tour which the English Johnson misses. Boswell's elation in his "Roman" Auchinleck comes as the epic reward of Aeneas/ Boswell, the climax of an important pattern of reference to the Rome of the *Aeneid.* The tour's moment of beginning—the departure from Edinburgh (the Whig, Lowland, Presbyterian capital, at whose state of neglect, destruction, and decay Johnson has scowled, and Boswell and his Scots friends have felt ashamed)—brings the travelers to Inchkeith. Here they inspect the old fort which, more literally than the hills around Loch Moidart, is inscribed with the history of past events: the fort has "an inscription on it, *Maria Re.* 1564." The fort and its referencee to Mary Queen of Scots is a sorry survival (the island is overrun with "luxuriant thistles and nettles") of Stuart rule. As the party leaves Inchkeith, Johnson calls to Boswell:

> "Come now, pay a classical compliment to the island on quitting it." I happened luckily, in allusion to the beautiful Queen Mary, whose name is upon the fort, to think of what Virgil makes Aeneas say on having left the country of his charming Dido:
>> Inivitus, regina, tuo de littore cessi.
>> [Unwillingly, O Queen, I left your shore.]
> "Very well hit off!" said he.

Boswell's ready-witted response to Johnson's challenge is a parallel between himself and Aeneas that is at least as serious as it is jocular. The crossing from Leith to Inchkeith marks an important threshhold in the psychopolitical journey Boswell is making out of Lowland Scotland, away from sentimental attachments to an independent Scotland (here appearing as a romantic attachment to the "beautiful" Queen Mary), into a new national identity. The fort comes as the last of the sequence of institutions in and near Edinburgh that are emblems of Scotland's wasted grandeur and failed nationhood. In the Under-Parliament House, gazing on the Treaty of Union itself, Boswell "began to indulge old Scottish sentiments and to express a warm regret that by our Union with England, we were no more—our independent kingdom was lost." Boswell then quotes a series of fierce reproofs from Johnson: "Sir, never talk of your independency, who could let your Queen remain twenty years in captivity and then be put to death without even a pretence of justice, without your ever attempting to rescue her. . . ." Johnson's warmth here on behalf of Mary initiates a sustained sympathy for the Stuart line, that allies him with Boswell against Lowland, Whig, Presbyterian Scotland. He implies (it was one of the traditional English jibes at the Scots) a national failure of manhood: "and such a Queen, too!—as every man of gallantry of spirit would have sacrificed his life for" (suggesting subtly, with that "gallantry of spirit," an unfavorable comparison with the English court of Mary's victorious kinswoman Elizabeth I). Two days later at Inchkeith, Aeneas/Boswell makes it plain that he accepts his duty to abandon charming Dido/beautiful Mary. Aeneas-like he is summoned away to his higher cultural mission, to enter Britain, to become the biographer of Johnson. Mary's tragic death was but one step in the tragic death of old Scotland. Boswell's witty quotation from the *Aeneid* comes not, in fact, from the moment of

Aeneas's departure from Carthage, but from Book Six, in which the hero encounters Dido in the underworld: she is already dead.

The Scots, Boswell insists, will find national renewal in cultural fusion. The ethos of Augustan Rome/Johnsonian London is to be brought into union with Boswell's construction of the Scottish *Volksgeist,* alive as the spirit of the Highlands. One night on Coll, Johnson dresses as a Highlander: "however unfavourable to the Lowland Scots, he seemed much pleased to assume the appearance of an ancient Caledonian." The Highland and island men and women treated most admiringly in the *Tour* are presented by Boswell as proud Scots who have survived and adjusted to the new relation with England. The scornful characterization of Sir Alexander Macdonald (from whom Boswell feared violence when his treatment of him had been published) as rapacious and penurious emerges because he represents the Union in failure, an "English-bred chieftain." Macdonald's brother, Sir James, a gifted and promising man who died young (and the lengthy inscription on whose monument Boswell quotes in the published version of his journal) was on the other hand "a loss for all Britain" (*Life*), and a Scottish Marcellus.

As important as the installation of Johnson in "Roman" Auchinleck is the visit to the ruins of the cathedral at Iona (Icolmkill), site of the monastery from which St. Columba had sent out missionaries in the sixth century to convert Scotland and northern England. In this place, Boswell's thoughts move not only to Augustan Rome but to Catholic Rome. Old Scots and Catholic associations had been fused in Boswell's mind at least since the days of his student friendship with John Johnston of Grange. Boswell had long wanted to bring Johnson here as he had wanted to bring him to Auchinleck:

> As we were landing, I said to Mr. Johnson, "Well, I am glad
> we are now at last at this venerable place, which I have so long
> thought that you and I should visit. I could have gone and seen
> it by myself. But you would not have been with me; and the
> great thing is to bring objects together.
>
> *(Tour)*

In his letter to Garrick, Boswell had seen Johnson as a permanent London "object," and compared him to St. Paul's cathedral. On Easter Sunday in 1779, Boswell went to St. Paul's, and his journal entry records explicitly the imaginative religio-political union implied by the *Tour:* "At altar thanked GOD for uniting Auchinleck and St. Paul's—romantic seat of my ancestors and this grand cathedral—'in the imagination which Thou hast given me' " (4 April 1779). In the western islands of Scotland, Iona and St. Paul's are great objects brought together: Johnsonian, Augustan Rome, and the Rome of the past and of Boswell's grand tour, where he brought himself near to Cardinal York, the Pretender's younger son, and urged himself to "think of Grange and old Scots kings and Chapel of Holyrood." Now at Iona, he thinks again of John Johnston of Grange and (as he had long planned to do) he wrote to him: "I promised to write to you from this venerable spot. . . . The sanctity of the place and the ruined monuments of religion and learning now arround me have thrown me into so excellent a frame that our long friendship has the most lively impressions upon my soul." But as he writes, Johnson enters, and Boswell tells Johnston that "it is grand to see the Rambler stalking about as I write." The associations with Johnston are remembered; those with Johnson are actual. Johnson displaces Johnston: St. Paul's Church is a permanent London object, but Iona is ruined. In Boswell's published journal, union is enacted in the text itself, when Boswell excerpts from Johnson's own *Journey* his account of the same solemn moment: the Boswellian and Johnsonian texts are the same. Johnson concludes this famous passage: "That man is little to be envied, whose patriotism would not gain force upon the plain of *Marathon,* or whose piety would not grow warmer among the ruins of *Iona*!" All distinctions of time, place, and individual personality, of local versions of Christianity, and of local versions of patri- otism, vanish in the sanctity of Iona: "Scottishness" and "Englishness" are cut down on the plain of Marathon.

When Queen Mary next appears in the *Tour,* Boswell has lost all interest in her beauty, and she has become openly an argument against Stuart claims to the throne of Britain. Despite the "kind of *liking*" he and Johnson have for Jacobitism, Boswell cannot find

> the firm feudal hold for which I wish and which my imagination
> figures. I might fix my eye at the point of James IV, from whom
> my ancestor Thomas Boswell got the estate of Auchinleck, and
> look no further, had I a line of males from that Prince.
>
> (*Tour*)

Mary violates Boswell's "high notions of male succession," and his own idealized Auchinleck provides a more satisfying succession of male rule than Stuart history. In this passage, Boswell frankly declares that he would not have gone to Prince Charles Edward's aid. Johnson's arguments "of right being formed by possession and acknowledgement of the people" have settled his mind, and "I now have no uneasiness."

In the revised version of the journal published after Johnson's death, Boswell concludes his account of Prince Charles Edward's wanderings with

a fulsome declaration of loyalty to George III. Some twenty years after his
minuet in Brunswick, Boswell could report to his readers that in the Highlands of Scotland "the plant of loyalty is . . . in full vigour, and the Brunswick graft now flourishes like a native shoot" (*Life*). "Great George our
King" provided a satisfactory conclusion to the unsatisfactory succession of
rulers since the Revolution, because he is monarch of all the Britons:

> Having related so many particulars concerning the grandson of
> King James the Second; Having given due praise to fidelity and
> generous attachment, which, however erroneous the judgement
> may be, are honourable for the heart; I must do the Highlanders
> the justice to attest, that I found every where amongst them a
> high opinion of the virtues of the King now upon the throne,
> and an honest disposition to be faithful to his majesty, whose
> family has possessed the sovereignty of this country so long, that
> a change, even for the abdicated family, would now hurt the best
> feelings of all his subjects.
>
> (*Life*)

George III, like Boswell, "gloried in being *born a Briton*." By "this country"
Boswell means neither Scotland nor England but Britain. But the most
revealing expression here is "generous attachment." The quality for which
he praises the Highlanders and their now abandoned devotion to the Stuarts
he would transfer, a couple of pages later, to all Britons and their new
devotion to George: "I would have every breast animated with the *fervour*
of loyalty; with that generous attachment" (*Life*). Writing years earlier in
his journal of the tour, Boswell had used the same expression to denounce
a ruler between whom and his people this quality did not obtain, Sir Alexander Macdonald, who—George's polar opposite, the Union in disarray—
"is wrong in everything and has no generous attachment." Four years after
the tour, while visiting Dr. Taylor at Ashbourne, Boswell and Johnson
recalled their journey to the Highlands and the Hebrides "with wonderful
pleasure." Much moved one night by music, Boswell was conscious of a
"generous attachment to Dr. Johnson as my friend and preceptor . . . I
could have defended him at the point of my sword." Here, military action
in defence of an admired great man is only an affectionate filial fantasy. The
phrase reappears in the account of the visit to Ashbourne in the *Life of
Johnson,* but it works there as a signal that the Boswell-Johnson "co-partnery"
has been fulfilled as the successful literary biographical association to which
Boswell had long aspired; and that those aspirations had been fashioned by
complex personal, dynastic, and national historical relationships he would
now reinscribe as generous attachments.

ROBERT J. GRIFFIN

Reflection as Criterion
in The Lives of the Poets

The Lives of the Poets are considered by many to be Johnson's best work. Boswell thought them "the richest, most beautiful, and indeed most perfect production of Johnson's pen." Although Boswell is often given to hyperbolic superlatives, especially when the subject is Johnson, more recent critics have not disagreed. George Sherburn, for example, is quite sure: "His last work . . . has easily survived as his best." In my view, however, there are several reasons for thinking *The Rambler* at least as good, and possibly better.

One might consider, for example, Johnson's way of measuring an achievement according to the difficulty it overcomes. Since the *Lives* employ principles which *The Rambler* had first set down, the relation between them seems to be somewhat parallel to Johnson's view of the crucial difference between Homer's poem and Milton's: *Paradise Lost* is "not the greatest of heroick poems only because it is not the first." One might object that generic differences render this comparison inappropriate. But then there is no question that *The Rambler* is written in the more elevated style. Robert Folkenflik demonstrates convincingly that Johnson deliberately chose the middle style for the *Lives* as more suited to narrative in biography and criticism. Wimsatt's point, that the very mass of factual detail requiring negotiation in the *Lives* prevented Johnson's "logic from taking hold of the theme and carrying it into the realm of elaborate generality," illustrates the difference well. *The Rambler* presents, for the most part, an abstract and elevated chain of reasoning; individualized portraits employed as concrete examples are allegorical, as their Latin names signify. The *Lives,* however, chronicle the fortunes

Published in this volume for the first time. © 1986 by Robert J. Griffin.

of real individuals. *The Rambler* is thus a more coherent and sustained achievement, whereas *The Lives of the Poets* seems sketchy in comparison.

But let me paraphrase Johnson: it is not to be inferred that of literary excellence the *Lives* has only a little, because *The Rambler* has more. My intention is not really to depress the stature of *The Lives of the Poets,* but simply to approach them by articulating my sense of their difference from the essays which have been undervalued. There are flats in *The Rambler,* it is true, but it should also be recognized that much in the *Lives* is hackwork redeemed only by the unique pleasures of Johnson's style. There are fifty-two lives, but no more than six or seven are really considered major; many never rise above the level of a perfunctory recitation of facts. The *Lives,* as Bate says, *are* a masterpiece. But their real strength lies, I feel, in the criticism. Herbert Croft could, regrettably, write a life of Young in Johnson's place; but Johnson, thank God, did not allow Croft to write the criticism of Young's poems. It is the criticism which spread an indeterminate amount of influence. G. B. Hill's footnotes, which are themselves a course in literary history, recurrently cite opinions by Cowper, Coleridge, Wordsworth, Southey, and Tennyson among others, which either agree substantially with Johnson, or in disagreeing with him confirm nonetheless his authority to set the terms, and cite the passages for debate. Johnson may be a master of biography, but we are interested in the lives because the men were poets; the *Lives,* taken as a whole, is literary history, and authoritative literary history at that.

Critics have noticed that the *Lives* are unmanageable; because they are so many things, it is difficult to say something coherent about them. The same is true from the point of view of reflection. *The Rambler* is predominantly meditative, and is frankly directed toward inducing reflection. *Rasselas* tells a story, but it is a story about the process of acquiring knowledge and reflecting upon it. What can be said about the *Lives* is that their informing principle is evaluation; they can be seen, in other words, as a series of judgments about life and art. Reflection has already taken place, in the sense that the principles of judgment are not discussed, but are either invoked where necessary, or simply assumed. For instance, the short dissertations on pastoral, sacred poetry, letter-writing, or epic, are informative in themselves, but their purpose is to provide explicit premises for judgment. Accordingly, my problem is to ascertain to what degree in the *Lives* reflection is a criterion for judgment. Before deciding that, however, questions of form and method should be investigated.

Although the *Lives* do not demonstrate the sustained reflective movement of the esssays, they show, as most prose must, a chain of discursive reasoning. And, indeed, visible marks of Johnson's process of thinking are evident. A reference to induction, for example, appears in Johnson's comments on Dryden's learning: "The atoms of probability, of which my opinion has been formed, lie scattered over all his works." Here—as in the phrase "the train of my disquisition has now conducted me"—the reflexive reference to method has become part of the rhetorical strategy. We are asked to accede to Johnson's view of Dryden's learning because of the comprehensive rigor of his induction. As elsewhere in Johnson's works, the appeal to the independent process of reasoning is often invoked in the *Lives*. Dryden's middle way between the looseness of paraphrase and the closeness of metaphrase had been defended by reference to the authority of Horace, "but reason wants not Horace to support it." Dryden's praise for Roscommon's principles of translation is considered by Johnson to be no more than civility, "for when the sum of Lord Roscommon's precepts is collected it will not be easy to discover how they can qualify their reader for a better performance of translation than might have been attained by his own reflections." Reflection both "collects" the sum of precepts, and then refers to itself for its authority.

As elsewhere, the self-consciousness of Johnson's reasoning process is, in many ways, constitutive of form. In *The Rambler*, thinking about thinking determines both subject and form; in *Rasselas*, this process is dramatized in a narrative itself skeptical of narration. In the *Lives*, this process takes the form of what Lipking calls "perpetual commentary." Referring to Bayle's *Dictionary*, Lipking writes:

> *The Lives of the Poets* employs a version of Bayle's perpetual commentary in which a review of previous commentaries furnishes a train of thought from sentence to sentence—we must remember that the first of the *Lives* opens, not with a statement about Cowley, but with a critique of Sprat's "Life of Cowley." Formally it is perpetual commentary, not moral or critical philosophy, that governs the structure of Johnson's literary biography.

Lipking notes that while Johnson often ruthlessly suppresses references to his sources, he gains a "unified vision" resulting from the independence of his judgment. What is interesting from my point of view is that, in the *Lives*, Johnson is participating in a dialogue, not only with previous biographers and critics, but also with the poets themselves. This is commentary not primarily as reflection upon experience, though that certainly is present, but commentary as reflection upon *literary* experience, the critical mind confronted with a text.

Lipking cites the opening of the *Life of Cowley* as an example of "perpetual criticism," but the opening of the *Life of Butler* is likewise instructive:

> Of the great author of *Hudibras* there is a life prefixed to the later editions of his poems by an unknown writer, and therefore of disputable authority; and some account is incidentally given by Wood, who confesses the uncertainty of his own narrative: more, however, than they knew cannot now be learned, and nothing remains but to compare and copy them.

As one could guess from Johnson's questioning of the authority of the texts before him, comparing and copying is done in the same way he collated and commented upon Shakespearean texts in order to determine the best reading of the given "facts." Where the data is inconclusive it is apparent that the true content of a passage is its value as an example of critical thinking:

> Wood has his information from his brother, whose narrative placed him at Cambridge, in opposition to that of his neighbors which sent him to Oxford. The brother's seems the best authority, till, by confessing his inability to tell his hall or college, he gives reason to suspect that he was resolved to bestow on him an academical education; but durst not name a college for fear of detection.

The questioning of the provenance and possible motive for any testimony is typical of a method which tries to bottom at the truth of a matter, looking it over from all sides. Whether by conscious design or not, the method is contagious; nothing prevents us from turning it upon Johnson himself; in fact, at times he seems to invite it. Johnson always notices, for example, when a man's reputation as a poet has been made because of his position in government. Halifax was one of these, but Johnson's dialectical rigor offers a qualification:

> To charge all unmerited praise with the guilt of flattery, and to suppose the encomiast always knows and feels the falsehood of his assertions, is surely to discover great ignorance of human nature and human life. In determinations depending not on rules, but on experience and comparison, judgement is always in some degree subject to affection.

Here Johnson attacks the cynical reading of Halifax's literary success by, interestingly enough, observing that judgment can be corrupted also by affection. The recognition of the frailty of human judgment is stated objectively, but it amounts to an admission of an awareness of the possibility that one's own judgment could be determined to some degree by either affection or disaffection. In view of the admitted fallibility of judgment, what becomes important, it seems to me, is the demonstrated rigor and dialectical balance of the process of arriving at any given judgment. Even where the conclusion is disputable, as most are, the integrity of the process makes any given conclusion at least plausible. To the extent that the process underwrites the judgment, Johnson remains, as Eliot said, a dangerous man to disagree with. Johnson must be refuted methodically, not simply dismissed on the grounds that taste shifts, for the shift itself is part of a larger dialectic in literary history, within which Johnson occupies an important moment.

It is not surprising that the most salient forms of Johnsonian reflection [studied elsewhere] are found in the *Lives* as well. The inductive move toward generalization, and the subsequent deductive move based on generalization is a method consistently applied. The very form of biography as Johnson inherited it—the narrative of a sequence of facts followed by a generalized "character"—is in itself a form of induction. It is not a question of adding a column of figures into a sum, for the whole, greater than the parts, must be divined. As Folkenflik has stated: "The life presents process; the character, essence." This intuitive ability to divine the character of a man from his life, or his poetical character from his writings, is one of Johnson's greatest strengths. The famous comparison of Dryden and Pope, for example, is formally a series of deductions based on an extensive power of induction.

The delineation of a poetical character is a form of reflection equivalent to the argument from design in philosophy. Criticism discovers the mind of the author in his works, just as philosophy considered the mind of a Creator through His creation. The old analogy which made God a poet hovers in the background. But this method of tracing certain qualities in poetry back to the mind of the poet, forming generalizations about the poetical character of the author, and using them deductively, is ubiquitous in the *Lives*. A series of illustrations should bring home the point.

Paradise Lost, at one point, is rated, not as a poem, but according to where it stands "among the productions of the human mind." A consideration of the "sentiments" of *Paradise Lost* leads naturally to their author: "The thoughts which are occasionally called forth in the progress are such as could be produced only by an imagination in the highest degree fervid and active, to which materials were supplied by incessant and unlimited curiosity." Speaking of Dryden, Johnson observes that "every page discovers a mind very widely acquainted both with art and nature, and in full possession of great stores of intellectual wealth." In the conclusion to the *Life of Waller,*

we find the transition from a characterization of the poetry to the quality
of mind that produced it:

> The general character of his poetry is elegance and gaiety. He is
> never pathetick, and very rarely sublime. He seems neither to
> have had a mind much elevated by nature, nor amplified by
> learning. His thoughts are such as a liberal conversation and large
> acquaintance with life would easily supply.

We will be led shortly to focus on the value Johnson placed on reflection
in a poet, but it is sufficient at present to note that Waller, in Johnson's
view, did little with his materials. What he knew was widely available, and
was little altered by any operation of his own mind, either natural or acquired
through study. The poetical character of Dryden, while delivering an opposite judgment, reveals nonetheless the same method of judging:

> In a general survey of Dryden's labours he appears to have had a
> mind very comprehensive by nature, and much enriched with
> acquired knowledge. His compositions are the effects of a vigorous
> genius operating upon large materials.

By comparing the appearance of great abilities with the uneven quality of
the work, Johnson concludes further that Dryden lacked diligence, and that
his goal was rather expedience than perfection: "He did not keep present to
his mind an idea of pure perfection; nor compare his works, such as they
were, with what they might be made."

Because Johnson's method is consistent, and his standards of judgment
stable, an implicit order ranking the poets emerges. A survey of Addison's
poetry, for example, implicitly places him in relation to Dryden: "He did
not trust his powers enough to be negligent." Milton combined genius and
learning with the diligence of Pope, whereas in Rochester's works "may be
found tokens of a mind which study might have carried to excellence."

The basic assumption of the argument from design is that, behind the
phenomenal appearance, there is a noumenal intelligence. In criticism, the
assumption is simply that there is a mind behind the text. As much as depth
psychology has questioined the role of the conscious mind in creative activity,
or has put in question the coherence of the personality, we still cannot do
without this basic inference. We still must construct a "Milton" or a "Keats"
in order to discuss literature at all. The limitations of such an inference are
also known to Johnson, and his method takes them into account. Comparing
two accounts of the reasons for Cowley's retirement, one which represents
his hopes disappointed at court, and another which shows him weary of

business and eager for the pleasures of solitude, Johnson observes: "So differently are things seen and so differently are they shewn; but actions are
visible, though motives are secret. Cowley certainly retired." A similar
caution is articulated in the *Life of Addison:* "The fact is certain; the motives
we must guess." The question of intention appears to be beyond the grasp
of certainty. But rather than clutter his text, and cripple each judgment
with repeated qualifications, Johnson simply discloses the rules he plays by
on certain occasions, and allows his reader to infer the rest. Johnson may
be correct about Dryden, for example; there is the question of probability;
but the speculative nature of inference is admitted, explicitly and implicitly,
throughout a text infamous for authoritarian pronouncements.

The recognition that much human knowledge is probable rather than
certain leads one to consider the limitations of thought as inherent in its
conditions. The very structure of reflection implies indirectness and mediation. Johnson's remarks on the historical setting of *Hudibras* reveal an awareness of what is inevitably lost when one is confronted with a representation.
Johnson notices how much of the humor of *Hudibras* is lost because manners
have changed; he asserts that, while "general passions are co-extended with
the race of man," accidental and peculiar forms of life "perish with their
parents":

> Much therefore of that humour which transported the last century
> with merriment is lost to us, who do not know the sour solemnity,
> the sullen superstition, the gloomy moroseness, and the stubborn
> scruples of the ancient Puritans; or, if we know them, derive our
> information only from books or from tradition, have never had
> them before our eyes, and cannot but by recollection and study
> understand the lines in which they are satirised. Our grandfathers
> knew the picture from the life; we judge of the life by contem-
> plating the picture.

The question raised here concerns the distance and unreliability of mediated
knowledge. The length of the distance and the degree of the uncertainty
depend, of course, upon the kind of knowledge which is sought; passions
are recognizable across centuries, whereas the manners they are bound up
with are obscure. It may be argued that all knowledge is ultimately mediated,
that both nature and human culture are themselves representations mediated
to our understanding by various signs. Thus we are always, and inescapably,
"contemplating a picture," and we see it, or what it represents, only darkly
as in a glass. Yet Johnson's observation makes a distinction—the glass is
perhaps a little less dark when the object is "before our eyes" and animated

with life, as opposed to a representation a century old. The problem of mediation remains, but it is less of an issue, if it was an issue at all for Johnson. The past appears to be problematical in this way, not the present.

What seems certain is that the development in the eighteenth century of a criticism based on historical perspective was an attempt to address some of the limitations involved in the "contemplation of pictures." What emerges is a more authoritative literary history. The same skepticism with which Johnson interrogates the provenance of any testimony is applied also to the provenance of any written artifact: "Those who have no power to judge of past times but by their own, should always doubt their conclusions." This assertion is part of Johnson's argument against the reputed small sale and silent reception of *Paradise Lost*. Johnson knew the worth of the poem, knew that Milton knew it, and, apparently certain that others must have known it too, casts about for the truth. The truth of the sale numbers, as Johnson sees it, is that fewer men were educated, and that women were totally excluded from learning at that time. The means of advertising and reviewing literature were likewise few, and, since literature was patronized by the court, "who that solicited favour or fashion would venture to praise the defender of regicides?" Given these adverse conditions, Johnson did not consider the sale of *Paradise Lost* as small, especially when compared to the sale of editions of Shakespeare; on the contrary, the sale is "an uncommon instance of the prevalence of genius," for it actually increased "till the Revolution put an end to the secrecy of love." Dryden's short epigram praising Milton above Homer and Virgil, which appeared in 1688, may have been one piece of Johnson's evidence.

Johnson also uses the historical method to attempt to assess the achievement of an author in terms of the difficulty he faced, for "that which is easy at one time is difficult at another." Addison's achievement, for example, is viewed in the context of a society which, on the whole, lacked literature and civility, and in which wit had most recently been the exclusive property of the rakes. We are reminded in the *Life of Prior* that battles, now celebrated by gazetteers, were then fit subjects for poetry. If the historical component of criticism seems only too obviously necessary today, even in the face of attacks by a purely rhetorical methodology, perhaps that is because Johnson made such good use of it.

Another characteristic way in which Johnson seeks to delimit the valid ground for inference is found in his approach to the muddy ground which links yet separates man and poet. Since Folkenflik was the first to write extensively on this subject, it is useful to begin with a brief review of his arguments. Noting that "life and work are essentially different things,

though conduct and poem are products of the same agency," Folkenflik goes
on to define three ways in which Johnson separates life and art. First, Johnson
consistently dissents from the doctrine of the *bonus orator,* the view stretching
from Isocrates, Cicero, and Quintilian into the Renaissance that a good
speaker must first be a good man. The disjunction between rhetoric and
action is a recurrent theme of the early *Life of Savage.* Related to the *bonus
orator* concept, but broader in that it does not focus on moral character alone,
is the idea that an author's personal characteristics and idiosyncrasies can be
found in his poem. The famous anecdote which explodes this notion is found
in the *Life of Thomson.* Lastly, Folkenflik argues that Johnson keeps the life
and the work apart in order to arrive at a more objective evaluation of the
work. Thus Johnson notices cases in which the poetry derives its reputation from the character of its author (Granville), or in which the minor
pieces of a great writer are overvalued (Milton), or, in a strange reversal,
how contempt for the poetry led to contempt for the man as physician
(Blackmore).

All three of these ways of separating life and work, it should be noted,
represent limitations on the use of inference: these things are what *cannot*
by concluded about an author by applying the argument from design. The
strictness of Johnson's method is communicated along with the subject
matter, for when Johnson departs into "fancy," which is rare, he usually
alerts his reader. Two examples come to mind: *Life of Milton* ("Fancy can
hardly forbare to conjecture with what temper Milton surveyed the silent
progress of his work"), and *Life of Pope* ("Who does not wish that Dryden
could have known the value of the homage that was paid to him, and foreseen
the greatness of his young admirer?")

Folkenflik also studies the connections Johnson allows between the artist
and his art. Of these I wish to focus on only two: the notion that genius is
dependent upon experience for its materials, and the related idea that, in
drawing a poetical character, Johnson focuses on only the abilities of the
man as poet. Both of these ideas reveal the extent to which Johnson uses
reflection as a criterion for judgment. Here it is not simply reflection applied
as a means to arrive at a certain conclusion, but also reflection used to
determine how reflective a poet is. Reflection here is neither the sole measure,
nor the highest, for it is only one component in the coalescent power called
"genius," but, as might be expected, the better poets are more reflective
than the others.

We must [turn now] to the proposition implied by *Rambler* No. 151,
that literature presupposes reflection. In Johnson's scheme, the age of recollection and narrative follows an age in which sense-experience is organized

by reason. Focusing on Johnson's definition of genius as "that energy which collects, combines, amplifies, and animates" (*Life of Pope*), Hagstrum has noticed that all of the verbs, with the possible exception of "animates," refer "directly to the materials of life and outside experience." While noting that it is not new to require the poet to be learned, Hagstrum places Johnson's emphasis firmly within the empirical tradition:

> Baconian philosophy and Lockean psychology provided him with a new touchstone for determining the rank of a poet: has he, like the natural philosopher, collected accurate and extensive data? has he exercised the empirical faculty in gathering from abroad? have the senses stocked the mind with fresh and original impressions of reality?

Hagstrum has been correctly criticized for his use of the term "empirical faculty" in opposition to "rational faculty." Both terms, of course, are collapsed in Locke's theory of reflection—reflection is rational, but it must have sense-experience to work upon before it knows anything. Hagstrum's central point, however, seems valid. That one of Johnson's touchstones for the poet is reflective breadth and depth is an idea I wish to expand upon.

Johnson's views on pastoral are notorious, but his grounds for dissatisfaction are not eccentric:

> It seems natural for a young poet to initiate himself by Pastorals, which, not professing to imitate real life, require no experience, and, exhibiting only the simple operation of unmingled passions, admit no subtle reasoning or deep inquiry.

The same criterion is applied to Congreve's first play, *The Old Batchelor.* Since light comedy is supposed to imitate manners in common life, "it apparently presupposes a familiar knowledge of many characters and exact observation of the passing world." What is concluded, however, is that Congreve took his characters from other poets, though there is evidence of "a mind vigorous and acute." Thus, even in an artificial performance, ability is discovered. Pope's *Pastorals,* another example, demonstrate "close thought" in their references to the times of day, the seasons of the year, and the periods of human life. Ambrose Philips's *Pastorals,* on the other hand, "are not loaded with much thought." At the other end of the scale from Philips is someone like Young whose poetry "abounds in thought." *Night Thoughts* is "variegated with deep reflections and striking allusions," and is described as "a wilderness of thought in which the felicity of fancy scatters flowers of every hue and every odour." What I find interesting here is that in the phrase "wilderness of thought" Johnson appears to be troping upon Milton's description of Eden as a "wilderness of sweets" (*Paradise Lost*, V, 294). The value of the pastoral *locus amoenus* thus is transferred by Johnson's phrase to the philosophical poem. Thought not only replaces pastoral, it also becomes a kind of pastoral, setting up the dialectic explored in *Rasselas*.

The issues explored in *Rasselas*, however, are never explicitly taken up in the *Lives*. Here, the high value Johnson places on poetry is generally related to the concentration of knowledge it contains. Contrasting moral and scientific knowledge in *Milton*, Johnson recommends that poets, orators, and historians be read most at school because they supply "most axioms of prudence, most principles of moral truth, and most materials for conversation." Perhaps one of the reasons Johnson admired Dryden was for "those penetrating remarks on human nature, for which he seems to have been peculiarly formed." Dryden is a good example of the poet as thinker, for his poetry shows "proof of a mind at once subtle and comprehensive." Everywhere in Dryden's work Johnson finds a broad knowledge of human nature:

> Dryden knew more of man in his general nature, and Pope in his local manners. The notions of Dryden were formed by comprehensive speculation, and those of Pope by minute attention. There is more dignity in the knowledge of Dryden, and more certainty in that of Pope.

By means of "comprehensive speculation" Dryden reaches a level of universality which constitutes the dignity of his verse. He has what Johnson felt Cowley completely lacked, "the grandeur of generality." Following Longinus, Johnson defines the sublime as "comprehension and expanse of thought," adding that "great thoughts are always general." But when Johnson attempts to locate the cause of Dryden's comprehensiveness, he concludes that, although Dryden had read widely, "he had a more pleasant, perhaps a nearer way to knowledge than by the silent progress of reading," which was the operation of his own mind—his quickness, memory, judgment, vigilance, "and a habit of reflection that suffered nothing useful to be lost."

It is the habit of reflection which leads the poet, in his survey of life, to "axioms of prudence" and "principles of moral truth." The wider the survey, the more extensive view of human nature the poet attains. Cowley, whose induction was apparently not very comprehensive, wrote upon "narrow views" failing to represent general nature:

> Cowley, like other poets who have written with narrow views and, instead of tracing intellectual pleasure to its natural source

in the mind of man, paid their court to temporary prejudices, has been at one time too much praised and too much neglected at another.

Knowing the world means knowing also the "mind of man," and that is known by turning the mind upon itself, and using what is found there for grounds of inference about the mind generally, exactly Imlac's advice to Rasselas. As opposed to Cowley, Dryden's critical precepts are valid because they "depend upon the nature of things and the structure of the human mind."

The view that reflection is essential to the poet is again made explicit in the *Life of Otway,* a dramatist Johnson considers second only to Shakespeare in the power of moving the audience. Otway's failure as an actor leads Johnson to consider the differences between poet and actor. Johnson conjectures that "the attention of the poet and the player have been differently employed—the one has been considering thought and the other action; one has watched the heart, the other contemplated the face." I don't pretend that Johnson is fair to the actor; I only notice that the distinction is made in terms of reflective depth. The actor mimics surfaces, whereas the poet is introspective, inquiring after causes, and tracing effects. And although Johnson's distinction separates surface and depth, it is clear that the poet's knowledge involves both, as we see when Johnson says of Addison that he "had read with critical eyes the important volume of human nature, and knew the heart of man from the depths of stratagem to the surface of affectation."

It is clear, then, that reflection, essential to the poet, is an important standard in Johnson's evaluations. Otway "conceived forcibly and drew originally by consulting nature in his own breast"; the metaphysicals, however, "neither copied nature nor life; neither painted the forms of matter nor represented the operations of the intellect." Wit, for Johnson, is not happiness of language, but "strength of thought," and a poem, in his view, which is not addressed to the understanding, but to the fancy, should never be lengthy because it will not hold our attention. One of the highest compliments Johnson pays to Milton is to say "he was naturally a thinker for himself."

The conception of mimesis implied by the criterion of reflection as Johnson uses it is not naïve, for it presupposes a mind interpreting experience, a mind, in fact, whose character can be assessed in part by the very amount of experience it assimilates and transforms. But the continual interpretation of the world by an active mind is only part of the creative process.

Art accomplishes its commentary on the world by inventing fictitious, if recognizable, other worlds. In the "Drury Lane Prologue" we were told that Shakespeare "exhausted worlds and then imagined new"; here we are told of Milton that "reality was a scene too narrow for his mind." Fiction, however, should not deny the world of experience for "the legitimate end of fiction is the conveyance of truth"; and therefore, "poetical action ought to be probable upon certain suppositions." What emerges, then, is a view of the creative process analogous to the paradigm of reflection I have been expositing. Once general principles and axioms have been reached, they are then used deductively, as it were, to create new worlds whose virtue, and whose power of pleasing arise from the conjunction of truth with novelty. In Imlac's phrase, the poet sends imagination out on the wing, but he does so, Johnson requires, in order to convey truth more effectively: "Poetry is the art of uniting pleasure with truth, by calling imagination to the help of reason."

A key verb in Johnson's definition of genius, the one we left temporarily aside, is "animates." This word refers to the power of representation. Johnson uses it in this sense when he says, for example, that Arb 'mot was "able to animate his mass of knowledge by a bright and active imagination." Animation is what Johnson means when he discusses Milton's knowledge in relation to his imagination: "To put these materials to poetical use is required an imagination capable of painting nature and realizing fiction." In two other places where Johnson discusses Milton's use of his learning, the descriptions turn on alchemical metaphors: "The heat of Milton's mind might be said to sublimate his learning, to throw off into his work the spirit of science, unmingled with its grosser parts"; "An accumulation of knowledge impregnated his mind, fermented by study and exalted by imagination." Perhaps what can ultimately be said about this intellectual alchemy is that it begins and ends in the mystery of genius. Imagination is required, it is true, to project one's point of view into the future, or to complete any induction at all. But the difficulty of creating a valuable work of art seems beyond the powers of ordinary reason. Johnson addresses this issue in the *Life of Butler:*

> It is indeed much more easy to form dialogues than to contrive adventures. Every position makes way for an argument, and every objection dictates an answer. . . . But whether it be that we comprehend but few of the possibilities of life, or that life itself affords little variety, every man who has tried knows how much labour it will cost to form such a combination of circumstances,

> as shall have at once the grace of novelty and credibility, and
> delight fancy without violence to reason.

The deconstruction of the difference between philosophy and literature, and
thus between criticism and literature, with reference to the metaphorical
grounds of language seems to me a valid move. But from another perspective,
that of Johnson's criterion of difficulty, the privileging of the poet makes
perfect sense. Although Johnson knew that the poet needed to be a critic
of his own work to succeed, it is doubtful whether the critic is likewise
required to be a poet. The crucial difference, as the quotation makes clear,
is the difficulty of forming a narrative, as opposed to forming an argument.
While there may be no absolute distinction between the language of the
poet and that of the philosopher, the distinction, based not on materials
but on the difficulty of what is attempted with those materials, seems worth
preserving. No one could say that Johnson mystifies the poet, for he continually debunks the poets he reviews; nor could anyone say that Johnson
is intimidated by the great work of art. His critical standpoint thus makes
his respect for the work of genius that much more convincing.

There is a crucial problem with poetry, however, which is focused by
the union, or joint effort, of imagination and reason. If imagination is
supposed to provide the pleasure, while reason assures instruction, the danger
is always present that the desire to please will overcome the duty to instruct.
Since poetry is not reducible to precepts, the tension between Johnson's
prescriptions for poetry as moral statement and as aesthetic object is clearly
felt, perhaps nowhere more so than in the *Life of Dryden,* where an admiration
for genius and a disgust for the degradation of genius are alternately
expressed.

If a consequence of viewing poetry as a pleasing instruction is a tension
between the moral and aesthetic components of art, it is nonetheless true
that the primary appeal of art for Johnson is found in its power to sustain
interest:

> Works of imagination excell by their allurement and delight; by
> their power of attracting and detaining the attention. That book
> is good in vain which the reader throws away. He only is master
> who keeps the mind in pleasing captivity; whose pages are perused
> with eagerness, and in hope of new pleasure are perused again;
> and whose conclusion is perceived with an eye of sorrow, such
> as the traveller casts upon departing day.

The principle is invoked here in order to defend Dryden's *Aeneid,* but it may be taken as emblematic of the defense of Dryden's poetry generally. Johnson invites such an extension, not only by bringing the general principle to bear, but also by his references to other writers:

> By his proportion of this predomination I will consent that Dryden should be tried: of this, which, in opposition to reason, makes Ariosto the darling and pride of Italy; of this, which, in defiance of criticism, continues Shakespeare the sovereign of the drama.

The significant phrases here are "in opposition to reason," and "in defiance of criticism." Reason and criticism are not equivalent terms, although they overlap. Both are subordinated in Johnson's view to the power of pleasing, not absolutely, but relative to the effectiveness of poetry. Reason, apparently, is a larger category than criticism, in that reason forms and tests principles of all kinds, whereas criticism is concerned solely with the principles of the art of writing. This sort of distinction directs the judgment of *All for Love,* for, although that work has the "fewest improprieties of style or character," it has "one fault equal to many, *though rather moral than critical"* (my emphasis). The fault, in Johnson's view, is to recommend for imitation "conduct which through all ages the good have censured as vicious, and the bad despised as foolish." The moral argument may be part of Johnson's criticism of Dryden's play, but the uses of "moral" and "critical" imply their separation.

Criticism appears to focus primarily on the aesthetic quality of technical excellence. Thus, although the allegorical scheme of *The Hind and the Panther* is considered absurd, it is confessed "to be written with great smoothness of meter, a wide extent of knowledge, and an abundant multiplicity of images." The aesthetic emphasis of the critic, moreover, is clearly stated in Johnson's opinion of Burnet's biography of Rochester, a book "which the critick ought to read for its elegance, the philosopher for its arguments, and the saint for its piety." Isaac Watts, like Burnet, combined moral with aesthetic virtues. The learning and acuteness of the Dissenters had been blunted by "coarseness and inelegance of style," until Watts "showed them that zeal and purity might be expressed and enforced by polished diction." Similarly, a poet like West combined the characters, apparently distinct things, of "Poet and Saint."

The pious book which is poorly written will carry no force, but the reverse seems not to be true. Elegance of expression and power of wit are attractive in themselves. Johnson never loses sight of what he calls "the moral effect of fiction," which he invokes in order to evaluate Richardson's expansion of Rowe's Lothario into Lovelace. Richardson's version is better, we are told, because it had the power "to make virtuous resentment over-power all the benevolence which wit, elegance, and courage naturally excite, and to lose at last the hero in the villain." Yet, however it may be that the best poetry combines a vivid imagination with a resolute moral purpose, there is much in poetry that gives Johnson a purely aesthetic pleasure. Watts was "one of the few poets with whom youth and ignorance may be safely pleased." Dryden may not have been a saint, but he was a far better poet. If Shakespeare was great "in opposition to criticism," Dryden evoked no such critical qualms.

From the point of view of reflection, the problems raised by the *Life of Dryden* are particularly perplexing because Dryden, who had the "habit of reflection," also seems to have lacked the kind of reflectiveness associated in *The Rambler* with the moral conduct of life. What may be discovered is that the evaluations in the *Lives* imply, as they did in *The Rambler,* a hierarchy based on degrees of reflection. As we have seen, the kind of reflection Dryden employed led him to knowledge of the world, and to fundamental insights about human nature; the metaphysicals missed this knowledge of general nature, even though "to write on their plan it was at least necessary to read and think," and even though, in reading them, "if the imagination is not always gratified, at least the powers of reflection and comparison are em-ployed." Thus, although the metaphysicals thought, and their poetry stim-ulates thinking, their poetry is weakened by the lack of the general principles which Dryden attained. Dryden, however, falls short of another level of reflection because of his vanity, his willingness to please, and the subsequent debasement of his genius.

Johnson had used the phrase "reigning error" in the *Life of Savage* to describe the faulty principle upon which Savage lived his life, a principle the enunciation of which illuminated the tragic consistency of Savage's flight from reflection. Dryden obviously possesses a greater dignity than Savage, but it can be inferred from the *Life of Dryden* that Dryden too had a "reigning error," which was that he wrote "only to please." The Restoration theaters, to which Dryden tailored his plays, are described by Johnson as "mansions of dissolute licentiousness" which were "avoided by those who desired the character of seriousness or decency." Johnson is at pains to notice that Dryden's personal character has never been questioned, for "he abetted vice and vanity only with his pen":

> His works afford too many examples of dissolute licentiousness
> and abject adulation; but they were probably, like his merriment,

artificial and constrained—the effects of study and meditation, and his trade rather than his pleasure.

This appearance of extenuating Dryden's fault, however, is followed dramatically by the most damning paragraph imaginable:

> Of the mind that can trade in corruption, and can deliberately pollute itself with ideal wickedness for the sake of spreading the contagion of society, I wish not to conceal or excuse the depravity.—Such degradation of the dignity of genius, such abuse of superlative abilities, cannot be contemplated but with grief and indignation. What consolation can be had Dryden has afforded, by living to regret, and to testify his repentance.

Actually, the question of the degradation of the dignity of genius arises earlier when one of Dryden's dedications is described as written "in a strain of flattery which disgraces genius, and which it was wonderful that any man that knew the meaning of his own words could use without self-destestation." Milton, we were told, set his expectations for himself according to a survey of his abilities; Dryden, no doubt, knew his abilities also, but that knowledge was not sufficient to become a standard unto itself. Genius did not imply, as Johnson so clearly felt it should have, the kind of standards which, upon reflection, would guide and guard its use. Instead, its use, being debased, brought no "self-detestation."

Johnson here implicitly judges Dryden according to a standard of reflection higher than that which Dryden attained. That standard includes, of course, a check on the vanity which appears to be an occupational hazard for authors. Johnson's use of the almost formulaic phrase "not sufficiently considered" in debunking Dryden's self-recommendations makes the point: "It was throughout his life very much his custom to recommend his works by representations of the difficulties that he had encountered, without appearing to have sufficiently considered that where there is no difficulty there is no praise." In these instances Johnson describes the moral failures which conspired, as he felt, to mar Dryden's writing. But when the discussion is shifted to purely aesthetic grounds, Dryden elicits the highest praise. The vanity evident in Dryden's prose is seen now from a softened perspective:

> He may be thought to mention himself too frequently; but while he forces himself upon our esteem, we cannot refuse him to stand high in his own. Every thing is excused by the play of images and spriteliness of expression.

The forgiveness that Dryden's style elicits from a reader with the strictest standards for moral and religious purity alerts one to the fact that Johnson's view of Dryden's greatness focuses almost exclusively on formal and rhetorical achievements. The plays Dryden wrote in 1678, for example, allowing even the charges of plagiarism, show "facility of composition," "readiness of language," and "copiousness of sentiment." In summarizing Dryden's achievement at the end of the *Life,* we are told that Dryden enriched the language with a variety of models, refined it with his diction, and improved poetry generally through his versification. With all of his faults, as we know, Dryden gave Johnson a more sublime form of pleasure than he received from Pope.

At this point we should define more distinctly if we can the degrees of reflection. On the one hand, there is the process which constructs an empirical picture of the world, which is constantly revised in that the process is open-ended; the more the process assimilates, the more comprehensive the views obtained. At some point, however—a point I would hesitate to specify, another kind of thinking which formulates attitudes toward what it knows comes into play. I hesitate to specify the point at which this shift occurs, because just as experience affects attitude, so attitude helps to determine experience. The hypothetical distinction between fact and value seems useful, however, because although they are not mutually exclusive, one can think of cases in which fact and value are not identical. Socrates' claim that knowledge and virtue are the same thing, notwithstanding, knowledge can be completely amoral. In this sense, it is like the lumber in Boswell's metaphor, which in Johnson was converted to living wisdom. It may be, as *The Rambler* holds, that he who thinks deeply, thinks morally, because thinking educates, or leads one out from the purely egocentric point of view, and thus accomplishes in the moral world the equivalent of the Copernican revolution in the scientific world. But the other possibility, which *The Rambler* also recognized, is that there is commonly a disjunction in the human world between knowledge and action, as also between rhetorical power and action. The rhetorician may be cynical or sincere, but, regardless of his attitude toward what he knows, there is a purely formal aspect of his performance which determines its effectiveness. Nothing new here, of course. I simply restate what is known in order to suggest that, just as there is a moment in the process of reflection which is premoral, or even amoral, there seems also to be a purely aesthetic form of reflection which is a factor in Johnson's evaluation of the poets. It is a criterion used throughout, but it can be seen most clearly in the *Life of Pope.*

Johnson views Pope's life with at least as much irony as he views Dryden's, possibly because Pope's vanity was at least equal to his predecessor's. Pope's threat in a letter, for example, to stop writing because the age deserves no more correspondence from him receives a classic Johnsonian response:

> The man who threatens the world is always ridiculous; for the world can easily go on without him, and in a short time will cease to miss him. I have heard of an idiot who used to revenge his vexations by lying all night upon the bridge. . . . Pope had been flattered till he thought himself one of the moving powers in the system of life. When he talked of laying down his pen, those who sat round him intreated and implored, and self-love did not suffer him to suspect that they went away and laughed.

There are ironies for reflection here. Pope was a man, we are told, who never took tea without a stratagem, and who played the politician, as a lady remarked, over cabbages and turnips; yet, through the exorbitance of his vanity, he is shown to have some affinity with that most vain and unreflective of authors, Swift's Hack. Just as Dryden's vanity betrayed him into a public contest with Settle, Pope's vanity betrays him into a war with Cibber, which Johnson thinks debases only Pope: "The dishonour of being shewn as Cibber's antagonist could never be compensated by the victory." The fault is defined as a lack of judgment: "Pope had now been enough acquainted with human life to know, if his passion had not been too powerful for his understanding, that from a contention like his with Cibber the world seeks nothing but diversion, which is given at the expense of the higher character." The high and the low are leveled by a common human failing: Johnson had noted earlier of the dunces that the world could only laugh at their injuries, "for no man sympathizes with the sorrows of vanity."

My point, of course, is not to rehearse the old chestnut about vanity as Johnson's central theme. I hope it has been demonstrated by now that the theme of vanity is essentially only one manifestation of the theme of reflection. My point is simply that one implication of the *Life of Pope* seems to be that what separates Pope from dunce is not necessarily any inherent moral superiority, but rather the ability of the genius as poet. Johnson admits that a satire on bad writing has the positive effect of improving judgment and putting down pretension, but he also states that Pope's motives were revenge, petulance, and malignity. Johnson's comments on the *Essay on Man* are a good example of the possibility of a division between content and form. For while the *Essay* was "a work of great labour and long consideration," Johnson judged it finally to be no more than "wonder-working sounds":

This *Essay* affords an egregious instance of the predominance of genius, the dazzling display of imagery, and the seductive powers of eloquence. Never were penury of knowledge and vulgarity of sentiment so happily disguised.

If we return to the comparison with Dryden, it appears that Pope's peculiar virtue, according to Johnson, is that he exemplifies in his style the aesthetic equivalent of reflection, which Dryden to some degree neglected, and which Johnson finds a new name for," *poetical prudence.*" This poetical prudence consists first in Pope's peculiar combination of natural faculties with a disposition to labor. More specifically, "the constituent and fundamental principle" of Pope's intellectual character was "Good Sense, a prompt and intuitive perception of consonance and propriety." Pope likewise had genius, and great strength of memory, but to all these "benefits of nature" he added the improvement of "incessant and unwearied diligence."

The dichotomy of genius and labor, soil and cultivation, that recurred in *The Rambler* appears frequently also throughout *The Lives of the Poets.* In a different context, the exposition of the critical equivalent of the argument from design, I have already cited examples of Milton, Dryden, Waller, and Rochester, who were measured by their ratio of genius in proportion to study. Cowley, who had a mind "capacious by nature and replenished by study," would be another example. What this criterion implies is that, just as Locke divided epistemology into sensation and reflection, Johnson distinguishes in his criticism between nature and reflection. Set against the endowment of genius that any given author begins with is the demand of the "toil of thinking." In the *Lives,* the recurrent word for this activity is "diligence." Diligence is associated with the direct contemplation of experience, and also with the activities that enlarge that contemplation, such as study and reading; these forms of labor are necessary to the preparation of the poet, but another form of diligence is the effort of composition itself, especially the process of revision. An example which seems to involve all of these senses of "diligence" is Johnson's comment on Pope's *Moral Essays,* that they "are the product of diligent speculation upon human life; much labour has been bestowed upon them, and Pope seldom laboured in vain."

Just as Locke had said that the continual practice of reading enables one to intuit meaning more quickly, Johnson implies nearly everywhere that continual practice in composition leads to increased "facility." Once Dryden, for instance, began to settle "his principles of versification" by writing several tragedies in succession, "he soon obtained the full effect of his diligence, and added facility to exactness." But revision, a further degree of diligence, was another matter:

As he had studied with great diligence the art of poetry, and
enlarged or rectified his notions by experience perpetually increasing, he had his mind stored with principles and observations:
he poured out his knowledge with little labour; for of labour,
notwithstanding the multiplicity of his productions, there is sufficient reason to suspect he was not a lover. To write *con amore,*
with fondness for the employment, with perpetual touches and
retouches, with unwillingness to take leave of his own idea, and
an unwearied pursuit of unattainable perfection, was, I think,
no part of his character.

All of the elements are there—diligence in study, principles formed and
refined by experience—except the diligence of revision and what that implies, the vision of an ideal perfection. By nature above rules, Dryden
possessed an "original rectitude," but that phrase describes only the natural
choice of a correct diction (another example, by the way, of the purely
aesthetic character of the activity I have been describing). For, while Dryden
was by nature greater than Pope, Pope and Milton are examples of more
diligent *artists,* and thus "every writer since Milton must give place to Pope."

An observation in the *Life of Milton* shows furthermore that diligence
applied in the tedious labor of revision also results in facility. Of the many
corrections found in the Cambridge manuscript of Milton's early poems,
Johnson remarks: "Such reliques shew how excellence is acquired: what we
hope ever to do with ease we may learn first to do with diligence."

In Pope's method we find that revision is interwoven in the process of
composition itself. One of the ways Pope's "incessant and unwearied diligence" manifested itself was in preserving and reworking fragments of verse
that later would find their place within the larger fabric of a complete poem.
The analogy of this method to the process of formulating and concatenating
principles into an open-ended system is only too obvious. The description
of Pope's method, in fact, could suitably describe reflection also, for that
method was "to write his first thoughts in his first words, and gradually to
amplify, decorate, rectify, and refine them."

This continual process of reseeing and rewriting, together with Pope's
natural abilities, defines only one aspect of poetical prudence. For that
prudence consisted additionally in writing always in the same mode, so that
what had been learned would always find future application:

Of this uniformity the certain consequences was readiness and
dexterity. By perpetual practice language had in his mind a
systematical arrangement; having always the same use for words,
he had words so selected and combined as to be ready at his call.

This increase of facility he confessed himself to have perceived in the progress of his translation.

What seems most interesting in the concept of poetical prudence, however, is the way that "facility" turns into "felicity," a term Johnson reserves for the happiest moments of genius. The famous passage from *Cooper's Hill,* for example, the one Pope parodied in "Flow, Welsted, flow," has not been praised above its merit: "It has beauty peculiar to itself, and must be numbered among those felicities which cannot be produced by wit and labour, but must arise unexpectedly in some hour propitious to poetry." Felicity here—as in the comment that Waller's style was attained "by a felicity like instinct"—is a manifestation, not of art and labour, but of nature. Its appearance is almost serendipitous, as seems clear in Johnson's judgment that *The Rape of the Lock* is Pope's best work: "Those performances which strike with wonder, are combinations of skilful genius with happy casualty; and it is not likely that any felicity, like the discovery of a new race of preternatural agents, should happen twice to the same man."

Yet, as the element of "skilful genius" in the combination implies, it seems that felicity only occurs to those already well practiced, and can even be attained in some degree through revision. Blackmore, for instance, the very opposite of Pope, was a poet who "had never elevated his views to . . . ideal perfection," and who "waited for no felicities of fancy; but caught his first thoughts in the first words in which they were presented." *Creation,* however, has "the appearance of more circumspection . . . it has either been written with great care, or, what cannot be imagined of so long a work, with such felicity as made care less necessary." The alternative explanations, either care or felicity, point to a blurring of the line separating art and nature.

A similar shading off of facility into felicity occurs in Johnson's opinion of *Eloisa and Abelard,* "one of the most happy productions of human wit." The subject has been "judiciously chosen," and "diligently improved": "Pope has left nothing behind him which seems more the effect of studious perseverance and laborious revisal. Here is particularly observable the 'curiosa felicitas,' a fruitful soil, and careful cultivation." Felicity here, therefore, is the combination of nature and reflection.

It is not quite accurate, nonetheless, to say that felicity occurs when art becomes indistinguishable from nature, if only because what we mean by "nature" is mediated by art from the beginning. In this case, for example, the subject that proved such "fruitful soil" was "judiciously chosen." Allowing for this qualification, however, Johnson seems to feel that the best art approximates nature, or at least hides its artfulness. He says pejoratively of Gray's odes: "His art and his struggle are too visible, and there is too little appearance of ease and "nature." Some idea of what is meant by "nature" in this context can be inferred from its coupling with "ease" and its relation to "appearance." This is not nature as talent, but the *sprezzatura* of the accomplished artist.

If Pope, however, best exemplifies the aesthetic form of reflection, there are ironies to this purely poetical kind of prudence, ironies related, of course, to the tension between life and art. Pope, we are told, did not publish hastily, but kept his works by him for two years: "He knew that the mind is always enamoured of its own productions, and did not trust his first fondness." This reflexive restraint of vanity practiced in the realm of art was not, as we have seen, always practiced in life. Perhaps it *is* easier to write than live.

At this point, a review is called for in order to move toward conclusion. Reflection is a criterion of judgment in *The Lives of the Poets* in two distinct, yet continuous, senses: reflection is necessary for the knowledge the poet needs before he begins to write, for "knowledge of the subject is to the poet what durable materials are to the architect"; and secondly, reflection is required in the process of composition and revision. In this purely poetical form, the process moves from diligence, to facility, and finally to a felicity which approximates nature, meaning that element in poetry which cannot be accounted for by reason or rational process.

Yet, as much as it would appear that the effects of diligence can repair the defects of nature, it is also true for Johnson that diligence is not enough. Prior is an appropriate example:

> What he had valuable he owes to his diligence and his judgement. His diligence has justly placed him amongst the most correct of the English poets. . . . He had apparently such rectitude of judgement as secured him from every thing that approached to the ridiculous or absurd; but as laws operate in civil agency not to the excitement of virtue, but the repression of wickedness, so judgement in the operations of the intellect can hinder faults, but not produce excellence. Prior is never low, nor very often sublime. . . . He has many vigorous but few happy lines; he has every thing by purchase, and nothing by gift; he had no 'nightly visitation' of the Muse, no infusions of sentiment or felicities of fancy.

Similarly, it is seen as a limitation in Dryden that "he studied rather than felt, and produced sentiments not such as Nature enforces, but meditation supplies." What is wanted is the "pathetick," the power in a representation of moving the affections, and this, apparently, no amount of thinking can supply.

Chronology

<table>
<tr><td>1709</td><td>Samuel Johnson born September 7 in Lichfield, Staffordshire.</td></tr>
<tr><td>1717</td><td>Enters Lichfield Grammar School.</td></tr>
<tr><td>1728–29</td><td>Attends Pembroke College, Oxford, but does not take a degree.</td></tr>
<tr><td>1733</td><td>Translates Lobo's Voyage to Abyssinia.</td></tr>
<tr><td>1735</td><td>Marries Elizabeth Jervis Porter, a widow.</td></tr>
<tr><td>1736</td><td>Opens a school at Edial, and begins Irene.</td></tr>
<tr><td>1737</td><td>Moves to London, along with David Garrick; his wife joins him soon after.</td></tr>
<tr><td>1738</td><td>Begins writing for Gentleman's Magazine, and publishes "London."</td></tr>
<tr><td>1739–43</td><td>Earns living writing miscellaneous journalistic pieces, some of which are biographical sketches.</td></tr>
<tr><td>1740</td><td>James Boswell born October 29 in Edinburgh.</td></tr>
<tr><td>1744</td><td>Johnson publishes The Life of Mr. Richard Savage.</td></tr>
<tr><td>1745</td><td>Johnson publishes proposals for an edition of Shakespeare.</td></tr>
<tr><td>1746</td><td>Johnson signs a contract for the Dictionary.</td></tr>
<tr><td>1749</td><td>Johnson publishes The Vanity of Human Wishes. His Irene is produced by Garrick.</td></tr>
<tr><td>1750–52</td><td>Johnson founds and does most of the writing for The Rambler, a periodical.</td></tr>
<tr><td>1752</td><td>Johnson's wife dies, leaving him to care for her blind friend, Anna Williams.</td></tr>
</table>

1753–58	Boswell attends the University of Edinburgh.
1755	Johnson receives an honorary degree from Oxford, and publishes the *Dictionary*.
1756	Johnson issues further proposals for an edition of Shakespeare.
1758–59	Boswell studies law at the University of Edinburgh.
1758–60	Johnson contributes the *Idler* series of essays to the *Universal Chronicle*, a weekly periodical.
1759	Johnson's mother dies; he publishes *Rasselas*. Boswell studies civil law at the University of Glasgow.
1760	Boswell makes his first visit to London, and converts for a short time to Roman Catholicism.
1762	The King awards Johnson a yearly pension of £300.
1763	Boswell meets Johnson in a bookstore. Boswell collaborates with Andrew Erskine in publishing *Letters between the Honourable Andrew Erskine and James Boswell, Esq.* He goes to Utrecht to study civil law.
1764	Johnson and Sir Joshua Reynolds found The (Literary) Club. Boswell goes on a Grand Tour of Germany and Switzerland, and meets Voltaire and Rousseau.
1765	Johnson publishes his edition of Shakespeare. He meets the Thrales.
1765–66	Boswell continues Grand Tour, and meets Pasquale Paoli in Corsica. He returns from Continent, is admitted to the Scottish bar, and begins practice in Edinburgh.
1768	Boswell publishes *An Account of Corsica*.
1769	Boswell marries Margaret Montgomerie.
1773	Boswell's daughter Veronica born; he is elected to The Club. Boswell and Johnson tour the Highlands and the Hebrides.
1774	Johnson publishes *The Patriot*, and tours Wales with the Thrales. Boswell's daughter Euphemia born.
1775	Johnson publishes *Journey to the Western Islands of Scotland*. Boswell's son Alexander born.

1776   Boswell's son David born.

1777   Johnson begins work on *The Lives of the Poets.*

1777–83 Boswell contributes a series of essays, *The Hypochondriack,* to *The London Magazine,* a periodical.

1778   Boswell's son James born.

1779   Johnson publishes the first four volumes of *The Lives of the Poets.*

1781   Johnson publishes the final six volumes of *The Lives of the Poets.*

1782   Boswell's father dies and he succeeds as Laird of Auchinleck.

1783   Johnson has a stroke, from which he recovers.

1784   Johnson dies on December 13 and is buried in Westminster Abbey.

1785   Boswell publishes *Journal of a Tour to the Hebrides.*

1786   Boswell moves to London, where he is admitted to the English bar.

1788   Boswell is appointed Recorder of Carlisle.

1789   Boswell's wife dies.

1791   Boswell publishes *The Life of Samuel Johnson, LL.D.* and *Memoirs.*

1795   Boswell dies in London on May 19.

Contributors

HAROLD BLOOM, Sterling Professor of the Humanities at Yale University, is the author of *The Anxiety of Influence, Poetry and Repression,* and many other volumes of literary criticism. His forthcoming study, *Freud: Transference and Authority,* attempts a full-scale reading of all of Freud's major writings. A MacArthur Prize Fellow, he is general editor of five series of literary criticism published by Chelsea House.

W. K. WIMSATT was Professor of English at Yale University from 1955 until his death in 1975. Best known for his works written in collaboration with Monroe Beardsley, *The Verbal Icon* and *Hateful Contraries,* his achievement as a scholar of Johnson and Boswell is formidable.

FREDERICK A. POTTLE is Sterling Professor of English Emeritus at Yale University. He has long been acknowledged as the dean of Boswell scholars, and as coeditor of Boswell's Private Papers (Yale editions) and author of the definitive biography of Boswell's early life (*James Boswell: The Earlier Years 1740–1769*) he has radically reshaped our understanding of Boswell's life and literary career.

WALTER JACKSON BATE is Kingsley Porter Professor at Harvard University. His works on the life of Johnson (*The Achievement of Samuel Johnson* and *Samuel Johnson*) are among the best in this century.

PAUL FUSSELL is Donald T. Regan Professor of English Literature at the University of Pennsylvania. His other books include *The Rhetorical World of Augustan Humanism* and *The Great War and Modern Memory.*

LEOPOLD DAMROSCH, JR., is Junior Professor of English at the University of Maryland. His other publications include *Samuel Johnson and the Tragic Sense* and *Symbol and Truth in Blake's Myth.*

FRANK BRADY is Professor of English at the Graduate Center of the City

University of New York and chairman of the Editorial Committee and coeditor of the Yale editions of the Private Papers of James Boswell. His books include *Boswell's Political Career* and *James Boswell: The Later Years 1769–1795*.

ROBERT BELL is Associate Professor of English at Williams College. He is the author of several articles on eighteenth-century topics.

WILLIAM C. DOWLING is Associate Professor of English at the University of New Mexico, and he is Associate Professor at the Institute for Advanced Study in the Humanities at the University of Edinburgh. His other books include *Language and Logos in Boswell's "Life of Johnson."*

JOHN BARRELL is Lecturer in English at King's College, Cambridge. His other works include *The Idea of Landscape and the Sense of Place, 1730–1840: An approach to the poetry of John Clare*.

LAURA QUINNEY teaches English at Cornell University, and is writing a book on Johnson. Her essay on Kafka appears in the Chelsea House volume *Modern Critical Views: Franz Kafka*.

GORDON TURNBULL is Assistant Professor of English at Yale University and research assistant on the Yale editions of the Private Papers of James Boswell.

ROBERT J. GRIFFIN is Assistant Professor of English at Bowdoin College, and is finishing a book on Johnson's criticism. His essay on Pope appears in the Chelsea House volume *Modern Critical Views: Alexander Pope*.

Bibliography

DR. SAMUEL JOHNSON

Alkon, Paul. *Samuel Johnson and Moral Discipline.* Evanston, Ill.: North-western University Press, 1967.

Bailey, John. *Dr. Johnson and His Circle,* revised by L. F. Powell. Oxford: Oxford University Press, 1944.

Bloom, Edward A. *Samuel Johnson in Grub Street.* Providence, R.I.: Brown University Press, 1957.

Bronson, Bertrand H. *Johnson Agonistes and Other Essays.* Cambridge: Cambridge University Press, 1946.

Chapin, Chester. *The Religious Thought of Samuel Johnson.* Ann Arbor: University of Michigan Press, 1968.

Clifford, James L. *Young Samuel Johnson.* New York: McGraw-Hill, 1955.

Davis, Bertram. *Johnson before Boswell.* New Haven: Yale University Press, 1960.

Edinger, William. *Samuel Johnson and Poetic Style.* Chicago: The University of Chicago Press, 1977.

Gray, James. *Johnson's Sermons: A Study.* Oxford: Oxford University Press, 1972.

Greene, Donald J. *The Politics of Samuel Johnson.* New Haven: Yale University Press, 1957.

Hagstrum, Jean. *Samuel Johnson's Literary Criticism.* Minneapolis: University of Minnesota Press, 1952.

Hilles, Frederick, ed. *The Age of Johnson: Essays Presented to C. B. Tinker.* New Haven: Yale University Press, 1949.

————, ed. *New Light on Johnson.* New Haven: Yale University Press, 1959.

Hodgart, M. J. C. *Samuel Johnson.* London: B. T. Batsford, 1962.

Hoover, Benjamin. *Samuel Johnson's Parliamentary Reporting.* Berkeley and Los Angeles: University of California Press, 1953.

Lascelles, Mary, et al., eds. *Johnson, Boswell and Their Circle: Essays Presented to L. F. Powell.* Oxford: Clarendon Press, 1965.

Leavis, F. R. *The Common Pursuit.* London: Chatto & Windus, 1952.

———. "Johnson as Critic." *Scrutiny* 12 (1944): 187–204.

McAdam, E. L., Jr. *Dr. Johnson and the English Law.* Syracuse, N.Y.: Syracuse University Press, 1951.

Quinlan, Maurice. *Samuel Johnson: A Layman's Religion.* Madison: University of Wisconsin Press, 1963.

Sachs, Ariel. *Passionate Intelligence: Imagination and Reason in the Work of Samuel Johnson.* Baltimore: The Johns Hopkins University Press, 1967.

Sherbo, Arthur. *Samuel Johnson, Editor of Shakespeare, with an Essay on the Adventurer.* Urbana: University of Illinois Press, 1956.

Sledd, James H., and J. Kolb Gwin. *Dr. Johnson's Dictionary: Essays in the Biography of a Book.* Chicago: The University of Chicago Press, 1955.

Turberville, A. S. *Johnson's England.* Oxford: Clarendon Press, 1933.

Vesterman, William. *The Stylistic Life of Samuel Johnson.* New Brunswick, N.J.: Rutgers University Press, 1977.

Voitle, Robert. *Samuel Johnson the Moralist.* Cambridge: Harvard University Press, 1961.

Wimsatt, W. K. *Philosophic Words: A Study of Style and Meaning in* The Rambler *and* Dictionary *of Samuel Johnson.* New Haven: Yale University Press, 1948.

JAMES BOSWELL

Aaron, Daniel, ed. *Studies in Biography.* Cambridge: Harvard University Press, 1978.

Bailey, Margery, ed. *The Hypochrondriack.* With introductions. 2 vols. Palo Alto, Calif.: Stanford University Press, 1928.

Brady, Frank. *Boswell's Political Career.* New Haven: Yale University Press, 1965.

———. *James Boswell: The Later Years 1769–1795.* New York: McGraw-Hill, 1984.

Butt, John. *Biography in the Hands of Walton, Johnson, and Boswell.* Berkeley: University of California Press, 1966.

Chapman, R. W. *Johnsonian and Other Essays and Reviews.* Oxford: Clarendon Press, 1953.

———. *Two Centuries of Johnsonian Scholarship.* Glasgow: University of Glasgow Press, 1945.

Collins, P. A. W. *James Boswell.* London: Published for the British Council and the National Book League by Longmans, Green, 1956.

Dowling, William C. *Language and Logos in Boswell's* Life of Johnson. Princeton: Princeton University Press, 1981.

Finlayson, Ian. *The Moth and the Candle: A Life of James Boswell.* London: Constable & Co., 1984

Fitzgerald, Percy H. *Boswell's Autobiography.* London: Chatto & Windus, 1912.

————. *The Life of James Boswell.* 2 vols. New York: D. Appleton & Co., 1891.

Fussell, Paul, Jr. "The Force of Literary Memory in Boswell's *London Journal.*" *Studies in English Literature* 2 (1962): 351–57.

Golden, James L. "James Boswell on Rhetoric and Belles Lettres." *Quarterly Journal of Speech* 50 (1964): 266–76.

Lewis, Wyndham W. B. *The Hooded Hawk.* London: Eyre & Spottiswoode, 1946.

Longaker, John Mark. *English Biography in the Eighteenth Century.* Philadelphia: University of Pennsylvania Press, 1931.

Lustig, Irma S. "Boswell's Literary Criticism in the *Life of Johnson.*" *Studies in English Literature, 1500–1900* 6 (1966): 529–41.

McLaren, Moray. *Corsica Boswell: Paoli, Johnson and Freedom.* London: Secker and Warburg, 1966.

Mallory, George. *Boswell the Biographer.* London: Smith, Elder and Co., 1912.

Nicolson, Harold. *The Development of English Biography.* London: Hogarth Press, 1933.

Pottle, Frederick A. "The Incredible Boswell." *Blackwood's Magazine* 243 (1925): 149–56.

————. *James Boswell: The Earlier Years 1740–1769.* New York: McGraw-Hill, 1966

Quenell, Peter. *The Profane Virtues: Four Studies of the Eighteenth Century.* New York: Viking Press, 1945.

Roberts, S. C. *Doctor Johnson and Others.* Cambridge: Cambridge University Press, 1958.

Tinker, Chauncey Brewster. *Young Boswell: Chapters on James Boswell the Biographer.* Boston: Atlantic Monthly Press, 1922.

Wimsatt, W. K. *Hateful Contraries.* Lexington: University of Kentucky Press, 1965.

Acknowledgments

"Johnson's Theory" (originally entitled "Johnson's Theory—I" and "Johnson's Theory—II") by W. K. Wimsatt from *The Prose Style of Samuel Johnson* by W. K. Wimsatt, © 1941 by Yale University Press. Reprinted by permission.

"The Life of Boswell" by Frederick A. Pottle from *The Yale Review* 35 (Spring 1946), © 1945–1946 by Yale University. Reprinted by permission.

"The Treachery of the Human Heart and the Stratagems of Defense" by Walter Jackson Bate from *The Achievement of Samuel Johnson* by Walter Jackson Bate, © 1955 by Oxford University Press. Reprinted by permission.

"In Praise of *Rasselas:* Four Notes (Converging)" by W. K. Wimsatt from *Imagined Worlds: Essays on English Novels and Novelists in Honour of John Butt* edited by Maynard Mack and Ian Gregor, © 1968 by Methuen & Co. Reprinted by permission.

" 'The Anxious Employment of a Periodical Writer' " by Paul Fussell from *Samuel Johnson and the Life of Writing* by Paul Fussell, © 1971 by Paul Fussell. Reprinted by permission.

"The Vanity of Human Wishes" by Leopold Damrosch, Jr., from *Samuel Johnson and the Tragic Sense* by Leopold Damrosch, Jr., © 1979 by Princeton University Press. Reprinted by permission of the publisher.

"The Strategies of Biography and Some Eighteenth-Century Examples" by Frank Brady from *Literary Theory and Structure: Essays in Honor of William K. Wimsatt* by Frank Brady, John Palmer, and Martin Price, © 1973 by Yale University Press. Reprinted by permission.

"Boswell's Notes toward a Supreme Fiction: From *London Journal* to *Life of Johnson*" by Robert H. Bell from *Modern Language Quarterly* 38, no. 2 (1977), © 1977 by University of Washington. Reprinted by permission.

"A Plutarchan Hero: The *Tour to Corsica*" by William C. Dowling from *The Boswellian Hero* by William C. Dowling, © 1979 by the University of Georgia Press. Reprinted by permission of the University of Georgia Press.

" 'The language properly so-called': Johnson's Language and Politics" by John Barrell from *English Literature in History 1730–80: An Equal, Wide Survey* by John Barrell, © 1983 by John Barrell. Reprinted by permission of Hutchinson & Co., Ltd.

"Johnson in Mourning" by Laura Quinney, © 1986 by Laura Quinney. Published for the first time in this volume. Printed by permission.

" 'Generous Attachment': The Politics of Biography in the *Tour to the Hebrides*," © 1986 by Gordon Turnbull. Published for the first time in this volume. Printed by permission. The text, referred to as *Tour,* on which this essay is based is: *Boswell's Journal of a Tour to the Hebrides with Samuel Johnson LL.D., 1773,* ed. Frederick A. Pottle and Charles H. Bennett, new ed. with additional notes by F. A. Pottle (New York: McGraw-Hill, 1971), which prints all that has been recovered of Boswell's original manuscript journal. Quotations from Boswell's published version are from the 3rd ed., 1786, vol. 5 of the Hill-Powell *Life.*

Quotation has also been made from several of Boswell's earlier and later journals, as published in our century: *Boswell's London Journal, 1762–1763,* ed. F. A. Pottle (New York: McGraw-Hill, 1950); *Boswell on the Grand Tour: Germany and Switzerland, 1764,* ed. F. A. Pottle (New York: McGraw-Hill, 1953); *Boswell in Extremes, 1776–1778,* ed. Charles McC. Weis and F. A. Pottle (New York: McGraw-Hill, 1970); and, *Boswell: Laird of Auchinleck, 1778–1782,* ed. Joseph W. Reed and F. A. Pottle (New York: McGraw-Hill, 1977). See also: *The Correspondence of James Boswell and John Johnston of Grange,* ed. Ralph S. Walker (New York: McGraw-Hill, 1966), and Frank Brady, *Boswell's Political Career* (New Haven and London: Yale University Press, 1965).

The Boswell materials are printed with permission of Yale University and the McGraw-Hill Book Company.

"Reflection as Criterion in *The Lives of the Poets*" by Robert J. Griffin, © 1986 by Robert J. Griffin. This essay constituted chapter 4, "Samuel Johnson and the Act of Reflection," Diss. Yale 1985. Published for the first time in this volume. Printed by permission.

Index